WE ARE JUST CLAY

God's Hand in Life's Hard Circumstances

Carlton Marshall

ISBN 978-1-0980-7170-7 (paperback)
ISBN 978-1-0980-7171-4 (digital)

Christian Faith Publishing, Inc.
832 Park Avenue
Meadville, PA 16335
www.christianfaithpublishing.com

Printed in the United States of America

THIS BOOK IS DEDICATED TO none other than the Lord God Almighty, King of kings, Lord of lords, the one and only living Sovereign God. As much as I would like to dedicate it to my wife and children, I cannot. Maybe if I write another one. This book however is an effort to convey God's work upon my life thus far, a work still in progress and which, until I die, will always be in progress. I feel God, by His will and providence, has provided me with and revealed to me any story, views or thoughts I have expressed in this book. Some of the views I have expressed, may not conform to certain modern theological opinions, but I have proposed them for the reader's contemplation and consideration in order to hopefully motivate a righteous and cautious mindset in the matters of God and our conduct here in this world. These views are given out of a deep reverence for God and His holiness, to spur contemplation for the reader, and are simply a response out of love and gratefulness to Him. It is also an effort on my part, as weak as my human efforts as a writer may be, to display the majesty of God in His will and work upon the fallen human creation. Praise be to the Lord God Almighty, and it is my prayer this book will bring Him—and Him alone—glory and honor.

I WANT TO EXPRESS A special thanks to Fred Campbell and Ronald Weldon Self for the time they have selflessly given to me over the past several years to mentor me and mature me in my faith and understanding of Christ Jesus. Additionally I wish to thank the members of my Sunday school as well as others, both friends and family, who were willing to take the time to share both their own insights into scripture as well as to willingly dig through scripture with me in order to find God's truth. All of these persons were fulfilling God's purpose to love and bond in the unity of Christ Jesus and assisted me in my Christian walk. Thank you, each and every one.

CONTENTS

NORMAL DAY?

IT WAS THREE O'CLOCK IN the morning on October 17, 2007, and I was trying to move around quietly as I prepared to leave for work in order not to further disturb my wife. Although this was not my normal waking time, neither was it unusual for me. I was a police officer in Dallas, Texas, and had been one for twenty-one years. Throughout my career on the department, I had filled numerous positions that operated on a variety of shifts. Several of those assignments had rotating hours each month, along with call-back responsibilities, so I often found myself going to work at unusual hours. It was for me just another normal day.

My wife Susan had awakened when I did, but she was caught between going back to sleep or waiting till I left. My eight-and-a-half-month-old daughter was sleeping in the crib in our room, but my two-and-a-half-year-old son had apparently heard me moving around and wandered into the room to see me. I was just getting ready to shower, and he wanted to shower with me. He was daddy's little boy and always wanted to be with his dad. I certainly did not mind that. I loved my family and spending time with them, and so I let him shower with me. Of course my wife was fully awake now, and we talked excitedly about the three-week vacation we were taking together starting that day. We were not going anywhere, just staying home to do work on the house and farm and to spend time with the kids and each other.

The truth is I probably would not be taking this vacation except I had maxed out my vacation time earnings and was starting to lose it, that is, I was no longer earning any more since I had reached my max. It was the same for many officers. We would basically be forced to take a vacation and burn our time down so we could start earning it again. The vacation was actually supposed to start that day, and I did not even have to go to work, but I wanted to. I had always loved being a police officer. I had been called to it since I had been a teenager, maybe even before, and each day was a new adventure. I loved the job, and doing something you love and getting paid for it too was a bonus. I had of course worked patrol, which every officer starts out in but had moved to various assignments, including Internal Affairs and Homicide, before I began moving up in rank. Although I enjoyed the investigative assignments, I had always enjoyed patrol. Even though I had begun to rise to supervisory ranks, I still loved the streets and would regularly be out with my troops doing the work right beside them as much as I could, whether it was in the Gang Unit, Deployment, or any other assignment; I always like being with my officers and being involved hands-on as much as possible.

Maybe my reputation was one of the reasons I was where I was at. I had made lieutenant just over two years earlier and was now assigned to SWAT (Special Weapons and Tactics) where I was the unit commander of E-Unit. This morning we were running an IRS Federal Task Force warrant involving a drug cartel, and I wanted to be there. A federal multijurisdictional task force that had been investigating a drug cartel had been operating for about three years and was coming to a close of its investigation. There were several locations being served that morning all across the nation and state including many within the Dallas/Fort Worth area. Our unit had been requested to serve this particular warrant in an Oak Cliff section of Dallas where some still unidentified players were at and where one particular person of interest was suspected of being located.

This suspect had been operating in Grand Prairie, but when a warrant had been served there just over a week earlier, the officers had missed him. It was important this person be picked up, and agents were concerned that if attempts missed again, then the suspect would realize he was a target for arrest and likely try to disappear into Mexico. Thus it was decided to run the warrant on the house at 6:00 a.m. At that time of morning, it was highly likely the suspect would be in the home and fast asleep. The warrant briefing was at 4:00 a.m. at SWAT headquarters.

As I finished dressing and prepared to leave, my son crawled up into the bed with my wife, and she was going to try to sleep for a bit longer. I gave her a kiss goodbye and told her I would be back in just a few hours. My wife understood my job because she was also a police officer, but for the Irving Police Department. She is a strong and terrific person who had made many sacrifices in her own career after the children were born while continuing to support mine. She sacrificed things like not taking promotional opportunities or trans-fers to new assignments, which would have required shift changes or call back responsibilities. With our new young family, someone had to have stable and regular hours, and she elected to be that person so I could pursue my career. I did not realize at the time just how strong she really was, but I would soon find out. Her strength would be revealed in a huge unexpected storm, when what I thought would be my return home just a few hours later turned into something else.

The Situation

I left the house and headed to the station for the briefing. My sergeants were already there finalizing the warrant plans and trying to account for any unexpected situations. I arrived a little before 4:00 a.m. and sat in the detail room reviewing the tactical plan. We knew there was a baby in the house, so we were trying to adjust our plan accordingly, such as not using gas inside the house. Part of our plan entailed a port and cover operation on one window that was believed to be the bedroom where the prime suspect would be. I was con-cerned about the baby's location in the house and particularly the bedroom due to our porting the window. I wanted to take every reasonable precaution, trying to combine the officers' safety needs along with the concerns for the baby. After all, a baby cannot be held accountable for the environment its parents bring it into.

A lot of people talk about having an ominous feeling about something happening, hairs sticking up on the neck or something. I never felt that. If I did, I guess I ignored it. My job on this operation was a simple one. My assignment, along with supervising the warrant, was the discharging of a deflagration device commonly referred to as a "bang" for noise distraction and providing just a minor perimeter containment function. If something went wrong, such as the warrant turning into a barricaded person, being the unit commander, I would not be tied up on something essential and could easily drop back and set up command operations. The fact was however that I loved being in the action and working beside my troops. As the commander, I did not have to be involved in any actual function of the warrant. I could have just sat back and observed my team run it. However, I considered myself as a servant leader rather than a boss in that I would never ask my men to do something that I was not willing to do myself. Although I would have enjoyed being on the entry team, that was not my place. I had to relegate myself to minor functions so I could drop back and handle other situations if they developed, such as an "officer down" scenario. But I liked being involved with my team, so there I was taking this minor role in this warrant.

The truth is that even to this day, I do not remember this operation. I have no actual recollection of the events that transpired that morning. I vaguely remember my concerns for the baby and calling the case officer to try and pin that information down, but even that memory is hazy at best. Much of what I am writing about the warrant service is what was told to me by the SWAT operators and others who were with me that day. The last thing I actually really remember was taking my wife and kids to the State Fair the week before. I guess in some way my brain has blocked my ability to recall this incident in order to protect me emotionally, and I think that is probably a blessing.

After the warrant briefing, the various operators made sure they had the equipment they needed to perform their assigned duties. Then we all loaded up into the vehicles and headed out to serve the warrant. Things are quiet in the warrant van as each officer is concentrating on his job duties and contemplating all possible scenarios that might come up. They imagine each possible incident and what their response will be to each. This is referred to as Psychosomatic Thinking. Basically it is a sort of cognitive and behavioral functioning technique. By contemplating possibilities and your reaction to them in advance, it assists in a quicker and more deliberate response because your mind has already dealt with the situation before it ever occurred.

Upon arrival to the warrant location, the teams of officers rapidly deployed to their various assignments, and I also arrived to the rear of the house to conduct my perimeter support function. As the warrant quickly progressed, suddenly something seemed wrong. We knew the house had surveillance cameras, which was not uncommon, but that could not be helped. Although the house had cameras and they could potentially create problems for us, the warrant still had to be executed. It was learned later that one suspect was awake and monitoring the cameras when we arrived and saw the team's movements toward the house. When he saw the team approaching the house, he called out to the other occupants warning them that we were coming and thus the element of surprise had been compromised. As the entry team penetrated the front door, another team, Tim Houston and Matt Smith, conducted the port and cover operation on the bedroom window and, as expected, engaged a suspect in the room. They identified themselves as police officers and began giving verbal commands to the suspect, but something was not going well. The suspect had been awakened and alerted to our presence by the warning, and he was not obeying the commands. He was jumping around, moving his hands erratically and being noncompliant.

The non-cooperation of a suspect was not necessarily unusual at all, but I must have felt things were getting out of control. It is my understanding that the commands being given grew more intense than usual due to the suspect's behavior and I must have been concerned for the entry team, which I knew was headed to the room and the possibility that we might be getting ready to have a shooting. Although our job is inherently dangerous when dealing with these types of situations, we train hard and initiate our actions in such a manner as to successfully accomplish our enforcement action and take the suspects into custody with no loss of life if at all possible.

As I said, I do not recall the warrant that morning, but I know what my assignment was, and I know I would not have altered the assignment unless something severe was occurring and the need presented itself. I must have genuinely felt that a shooting was imminent, and I wanted to prevent it if I could. Probably as a result of this feeling of impending calamity, I suddenly altered my assignment. There is a tactical theory that a suspect facing one gun may decide to fight thinking they can beat the one gun, but when confronted by two or more guns, they recognize the futility of fighting and become cooperative and surrender. Based on the witness officer's reports, I approached the bedroom window next to the port and cover team and broke that window to gain a view of the room to possibly assist the port and cover team by introducing a second gun in order to help bring the suspect into submission to the commands. To do so would hopefully bring the warrant to a desirable conclusion with no loss of life. I broke the window with the palm of my left hand and, as is not uncommon, found the window covered from the inside with a curtain or blanket. As I reached up and pulled the obstacle out of the way in order to gain a view inside the room, a gunshot went off, and suddenly I was hit. *Suddenly I* was the "officer down."

The gunshot came from inside the house from a female suspect that Tim and Matt could not see. They had seen her roll off the bed with the baby, but they lost sight of her behind the bed and were fully engaged with the male suspect who was not cooperating. The female had hidden behind the bed on the floor and was concealed from their view. There is a chance if I had not broken that window and created that distraction, then Tim and Matt would have been the targets of her discharging the firearm, or maybe one of the entry team members once they were to make entry into the room and were potentially distracted by the same uncooperative suspect. As it was, when I broke the window and pulled the blanket back, I drew her fire. A .45 ACP bullet hit me in the vest right at the neck line, and since she was shooting from the floor toward the window in an upward trajectory, the bullet deflected upward from the impact with my vest and penetrated my neck. The path of the bullet is unknown to me for sure, but during the course of ricocheting around in my neck, it broke several vertebras as well as breaking my hyoid bone in the roof of my mouth before exiting my back just above my left scapula. I fell to the ground immediately. The call then went out that shots were fired and an officer was down.

When the officer down call was broadcast, officers Kung Seng and Josh Hertel who were conducting a port and cover on another window immediately left their assignment and came to my aid. They grabbed me and proceeded to drag me to the front of the house where the SWAT doctors Alexander Eastman and Jeff Metzler were located. Josh and Kung came to aid me without regard for their own safety. Although they knew someone was armed and had already shown a willingness to shoot at an officer, they still placed themselves in danger in order to evacuate me to a secure location. Within moments, the entry team made it to the room; and as they did so, Tim and Matt broke off their assignment and provided cover for Kung and Josh while they dragged me from the field of fire. Had they hesitated to act until the room had been secured by the entry team to get me to the doctors, the results might have been drastically different or even fatal. All of this occurred in about thirty seconds or less. That is how fast these warrants happen, particularly in smaller houses like this one.

It was no easy task to move me. I was a pretty big guy weighing in at 210 pounds in gym clothes. With all my SWAT gear, I was close to 260 pounds and was deadweight. I owe these guys a great debt that I may never be able to repay. If it wasn't for their quick action to get me to Alex and Jeff, I probably would have died right there. Along with breaking the three vertebrae in my neck and damaging my spinal cord, one of the two vertebral arteries that run through the vertebral column had also been severed; and as a result, I was bleeding out and suffocating in my own blood. However, due to their quick actions, I received immediate help from the doctors.

SWAT Docs

FOR JUST OVER THREE YEARS prior to my transfer to SWAT, the Dallas Police Department had been supporting a program called the City of Dallas Tactical Medical Support Team (now called the Dallas Police Tactical Medicine Program), which was initiated by Dr. Alexander Eastman and supported by his supervisor Dr. Paul Pepe. Though the proper name of the program was City of Dallas Tactical Medical Support Team, in casual conversation, we commonly refer to it as the SWAT Docs Program. In the SWAT Docs Program, real doctors or EMT's and in some cases like Dallas PD—actual surgeons are trained and ride with SWAT and Narcotics Division officers when running various warrants or conducting other police actions in which the potential for injury exists. These medical personnel are not there only for the officers, but also the victims, suspects, or any other person that might be harmed during or until the situation is brought to a conclusion. The doctors are prepared for and capable of conducting in the field triage when necessary even while the situation is still volatile. Thankfully their actual significant need is rare, and most of their time is spent checking on the condition of hostages and suspects at the resolution of the incident. These doctors carry a pager and respond to all callouts and other situations as needed just as the officers do. Here is the kicker: They volunteer to be part of the program. They do not get paid by the city. They are not city employees. They are real surgeons working in the trauma ward at a real hospital and taking care of patients. They do this job in the SWAT Docs Program in addition to their regular hospital duties. Until recently, they even had to drive their own personal cars to respond to these situations. Slowly, finally, the city has given them city cars to use when responding to calls so their personal cars are not subjected to unnecessary damages. These guys are real heroes who quietly work behind the scenes. Even before, but especially now, I can personally attest to the worthiness of this program. Every city should seriously consider a similar program for their units that operate in high-risk operations.

When Josh and Kung had gotten me to the doctors, I was unconscious, yet my eyes and mouth were still open. Alex stated that initially I looked okay with just a little blood showing on my lip, and he thought I had just been hit in the face with a breaching tool or something. But as he was looking at me, I tried to breathe, and blood gushed out of my mouth and out from under my neck protector, which was initially hiding the gunshot entry wound. I was bleeding profusely on the inside due to the severed artery, and I could not breathe because I had no airway. I was literally drowning in my own blood. Upon seeing this, Alex and Jeff took action without hesitation. They decided to perform on me a procedure called a cricothyrotomy in order to establish an airway while at the same time trying to stabilize my head and neck. The cricothyrotomy involved incising the cricothyroid membrane and placing a breathing tube through my neck and into my trachea. The doctors had to act quickly. There was no time to introduce any painkiller and certainly no time to wait in order to give it time to take effect. I was in the process of dying right there as they were watching. Jeff held me still with his hands and placed my head between his knees in order to keep my head immobilized while Alex cut into me in order to perform the cricothyrotomy. It was still dark when this occurred, and SWAT operators had to illuminate the procedure with the barrel lights attached to their Colt Commando Tactical Rifles. Only after the procedure was complete were the doctors able to start an IV and give me pain medication. When the ambulance arrived at the scene, Dr. Eastman rode with me to Methodist Central Hospital, which was the closest hospital with a trauma unit. I was then taken directly into emergency surgery. If the

CARLTON MARSHALL

SWAT doctors had not been there, I would have died for sure. It took the ambulance eight minutes to get there, and because of the severed artery, I was drowning in my own blood and would have had four minutes or less. The doctors were able to open an airway for me and get me stabilized enough so I could be transported to the hospital.

When I arrived at the hospital, upon taking me out of the ambulance, the bullet, which exited my shoulder, fell out onto the gurney. It wasn't long before a grandiose story of legend was going around that I was Superman and I had caught the bullet in my teeth and I spit it out as I stepped from the ambulance on my own power. Oh what dreams are made of, and boy do I wish it was true.

THE NOTIFICATION

THIS SHOOTING HAPPENED A LITTLE before 6:00 a.m. The department has a protocol for handling the notification of the immediate family of downed officers, particularly if the survival of the officer was questionable, as in my circumstance. According to the protocol, an officer and a supervisor are supposed to go to the home of the family member to inform them of the situation and drive them to the hospital or stay with them at the home if necessary till other family or friends can arrive for support if needed. Officers are supposed to be physically present during these notifications because people react differently when presented with this kind of news. Some will handle the notification highly stressed, but well, while others break down completely and cease to be able to function; others may become angry or even suddenly suicidal. The emotional gambit of how a person might react runs the full length of the spectrum. This procedure was put in place because of these highly emotional and sometimes volatile responses.

Somehow the ball was dropped on this incident. Susan as such was already up and preparing the kids for daycare when she received an anonymous phone call on the landline at about 6:30 a.m. She knew this was unusual because nobody called the house that early. If it had been me or one of her family, they would have called her mobile phone and not the landline. Irving PD has a similar notification policy in place, so she had no reason to think anything was wrong. She reasonably assumed it was just a wrong number. When she answered the phone, an unknown officer told her that I had been shot. When she questioned them, they could not tell her anything about my condition or even describe what happened. They simply told her that I had been shot and some officers were on the way to pick her up.

The officer who called was almost certainly someone we knew though possibly someone new to the Communications Division who was not familiar with the standard operating procedure or became anxious maybe thinking it was a good idea to ensure my wife was up and dressed for when the officers arrived so she could leave quickly. I tend to believe it was someone from the Communications Division because officers who were close to us generally had our cell numbers. The landline number was just for department records. I think who-ever they were, they had the sincerest and best intentions for both of us, but the desire to help was not well thought out. I think it is the desire of most anyone to be able to say goodbye to a loved one who they know are going pass. In some cases this is possible, but in reality, for many cases, it is not. The fact is, we are not in control in this world and we do not know what the future holds from one minute to the next. We habitually go about our business thinking we know what will happen, but the truth is we do not. That is why it is important that people know they are loved each time they leave, just in case that chance to express love and say goodbye does not pres-ent itself. I have seen delayed notifications in similar situations and watched the family become angry because they felt they had missed an opportunity for a final moment, and I understand the sentiment, but it just is not realistic for situations like mine. This desire exists even for officers and I think and hope it was the caller's intent to give Susan an opportunity to get to the hospital as quickly as possible just in case. In reality though, her seeing me, as with any other person in my condition, could not have happened because the doctors were busily working on me in the trauma ward, and her chances to see me were nil to none. Even if by some miracle she could, I would be out because of the drugs and would be oblivious to anything. That being the case, if she had been allowed access to me, possibly at least in her own mind, she might have had some comfort in being able to speak final words to me. These chances however are truly slim to nonexistent in reality, and the potential for adverse possibilities by an anonymous call far outweigh the potential benefits. The protocol was put in place for a reason. In her case, she was at home alone with the two babies. No one was there to be with her if she reacted badly. I can only thank God that she is a strong woman.

It was fortunate she reacted to the news in a strong self-disciplined manner, and her logic and police instincts kicked in rather than emotion. Susan is a smart person and is able to think clearly and rationally even under extremely stressful situations. Based on department protocol, she rationalized that I must not be hurt too bad because other than the impromptu phone call, officers would have been at the door to make the notification in person. Due to where we lived, she speculated the officers would be a while in arriving to take her to the hospital, and she also knew that the hospital was not a place for the children, and the best place for them right now was the daycare.

As it turns out, the officers arrived quicker than expected and pulled in just as she was headed out the door with the kids. They tried to keep her there, but as I said, she knew the kids were better off at the daycare than at the hospital, so she quickly gathered the kids and took them to their daycare facility and headed back to the house where the officers were waiting. As she was driving home, the news media was already reporting on the shooting. She heard the commentator on the radio announce that a Dallas Police Department lieutenant had been shot in the neck and was in critical condition at Methodist Central Hospital. This is how my wife was notified. The media, in their zeal to be the first to report the shooting, did so without regard for or verification of whether the family had been contacted or not. It should never have happened this way. When Susan got home, she quickly got in the squad car, and the officers drove her to the hospital. Little did she know at that time how this morning would forever change the course of our lives.

Her Arrival

Susan still had reserved hopes my injury was not as bad as it was being reported. She maintained a strong and controlled composure until while en route to the hospital a fellow officer contacted the driver of the squad car on the police band and asked if they were driving Code 3, which is emergency response with lights and siren? When he responded no, the officer told him to run Code 3, that they needed to get there quick. It was at this conversation Susan broke down. She knew then that things were worse than she had imagined, and this message to hurry was an indicator that I might indeed be dying or even dead upon her arrival.

When Susan arrived at the hospital, she was met by a sea of police officers. There is an amazing brotherhood bond that exists among officers. It is tremendously strong and very close, a unique bond that very few can understand except those in unique professions, like military personnel who have faced active combat, or firemen who have worked together in stressful life-threatening situations and such. Police share this bond with each other because of the unique nature of the job. We see and deal with the all aspects of humanity, the tragedies, the victims, the criminals. Day in and day out, officers place themselves in harm's way to protect the innocent and stand the line between right and wrong. The job is not always fun. Officers are tasked with many unpopular jobs including the ever-appreciated traffic enforcement, keeping the peace such as quelling loud parties, and other unpopular duties. They face anger by citizens for not being faster to respond to a call, for not being present to prevent the crime in the first place, or for taking undesirable enforcement actions based on law, or not taking enforcement action based on law. Criminals, of course, hate being arrested, and everyone tries to second guess an officer's decision. Police, however, do not make the laws. The laws are made by the people, but officers have the task of upholding and apprehending the violators of those laws that our citizens create. Although we are titled "law enforcement officers," it is the citizens who actually enforce the laws through the processes of our judicial system by a jury of peers. By holding a person guilty or finding them innocent, it is the citizen who enforces the law, but it seems like the police are always the beginning of that process and therefore they are always bearing the brunt of the blame and the title so to speak. Officers are often loved when needed or wanted but seem to be loathed and bothersome when not.

Unlike the nonsworn civilian population, police officers see both sides. People forget that officers used to be civilians before they entered law enforcement, and they are still civilians when off-duty. They are bound by the same laws as the public with very few exceptions, and those exceptions are only job and duty related. In fact, officers are actually held to an even higher standard than the public. So we see both sides of the coin, good and bad. Unfortunately, as a result of the nature of the job, we are exposed almost constantly to a lot of bad and very little good, which tends to push us closer together and which can result in causing us to alienate ourselves from the general public, who seem to question everything we do. So when an officer goes down in the line of duty, other officers gather to show respect and provide support. It does not matter if they know each other or not. It doesn't matter if they are from the same department or precinct or not. If they are law enforcement, then they are a brother or sister. They and their family are family.

Susan was quickly met by a good friend of mine, Sergeant Mike Milligan, who escorted her to a small room where several officers, many who were friends of hers from the Irving Police Department, were gathered. She was then briefed and informed that I was in surgery and they would all have to wait for further information. Officers then gathered around her to provide support as they were able.

Mike had worked for me on a couple of occasions at the department. He was a tremendous asset in those assignments, and although we had never really met until the last few years in our careers, it was a very short time before we became good friends, and I knew he was someone I could trust and rely on. Unknown to me at the time, Mike had taken upon himself the role of guardian over Susan. He stayed with her constantly and made sure to get her whatever she needed while they waited.

Several hours later, Dr. Darryl Amos, who had performed the surgery, came in the room and spoke with her. He informed her I had survived the surgery and was recovering and then concernedly explained the complications and possible risks I would be facing.

THE VISIT

I HAD SURVIVED AT THE scene and the transport to the hospital as a direct result of the quick actions of our SWAT docs Alex Eastman and Jeff Metzler, and I survived the trauma surgery by Dr. Darryl Amos, but I was still far from being deemed "going to survive." The bullet along with damaging the vertebra at and around the cervical spinal nerve 4 also caused one of the vertebral arteries to tear, which could cause additional complications. It then managed to exit my back near my left shoulder blade. I was still at death's door. For some reason, three days after the shooting, I developed spinal meningitis; and two weeks after the shooting, due to the vertebral artery being severed with the breaking of the vertebra, I suffered a massive stroke down my left side.

Initially the doctors believed that even if I survived I would be unable to speak due to the damage the bullet caused to my vocal cords and the subsequent reconstructive surgery. I had in fact not spoken for a while, and nobody even expected me to; but one day when my wife was sitting next to me and was picking off some dead skin or something that was on my arms, I spoke. Her picking at my arms and pulling off the dead tissue was kind of irritating, sort of like having the hairs pulled out, and I quietly told her to stop. Up until that time, I had not spoken.

I was in and out of consciousness during those first couple of weeks, but I had awareness of what was going on at least to some limited degree. Late one night a close friend of mine named Scott Eggleston had come up to visit me. Scott had worked for me for several years both in patrol and on an evening deployment team, and I sincerely believe much of the success I was credited with as a supervisor was due to his efforts. It probably happens that way for any successful supervisor because a supervisor is only as good as their troops. The supervisor may plan and direct but the troops implement that plan and their efforts often determine if the plan succeeds or fails. It is sort of like a good man usually has a good woman behind him who made him that man. I guess I happened to be in one of my alert phases at the time of his visit. I say "I guess" because I was actually still so drugged up I hardly remember the conversation, but still in my mind I must have sensed something bad was going to happen and possibly I would not be around much longer. That night before he left, I asked him for a favor; I asked him to take care of my wife and kids. Later that night at about four o'clock in the morning, I would suffer the major stroke.

Things were still very touch-and-go for a while, especially after the stroke occurred to complicate matters further, but eventually I began to stabilize. The doctors finally felt optimistic I would survive, but they were very uncertain just how much of me they would get back. The initial prognosis was quite grim. I would survive, but by *survive* they basically meant I would likely just "exist" between being confined to a bed or possibly being moved to a chair and pushed around. Between the spinal cord damage, the meningitis, and the stroke, I would likely have no decent mobility or function; and also due to the meningitis and its treatment, I would shortly go completely deaf.

Within a month, my wife was trying to get me moved to another hospital, but she was running into obstacles. Fortunately one of the visitors who came to see me during my incoherent phase was none other than Mr. Ross Perot. I did not know Mr. Perot personally, but I did know his reputation. Along with being very wealthy, he was also a quiet supporter of the police, fire, and military personnel. I knew of several donations and other assistance he had provided to police officers and military personnel while under tough situations. When looking for a hospital to move to, Zale Lipshy had agreed to take me, but my wife was having difficulty getting me released to them and was told it would take a few weeks to get through the "red tape." Upon the information being passed to Mr. Perot, that "few weeks" turned into a few hours, the red tape had been resolved, and I was on my way to Zale Lipshy the next morning.

By the time I had been admitted to Zale, I had become deaf. I was still not conscious most of the time and was very incoherent when I was awake and so was not even self-aware of being deaf. I did not talk much due to the damage to my vocal cords nor was I eating. I was actually being fed through a stomach tube because of the damage the bullet had caused to my throat and the trauma to it during the surgical reconstruction and any attempt to swallow food, even soft food, would be painful and possibly cause further damage. Medical staff and others would come in and talk to me, or rather, to Susan, and because I could not hear the conversation or the questions, I would just look at them. I could speak but rarely did so even when asked questions basically because I could not hear the questions. It was some time till somebody snapped on the possibility I could not hear and wrote on a dry-erase board that I finally actually responded. I read the question and responded verbally. Everyone seemed relieved. Apparently they were concerned I had suffered brain damage due to the extended time I was without oxygen during the original trauma at the scene of the incident. To find out I was actually just deaf almost broke out into a celebration.

Once it was discovered I was deaf and not brain damaged, everyone started writing me notes and questions. It was funny because some friends would write a long question, and I would only respond with a very short answer, usually only a yes or no, and it would almost exasperate my friends. I never was one for talking a lot, but that really revealed itself during that time. Eventually due to the technology of cochlear implants, basically a prosthetic for the ears, I would gain a very acceptable level of hearing ability. Though the implants allowed me "to hear", I was in fact still stone-cold deaf, and I would come to understand each person receiving these implants will hear at different levels. For example, I cannot hear music anymore as it should sound, and unfortunately I hear everything without distinction, so in a crowded or noisy environment, I have sensory overload; and as such, I understand nothing because everything is garbled. I even have trouble on the phone or when people are trying to talk to me from a distance, but for the most part, I can carry on conversations with people near me, say ten feet or less, as long as there is not too much background noise. If there is more than one person engaged in the conversation and all persons will take the time to talk one at a time, I am good. If multiple people are in the conversation and talking at once, my understanding of the conversation can be hit or miss. My hearing certainly has problems and is not perfect like God created hearing, but it is definitely better than being deaf.

It was during this time of being deaf that I began to become cognizant and alert most of the time. Though I was still on pain medication, I was not drowsy and zoned out like before. Still, I was immobile and deaf. When people were not in the room, all I could do was stare at the ceiling and think. The hospital had corkboard rectangular tile ceilings like you find in most hospitals and business buildings, and I would often make a game of trying to find figures in the ceiling's tiles, similar to people watching cloud formations and trying to see objects in them. I was not able to move at all during this time and could only lie flat on my back looking up. I had a television in the corner of my room, but I could not operate the remote control, and I also had a halo on, which prevented me from turning my head so I could watch it. Even if I could have watched it, I could not have heard it, so most of my alone time was just spent looking at the ceiling and thinking, thinking mostly about my life and the future.

It was while I could not move or hear that I did in fact hear. That is, I heard the voice of God. I cannot say it was an oral voice like two people talking out loud, but it was as real as if it were. It was not a vision and certainly was not a dream, but it was real. It was like an extended epiphany or moment of clarity, yet it was more than that and had what I can only describe as an audible dialogue—it was that real. This voice brought me back to when I had been baptized at the age of sixteen, and when for the next three years of my life, I had considered myself to have a great relationship with the Lord. I went to church every Sunday morning, evening, and Wednesdays, and to any other church function that might arise. I had a group of Christian friends I associated with both in school and out and a family that supported my decision for Christ. Things seemed to be going well.

Things seemed well, but shortly after graduation, I left for college; and when I did, I left my family, my church, and my friends; my entire Christian support group, and arrived at a party college not knowing anyone. My car was old and not very reliable, and parking spots near the dorms were a premium, so I rarely moved my car. There were not many churches within walking distance, and the ones I tried did not seem very receptive to having another college student. As a result, after a few efforts, I began to think I would be better off on my own, and I stopped going to church. During that time, I slowly began to meet other students and pursue college life. First Corinthians 15:33 in the Bible says, "Bad company corrupts good morals," and how true that is. It was not long before I began drinking in order to socialize and be better received at parties. Though I will not say having a drink of alcohol is a sin in itself, I will say as alcohol takes its inebriating effects, it facilitates sinful behavior, and as such, it was not long before even my sins that previously existed due to my immaturity in Christ began to expand into other areas. That spiral of sinful activity began there, and it would continue downward for the next twenty-five years.

I was a good guy, I did not do anything that society at large would have a problem with, but I certainly did plenty that God would take issue with. Though my sins started out small—that is, assuming of course sin can be graded, sin is never satisfied, and it continues to try to grow and expand wanting more and ever more often. Sin is always sinning and is always striving for more ways to fulfill sinful desires. It would be almost like being on heroin; sin can never get enough of sinning, and complete satisfaction would never be achieved until it killed you. It was not long before sin got hold of me, and I fell into what I call the "traps of justification." Satan is constantly baiting us, and he has fishing lines of temptations of every type all around us with justifications as the bait, and he is just waiting for us to bite so he can hook us. He lies constantly and is always willing to help you justify sin with such thoughts as "It's not so bad," "Everybody's doing it," "Who's going to know?" or worst of all, "God will forgive you anyway, right?"

It was while in the hospital room and I was unable to move or hear that God had finally gotten my attention. I realize now He had been trying to talk to me for years, but I was too busy and too wrapped up in my own pursuits to listen. Now, I was totally still and unable to do anything to distract me from God's efforts to speak with me. It was now at this time that God confronted me directly. He confronted me with my sins and particularly those sins I had justified to myself since the time I had accepted His Son Jesus Christ into my life. He revealed to me where I was in regards to my relationship to Him and where I should have been and how much my communion with Him had severely declined. I was still a child of God which was itself proven even by this confrontation, but I was a prodigal child. Although I had strayed in my relationship with God, my straying did not negate the fact that I was still His child. I was simply a child for whose return to a communal relationship He was seeking. Along with revealing how our relationship had declined, He also showed me that my heart had become so hardened and obstinate with sin that I had virtually stopped hearing the rebukes of the Holy Spirit. Because I had justified my sins, I had become engaged in sinful conduct willingly, purposefully, and habitually to the point of practicing sin and being almost arrogant about it. I would like to think that if I knew I was offending God, then I would have stopped, but because I had justified my sins to myself, I know that is not true. Since I justified my sin, I had in fact knowingly pushed God aside. Because my sin was purposeful and willing, it was of course also sin that had not been repented of. I was on the other side of the spectrum from where I should have been in my relationship to God. The apostle Paul talks about similar behavior the Corinthian church was tolerating from one of its members (1 Corinthians 5:1–2) and how the behavior of unrepentant and practiced sin should be mourned (2 Corinthians 12:21; James 4:1–9).

The conversation with God had a quality in it that caused me great fear. Not only did the realization of my sins and guilt stun me upon being confronted by them because I had not realized just how sinful I had let my life become, but I felt fear also because God had an ominous or almost sad and foreboding tone. He had the air of love, of a fatherly love that was combined with disappointment and pending consequences. He then asked me, "If you died today, how are you going to explain and answer for your sins to Me?"

In Ezekiel 33:3–5, God talks about the trumpet of warning and states, "Then he who hears the sound of the trumpet and does not take warning, and a sword comes and takes him away, his blood will be on his *own* head. 'He heard the sound of the trumpet but did not take warning; his blood will be on himself. But had he taken warning, he would have delivered his life." In the hospital room, God was sounding the trumpet of warning. I had been at death's door, but God in His mercy did not call my life to an end but rather He was confronting me and giving me one more opportunity. He was sounding the trumpet of warning, possibly my last warning.

As I saw all my past sins and the purposeful and willing way I had committed them, I realized I had no answer and no excuses. I was guilty of taking His grace for granted. As I realized all I had done and the abuse of grace I had committed, I just began crying like a baby, begging for forgiveness and repenting of them all. I heard the trumpet, and I chose to heed the warning. I continually begged for His forgiveness in between sobs and also begged for another chance. Though I had accepted Christ and had been baptized at the age of sixteen, now twenty-eight years later, I finally had a true heartfelt repentance. This time my heart had been broken because of my sin and not just my conscious, logical mind. My broken heart combined with my fear of the eternal consequences was overbearing. This time, in the hospital bed, I actually came to know God on a personal basis. He was talking to me plainly and clearly, and this time I truly and sincerely repented and submitted myself to Him with no reservations. I asked Him to please give me continuance in this life and another opportunity to do right and good for Him. Those prayers would continue for a few more weeks, and all I could do was wait for His response.

Though I felt and perceived it as an actual conversation at the time, now upon reflection, I have come to believe that it was God's Holy Spirit that was in an actual and literal conversation with my spirit. I believe that is why I could seemingly hear even though I was fully physically deaf and could not hear, I have no other reasonable explanation other than our God, who is in control of all things, had opened my hearing just for this conversation. That being said, I still believe it was a spiritual conversation because I doubt had anyone been in the room that they would have seen or heard anything other than maybe me sobbing like a baby. But God had gotten my attention, He was talking to me, and He was saying in effect Ephesians 5:14, "Awake, sleeper, arise from the dead, and Christ will shine on you."

INTERVENTION

FOR SEVERAL YEARS I HAD recognized much of the sin in my life. As I said, it was not such type sin activity that the world as a whole would have a concern with, but it was certainly something God would have heartache with. I was in violation of at least three of His "Thou shalt not" commandments on a regular—and often even willing—basis and then others occasionally. I was trapped in a cycle of sinful activity that just continued even though I had been faced with and had to deal with the consequences of those activities in several ways. Often I would pursue my sinful passions and, after the fact, regret having done so because I recognized it as offending God no matter how I might have justified it at the time I was engaged in it.

I have heard, that when we feel regret for our sin and its offense to God, that is a sign that the Holy Spirit is working in us and rebuking us and it is evidence we are a child of God. I believe that is true and it is part of God's sanctifying work. During these times when I was feeling remorse for offending God and/or facing stressful situations as a result of my activities, I would frequently pray to Him that He would help me get back into the relationship I had with Him in high school the first three years after my baptism and before being corrupted by my college experiences. Although I would pray for God to restore me, I myself made relatively little effort on my own to help in that restoration. I guess I just expected God to snap His fingers and announce, "Let it be done," and I would automatically be restored. After my prayers, I would just return to my regular activities and try to exert a little more self-control and try to be a little more obedient.

My self-powered attempts of obedience and self-control however would quickly end in failure and often result in a larger fall into my sin than before. I realize now that without keeping myself in communion with God on a regular and frequent basis, I was doomed to fail. Rather than relying on Him and turning to Him for strength and help when confronted with temptation, as He told His disciples in the Garden of Gethsemane to "watch and pray that you may not enter temptation" (Matthew 26:41), but instead trying to rely on my own power and abilities, my efforts were just failure and disaster waiting to happen. That was what got me into trouble at college, relying on my power instead of relying on God, and not staying in touch with Him but instead, continually mulling over my temptations until they snowballed and eventually came to fruition (James 1:14–15).

After years of going through this cycle, I finally settled down some when I met my wife. I did not stop everything however. I still engaged in some activities but had better control on others, though I certainly would not even imply complete control. A few years later, we had our first child named Joseph. Two years later, we had Jessica. After the birth of our children, my thoughts ran toward their upbringing, and my prayers to return to God became more frequent and intense.

My prayers to God came more often and were more heartfelt because I recognized my own habitually sinful and fallen person. I also knew because of my fallen state that I could not raise my children, whom I loved dearly, with a proper Christian foundation and influence. Actions tend to speak louder than words, and even if I told them one thing, when I then went and did another, the message would be communicated loud and clear, but it would be the wrong message. This time, after Jessica's birth, unlike in the past, I did more than just pray. This time, around February of 2007, I took action by actually looking for a church for the first time in almost twenty years.

I sought a church because I wanted my children to be raised with a strong Christian foundation, and I knew I was not capable to give them that foundation. Besides, even if I could, I knew it would not be long till they reached that age when their mother and I would be rather obsolete. We would be the uncool parents who did not know anything; we would be technologically and socially inept from their view, and our influence would be minimal. Instead, it would be their peer group, social and/or other media, and other factors that would be their main influence. I wanted my children to have a Christian foundation and Christian peers who could be there to assist them when many of life's challenges came along and talking to their parents would be embarrassing. Teens start thinking they know what life is about. To them adults are old and out of touch even though the parents may have faced many of the problems kids face today. The ease of access to sinful propaganda and opportunities is much more prolific today, and many adults may not realize just how accessible it has become, and how subtly, and increasingly the film industry and other media are influencing them as well as us. When our parents allowed one moral flaw to enter their lives, such as profanity on television, and then we subsequently in turn concede to one little infraction of our morals which occurs through the media or some such area, and we just shrug our shoulders in a seemingly help-less apathy, we have begun to compromise our values and have fallen down a slippery slope. That compromise affected our parents, affects us, and will subsequently affect our children, and as we continue to make further and further concessions within those areas, eventually those concessions become acceptable and we do not even recognize we have slipped because they are our new normal. It is especially hard to fight this propaganda, considering the amount of new technolo-gies that allow almost unrestricted access almost anytime and any-where. Drugs, sex, gangs, and other worldly snares often hyped up by various means would be out there waiting for my children, but there are much more subtle areas in which they would be influenced, and I hoped a Christian upbringing and their Christian peers, along with, of course, their own personal communion time with God, could help them overcome those challenges when faced by them.

Of course as adults we do have an understanding of many of the issues they are facing, and we have the experience of living through those issues or having observed other people dealing with them. If we are paying attention, we also recognize how Hollywood and society in general are changing our kids' perceptions. Some of the changes are for the good, but many are for worse. Our secular society, the news, the media, and other influences are often trying to influence how our children think and relate to the family and to others. As adults we have seen and been a part of successes and failures, but trying to give our wisdom and experience to our children and have them learn from us is often a huge effort in futility, especially when Hollywood subverts the role of the parents. I was confident that I would be a good father and be involved in my children's lives, but I was also certain that I would eventually drift into the realm of being "out of touch" and "uncool" or whatever the popular terminology is at that time, and the children's peers would become a major influence. I would try to raise my kid's right, but just how far and for how long would I be their influence? There is no doubt that they will have peers with secular values, but I wanted them to have peers with Christian values. During this effort to find a church, the challenge of the shooting would arise.

Initially when I began looking into churches in the early part of 2007, I went to several churches trying to find the right fit for my wife and children. After several months of looking at various ones, I finally found two that my wife and I were seriously considering. My family had gone to both several times over the last couple of months, and we were trying to choose our home church. A problem existed however with regard to my earlier prayers, which was that I was going to church for my children's sake and not my own. I was concerned about their welfare and not worried about myself because in my prideful and egotistical way of thinking, I already had my Christian beliefs no matter how weak and inaccurate they might be.

Although my heart was in the right place with regard to the children and trying to raise them with God, it was in the wrong place with regard to my own relationship with Him, and He was having no part of it. God was thinking way more thoroughly than I was.

Although it was my intention to raise my children in Christ, and in that effort He approved, it was my method that He disapproved. You see, God had a love for my children and their souls as much as He had a love for my soul, but my effort was flawed. Remember what I said about "actions speak louder than words"? Though I was going to church, I was going for my children's sake and not my own, and that was another disaster in the making. By not going to church for myself, I would just be going through the motions, and it would not be long till my zeal waned. Not only would I likely not live a Christian example to my children, but before long, we might stop going to church altogether, or maybe I would drop the kids off but not attend myself—or any number of scenarios bent for failure. I would be sending mixed signals, and those mixed signals would harm my children's growth in Christ, and my own relationship with Him would be no better. He was not going to allow that, and the correct path had to be established.

It was in the beginning of October 2007 when we were seriously trying to settle on our church selection. It would be coincidently, or maybe not, October 17, 2007, when I would be shot; and God would use that shooting to answer those prayers I had been praying both for my benefit as well as my kids'. God was answering in a manner completely unexpected, but I would eventually understand why.

As I reflected on this and the timing of the shooting, that it was just as we were seriously making a church decision, it is my opinion that like in the book of Job, Satan was making a bet with God and was trying to stop me from going to church and possibly getting myself back on the right track with God. You see, when we are apathetic or unresponsive to God's leadings, that apathetic attitude is just fine with Satan. He will still attack and create problems, but probably not too vigorously because we are already complacent and it would be easy for him to influence us, but when we start moving in God's direction, his attacks will intensify because he will see our movement toward God and recognize he is losing control of us, and his attacks are attempts to regain that control. We should hopefully recognize in advance that these attacks will occur when we decide to pursue God so we can seek the strength and protection from God which only He can provide in order to withstand them. Unfortunately most, because they are not already close to God, will not be aware of and braced for these attacks, but God knows your heart's desire and knows how to bring that desire to fruition. Some denominations believe in what some term as "once saved, always saved" while others do not, and the argument rages with both sides quoting scripture to support their understanding and view. But Peter in 1 Peter 5:8 says, "Be of sober spirit, be on the alert. Your adversary, the devil, prowls around like a roaring lion, seeking someone to devour" and Peter, shortly after confessing Jesus as the Christ was told, "Satan has demanded permission to sift you like wheat" (Luke 22:1). Peter was "sifted" by his fear and subsequent denial of Christ during His trial just before the crucifixion and the subsequent guilt he felt afterwards. But Peter, though he felt immense guilt and probably felt he was unworthy of Christ due to his denial of Him, later, upon being confronted by Jesus after His resurrection, came back stronger than ever. After my event and being confronted by God, I tend to believe in the doctrine of "once saved, always saved," though I prefer the reference of a friend of mine named Weldon, which he calls the "eternal security of the believer" because "once saved, always saved" lends itself to much abuse and misunderstanding. I believe in "the eternal security of the believer" because I now see how God has worked to get my life back in line with Him just as He did with Peter. Although a true believer may be drawn off the right course for a while, just as I was, they will eventually make a course correction when confronted with the reality of their lives, even if it means hitting rock bottom first. God knows all things and, as such, knows if a person is sincere or not and whether they will repent or not. Likely one factor involved is the sincerity of heart at the time of the profession of faith as to whether one is actually saved or not, but if it was sincere, Christ has entered the life, and He will save it. Even if the profession was less than sincere, God may work to cause the insincere professor to become sincere and repent at a future time. Though being saved, having our life secured in Christ, and reestablishing our communal relationship with God by Christ's redemptive work on the cross is the emphasis of our profession of faith, that eternal security from condemnation does not mean Satan could not hinder or alter our eternal standings. The Bible speaks of gaining various crowns by our conduct and actions in this life. If Satan could disrupt my spiritual relationship with Christ, he can make me pay an eternal cost even if I would not lose salvation itself. As the apostle Paul talked about 1 Corinthians 3:13–15, each person's work will become manifest; and if their work or deeds were not good, "he will suffer loss, though he himself will be saved, but only as through fire." With this realization, that I am eternally secure and nothing can forfeit that but my eternal life can still be impacted by my thoughts and actions in this life, I have personally decided to walk the remainder of my life as if I could fall from grace. I do not mean to live in fear of damnation, but to be humble in heart, being contrite for my sin, and wanting to maintain as reverent a heart and mind-set toward God as I can in order to avoid the complacency the "once saved, always saved" doctrine can breed in new, weak, or apathetic Christians, of whom I once was.

Having the assumption that my salvation is eternally secure, I had to move to the next scenario, which was even more likely. That scenario was that Satan was trying to stop me from getting my children into a relationship with God by preventing me from raising them in the church and with Christian principles. After all, theirs were two young uncommitted souls. How would he stop me, you ask? It would be easy; he would put me into such a state physically and emotionally that I would not or could not pursue God. I say "would not" because of God giving me free will, and if I became angry with Him, I could still choose not to pursue Him. I say "could not" because in my physical state it could be difficult for me to go or it would be easy to make excuses for not getting ready and go to church. I mean, how many able-bodied people do not make it to church regularly much less someone who has definite physical challenges?

I had considered that Satan was trying to kill me to stop me, but upon reading the scriptures, I have found that would be a simplistic and a mostly inaccurate statement. Satan might have personally wanted to kill me, but the fact is he was not *allowed* to because God would not let him. Satan's power of death is incumbent on God's will and permission. However, though God would not allow him to kill me, He would allow him to severely afflict me. God had purposes in allowing that affliction, and those purposes would be at the very least, God's discipline of His errant child in order to gain repentance and cause a course correction, as well as His wrath against sin itself. He may have had other purposes in mind as well. As the apostle Paul also told the Corinthian church regarding a wayward professor of Christ, "You are to deliver this man to Satan for the destruction of his flesh, so that his spirit may be saved in the day of the Lord" (1 Corinthians 5:5). However, prior to my affliction, God also took the time to make some arrangements in order to facilitate my survival.

Some people might think I am overreacting when moving toward a religious response due to my near-death experience. I am not sure how to respond to that claim but to state unequivocally that I do not feel I am over reacting, but instead, *properly responding* in the manner I should have from the beginning. Upon being confronted with my sinfulness, I now have a solid understanding of my need for Christ and His atoning sacrifice; and as a result, I have an utterly grateful response. I have simply seen the truth and have become zealous for God as compared to being cold before. But God's working on me through this shooting was only beginning.

SUSAN'S ORDEAL

I HAD NEVER GATHERED HOW truly strong a person my wife was until this incident and then those which would follow. After my shooting, the future for Susan as presented to her became rather hard, very depressing, and very bleak. All of a sudden, life had taken an arduous and burdensome turn. We went from a full, complete, and wonderful life with two beautiful children to a suddenly questionable future with promises of hardship. Instantly and without warning Susan had to take on the full responsibility of running the household, raising the children, working her job, and tending to an invalid husband. The dreams that we had, the bright future that was planned had abruptly come to a screeching halt. God tells us in James 4:14–15 to live for and depend on Him and not to plan too far in advance because we do not know what the future holds, and we certainly were not expecting anything such as this.

For over two months, Susan was at the hospital every day all day. While I was at Methodist Central, they had a hotel attached to the hospital where she stayed at night in order to be close, and then later she would still stay all day at Zale Lipshy and go home to sleep but return early in the morning. I was still in a lot of pain and so was medicated with morphine. I would slip in an out of consciousness, but during the day when I would become alert, I would always see Susan there watching over me. During the first month of my hospitalization the children were being kept by a friend named Barbara

Ahlmen, who had previously been their daycare sitter. She gladly volunteered to keep the children while Susan kept vigil.

In addition to the stress of the shooting and her constant vigil, there were events occurring that I had no knowledge of and issues that needed to be dealt with that I was completely unaware of. I would later learn that from the time of my shooting on October 17 till the end of the year, it would be a very stressful period for my wife, but I had no idea how stressful. She would not tell me the things she was facing because she did not want to worry me, but even if she had told me, I was in no condition to respond, give advice, or potentially even able to conceive or understand.

At the time I was shot, even though we were married, we had maintained separate checking accounts and bills. She handled her business, and I handled mine. Suddenly she was confronted with trying to organize all our bills, and she had to jump through several hoops to finally consolidate our accounts so she could have access to mine in order to pay all the bills and other outgoing expenses. We had never talked about our finances, which is something I now highly recommend all married couples do. I also did not have a will or power of attorney, so had I died, my finances and potentially portions of the homestead as well as other issues could have been in question. It is not fun to contemplate dying, so it is not something a lot of people give consideration to, but it has proven to be a very important issue. Discussing potential events such as these while making the necessary preparations by planning ahead are things that would make dealing with unexpected situations like this considerably easier on the spouse. We all think it will never happen to us, but unfortunately *never* sometimes happens, and it would be wise to be prepared for it.

It was in December that the stress really pounced on Susan besides my just being shot, having to complete the necessary paperwork for making medical decisions, and handling our financial matters. I had my grandfather living with us at the time of the shooting and was very close to him. After I got shot, Susan tried to keep taking care of him along with everything else she was faced with. Two friends of hers, Kim Vanderbean and Laura Doyle, voluntarily came to the house every day and took care of the animals and my granddad while she stayed at the hospital with me. Susan tried to hire a home health aide to look after my grandfather, but he was set in his ways and wanted no part of them. With all that was going on, she simply could not take care of him and eventually had to consider putting him in a retirement home for his own well-being. This caused her a great deal of stress because she knew how I felt about him and knew I had promised my grandmother on her deathbed that I would look after him. She also knew in his mind-set that he would not like a retirement home at all. She was afraid I would be upset with whatever she did. Fortunately, upon becoming aware of the situation, my Uncle Don and Aunt Mary volunteered to take him in. My grandfather had always appreciated and gotten along with them, so I cannot express how very grateful I am to them for taking him into their home.

Also unknown to me at the time was that my infant daughter Jessica had suffered a seizure one day while at the daycare. As usual, Susan was with me that day when the daycare called her and told her our daughter had suffered a seizure and informed her she was being transported to Children's Hospital by ambulance. Talk about stress! At first the cause of the seizure was unknown, but it was later identified as having been caused by a fever associated with an earache. Jessica later had to have tubes put in her ears due to her constantly getting earaches because of her sinus problems. This might not seem like a big deal, and maybe it was not in reality, but I remember Susan and I had to watch our daughter be put to sleep once for an examination, and it was one of the hardest things we had ever endured as we watched her be put to sleep and looking lifeless. This time Jessica would have to be put to sleep again for the tubes to be put in, and Susan would have to watch it alone. I know it was hard on her. Then on December 13, her mother passed away unexpectedly, and that event was quickly followed on December 16 with her horse—which she had since she was age eighteen—passing away. The end of the year of 2007 was not good to my wife. How she endured all this stress especially in such a close time frame, I will never know. She is truly an amazing woman and a source of strength and motivation for me. I love her with all my heart.

ANSWERED PRAYER

AFTER THE REVELATION IN THE hospital and my cry of repentance and for forgiveness, I could only wait for God's response. I had finally awakened back to God and had a new heart for Him. I had repented of my sins and begged for His merciful forgiveness. I was still bedbound and unable to move, but now it did not seem to matter as much because I actually felt at peace with God. Although my prayer of repentance and asking for forgiveness was I think God's key purpose in this shooting, upon obtaining my repentance, He would eventually, out of His goodness, provide many blessings and mercies in response to that repentance. Although my prayer and change of heart was important to God, He owed me nothing with regard to it, and I will not by any means take credit for the good that God would bestow. It is a fact that at the beginning of this when the shooting first happened, and I was still incoherent, there were many prayers being made by many people and many churches, even as I was to find out some from other countries. The Bible also shows God will respond to a situation if people will pray to Him where otherwise the lack of petitions and prayers by Christians would result in His inaction. There is no doubt in my mind that those prayers were heard because God has always put credence in the prayers of others for others. I therefore am also certain a large part of my outcome was due to those prayers of the righteous lifting me up to God. As the Bible says in James 5:16, The effective prayer of a righteous man can accomplish much (NASB). Because many people stood the gap and prayed for several weeks, I credit them for my soon-to-be revealed condition as a direct result of their prayers and His faithfully rewarding their petitions.

Due to my lack of mobility, it was the routine of the hospital physical therapists to come in and stretch and bend my legs in order to prevent my muscles and leg joints like the hips and knees from basically freezing or locking up and becoming unbendable when I would eventually be transferred to a wheelchair at some point, and it was during this time, a short time after the revelation and my repentance, that God's answer to the prayers would be revealed.

It was another routine morning when physical therapist Kim Wimberly came into my room to begin stretching my legs as she had done regularly for the past few weeks. This time however as she began stretching my leg, something would happen. On this day as she was bending my right leg, suddenly my thigh twitched. That twitch was not supposed to happen according to my diagnosis. All my nerve signals had been interrupted from my neck down, and that twitch was not supposed to occur. Upon seeing my thigh twitch, Kim put my leg down quickly then speedily rushed out of the room without even touching the other leg. She quickly rounded up Dr. Karen Kowalske, my physical therapy doctor, who responded by coming in and conducting a brief exam. Although I did not hear it myself, it is reported that she was beaming as she announced, "He is going to walk out of here."

God had responded to my prayers as well as the prayers of others yet again. His response in allowing my leg to twitch was a subtle indication that He was answering. It was also a positive proof to me, in my opinion, that God in His faithfulness had forgiven my sins because of my repentance, and He was giving me another chance in life. It was at this point, because of that thigh twitch, that my physical therapy would really begin. Once my legs showed signs of nerve connection, there was new hope for me, and Dr. Kowalske was going to pursue that hope with a vengeance. I was now going to be moved to a wheelchair, taken to the therapy gym, and tested and exercised every way possible in order to stimulate and connect muscle memory with whatever nerves were reconnecting.

Initially I had been outfitted with a power chair, which could be operated with a chin controller, but my progress in recovery of physical abilities in my upper extremities, especially my right arm and hand, soon negated the need for chin control, and I moved to a left hand controller so my right hand would be free for use since it was more functional. It was a good thing I was able to move from the chin controller because I was a terrible chin driver. Instead of concentrating on where I was going, I would turn my head to look at something and, by doing so, would cause a major change in course of the wheelchair and veer off my path. I think my wife and those assigned to me were thrilled to see me change control methods.

Unfortunately for me, during my bedbound time, I had developed a level 4 decubitus wound, a pressure sore that was the highest level, right on the rear tailbone area. The sore was about the size of a half dollar going all the way to the bone and was a constant and immensely painful irritant that impeded my therapy. In fact, when all things are considered, all the pain I had for various reasons, the pressure sore was the worst part of my entire hospital experience.

Once the therapy had started, I was transferred to a veteran physical therapist named Cheryl Oliver. Cheryl was a wonderful and kind person with a great sense of humor and loaded with patience, and we hit it off immediately. Initially in the beginning stages, I was taught to transfer to a therapy mat where I was stretched and then asked to preform various exercises on the mat. The pressure sore was so painful it severely impaired many exercises while on the mat, and so Cheryl had to work around it with optional exercises. Eventually I would graduate from the mat to a Standing Frame, where I was required to build up my supported standing strength to at least twenty minutes.

Shortly after I could stand in the Standing Frame for twenty minutes or longer, I graduated again and was placed in a LiteGait walker. Basically I would be suspended vertically in a harness with my feet touching the floor from a rolling device similar to a Hoyer lift but different. I would be asked to try to take steps as the dolly rolled. For a while Cheryl and some other therapist would have to move my legs for each step while an aide pulled the dolly forward; and someone else, often my wife, would follow with a wheelchair in case I had to sit down. After a few sessions on the LiteGait walker, my nerves in my leg muscles finally connected and started to step on their own. Very slowly, very ugly, but they began to move without aid. As those connections continued to improve and strengthen over the next few weeks, the harness that suspended me was lowered more and more until I was supporting a substantial part of my own weight.

I loved the days when we used the LiteGait walker because it gave me my first sense of a recovery since I could move my own legs some. Initially I think about 75 percent or more of my weight was supported by a harness, and I could only walk about fifty feet or so before I was exhausted. Later they lowered the harness so that I was supporting about 50 percent or more of my own weight, and eventually I could walk about eight hundred feet while doing so. Again the worst part of it was my pressure sore because the harness would rub directly on it, and the pain would be barely tolerable. Substantial efforts had to be made to cushion or try to alleviate the pressure, which the harness exerted on the sore. Even with all those efforts, the sore still managed to make its presence known. I would eventually have to sit not because I was tired but because I could no longer take the pain. I hated that pressure sore.

I was equipped with a "wound vac" for several months because of the sore and its treatment, and I noticed that several other patients also had the same vac. I asked a nurse about this and told her my impression about this sore was it had occurred because I had not been rotated every two hours as was recommended medically. These rotations were supposed to occur even at night. After the sore developed, besides the wound vacuum, I was also equipped with a special air mattress that had some type of rotation device that moved me and shifted my weight every ten minutes. This mattress was provided in order to prevent any other sores from developing and to try to keep the sore I had from worsening as well as to facilitate its healing. I was curious why I had not been provided with the mattress before the wound developed since it was obvious I could not rotate myself, and possibly due to staffing shortages or other events, I was not being regularly turned by the hospital personnel?

The response to my question was rather long and more complicated than I expected. I was told there were several ways the sore might have been initiated, which would have nothing to do with the rotation issue. It might have started at the initial time of injury when I fell and the loss of a substantial amount of blood. It might have started due to extreme blood loss and pressure being located on that less meaty area for an extended period of time due to being on a surgery table for several hours. Then of course there was potentially the inadequacy of the rotation.

Although the other possibilities were viable theories considering my injury, in my mind, the sore occurred because of or at least graduated to its level of severity due to lack of timely rotation. The sore probably began at the first hospital with it manifesting itself at the second hospital. Regardless, my question was why patients who were obviously incapable of turning themselves were not provided with these mattresses upon their admission in order to prevent the sores from occurring? The answer given was that most insurance companies refuse to pay for an air mattress or other preventive treatments until the sore manifests. Insurance companies are going to balk at paying the cost of the air mattresses if the medical need is not a necessity and assume or point the finger at the hospitals, accusing them of not having adequate staffing for the necessary rotations to occur in order to prevent them.

Hospitals, on the other hand, like any other business, try to function at their least operating expense, and that often means the staffing regularly falls short for various reasons or the staff become overtaxed due to unexpected events. Either way, the hospital staff is therefore generally overworked. As a result of shortages, they tend to shave routine duties in order to perform more immediately necessary tasks. The turning rotations then suffer by not occurring with frequency, if at all, and the insurance companies wind up paying probably ten times as much when the sore does develop. This does not take into consideration the other factors entirely outside the rotation issue that could cause a sore to develop.

Like everything else, it truly all boils down to money. I am not sure of the cost of these mattresses on a per-day or monthly rental, but I can only imagine insurance companies would save money in the long run by preventing the sores from occurring rather than pay the expenses that are incurred for their treatment after they manifest themselves. As the old saying goes, "An ounce of prevention is worth a pound of cure."

I can attest, these sores, along with being potentially deadly, can be very painful, and mine severely hampered my therapy. Other than fighting the pressure sore, which was the most painful part of being in the hospital, there was a mass of physical and occupational therapy. Even though the therapy was hard and very challenging, I rather enjoyed it. I was only given therapy for a couple of hours per day during the week with less than that on Saturday and none on Sunday. The weekends were the hardest for me because I wanted to be in therapy.

During the week, after my therapy time was completed, I was allowed to stay in the gym and exercise as long as therapists were around, and I did so daily. But on the weekends, I was not allowed to go to the gym and do any exercises by myself, and I was relegated to waiting for Monday to get back to business.

While I was at the hospital, there was another patient named Chase Frost, who was a volunteer firefighter out of Pennsylvania. He had been trapped by a cave-in while fighting a building fire and sustained third-degree burns over most his body. The burns were so bad he actually lost an arm and a leg. Chase had the same "fight and overcome" mentality that I had. He would also stay longer after his therapy sessions and continue to work out to get stronger and overcome his challenges. Chase and I fed off each other's determination to overcome our obstacles and became friends and brothers through our afflictions.

After I had started walking relatively well in the LiteGait walker, and I could support my weight for about thirty minutes in a Standing Frame, I was moved to the parallel bars where I could support my weight with my arms only and begin to learn to walk independently supporting my entire weight on my own. Eventually I would be able to use a walker to walk, and just as Dr. Kowalske predicted, I did indeed walk out of the hospital using my walker. I made a point of it. Even though by hospital regulations I had to be wheeled out in a wheelchair, once I was at the door, I insisted on walking out of the hospital with my walker the short distance from the door to my wife's truck. God had answered my prayers again as well as those of many others in a wonderful way, a way that was totally unpredicted, beyond expectations, and far more than I deserved."

DEPRESSION AND GRIEF

DURING THE INITIAL RECOVERY IN the first two or three months, I had little understanding of the actual extent of my injuries, but much less the effects those injuries would have beyond physical limitations. As I continued to recover, I continued to have an unrealistic hope. I knew I would never be the man I once was physically, but I envisioned more than I should have. I am not sure I completely grasp the totality even now, though I have come to understand certain aspects and accept certain realities.

Since there were the early signs of unexpected movement, which presented hope and promise, I had a mind bent on recovering. I had been injured before, though not to this extent, and recovered, so the early signs of improvement beyond the initial expectations gave me the mind-set that I could make a substantial recovery if I just tried and worked hard enough. That attitude may classify as delusional or absurd and unreasonable, but I had never faced or experienced an injury of this magnitude nor intimately been around people who had. I had successfully overcome many obstacles and traumas through hard work and perseverance and felt I could do the same with this. I was unwilling to accept defeat without at least going to war with my adversary, and even if I were to lose, not one inch of ground would be given up without a fight. This was the attitude I had in life toward any snag or hurdle I had faced. I do not think I was intentionally trying to avoid acceptance of the reality of the injuries, but I just did not comprehend the extent of them. I was not familiar with the extreme intricacies in which God had made our bodies, but upon seeing function of muscle twitches, which was not expected, and the shock of surprise by the hospital staff, I felt that my injuries could be beat.

The first few months were difficult to say the least, not only because of my physical injury but also the psychological aspect of having to be dependent on everyone for everything and the humility of certain situations such as the toileting issues; but for the most part, I was making notable progress in my recovery almost daily, and my attitude remained high. Although I had lost substantial weight, there were no mirrors in which I could casually view myself with, and so mentally I pictured myself the same physically. Having a normal picture of me physically in my mind also masked the extent of my trauma. Albeit, even though I had a positive attitude and was making physical progress in my recovery, there were times I would appear to suffer a setback. Those setbacks revolved around therapy by not being able to do something or at least not to the level I had just done it the week before, and this would cause me to become depressed and put me in a funk for a few days.

One day while I was feeling very down about myself, a therapist explained that what I was experiencing was a normal cycle. It was an ebb and flow of the body cycle, sort of like the ocean tides, that everybody goes through. For me, in my current situation, those cycles were just more noticeable to me since I was so weak and was trying to recover from such a severe injury. I thought about this and realized it had happened almost monthly when I was healthy, but I had never paid attention. I had been athletic and exercised since I was a young boy, and I recalled even prior to this shooting that I had very good days, average days, and also some bad days in the gym. There were days when I did not even feel like being at the gym and my level of performance was well below par.

As I understood this, I reflected that after a week where I experienced poor performance in my recovery efforts, the next week I usually came back much stronger and with additional improvement. Realizing that performance was cyclical for everyone, I no longer got depressed after a bad couple of days. The bad days would still frustrate me, but I no longer let the depression take over; instead, I began to look forward to the improvement I was expecting the next week would reveal.

During the initial rehabilitation period of eight and a half months, and even for about two years afterward, I maintained a pretty positive attitude about continuing to improve. For about two years after my release, even though progress had slowed, I was still making progress. But soon after this, things changed. After about two years, even after I managed to return to work in an office assignment and in a light duty capacity for a period of time, I seemed to have peaked in my recovery. That bothered me, but worse than that, I actually started to have a decline for some undetermined reason. This was disturbing to say the least, but I still tried to remain positive in my outlook. After all, I was still alive and was still functioning physically at a level that had been unexpected. I considered myself very blessed by the mercy God had extended to me to be alive and the grace He had given me to be functioning at my level. But over time, slowly, I began to see even further physical loss in ability. When my physical abilities started waning, though I continued to exercise, my mind lost its focus from recovering physically, and I then began to recognize and contemplate the losses in life I had sustained or felt I had sustained as a result of my disability. These losses in life were not only what I once could do, the loss of the future of things I had planned to do, but included losses in areas I had not expected as well.

Earlier I had stated that God had revealed at least part of the reason I had suffered my injuries. It was upon receiving that revelation that I repented, and after repenting, He had allowed me to recover far beyond expectations. I was passionately grateful for God's hand in my incident and am still so today. I cannot begin to explain the awe and feeling of thanksgiving I have. With all my losses considered and being weighed, in comparison to my spiritual renewal, I can and do still say I am very grateful for God's chastising discipline and the grace He has provided through it, both spiritually and physically. Also because of the renewed and vastly improved spiritual relationship with Him, I have that "peace that surpasses understanding," which the Bible talks about with regard to my condition. My chastisement at the price of my disability may seem harsh, but compared to the positive effect it has had upon me spiritually, I found it a very acceptable trade. However, that being said, for discipline to be discipline, there must be negative aspects. If being a quadriplegic in trade for a restored relationship with God was acceptable and there were no regrets, then that discipline might no longer necessarily be considered discipline. Does that make sense? There is not discipline/chastisement without there being grief or remorse attached with it. If you spank a child for bad behavior but they like being spanked, did they learn anything?

Initially I did not consider myself to be having any grief. I really had no recognition or understanding of grief other than mourning over someone's death, and my exposure to personal grief was very limited even in that aspect. But even while still in the hospital, in addition to the bouts of depression, which I was attributing to the regression of performance issues, I would also have sudden fits of anger at times, and those outbursts would come over relatively minor issues rather than major ones. Events that were quite intense and which should displease me, I would take calmly, then in contrast become angry over something rather miniscule. Other times I would break down and sob like a baby while not really understanding why. Many times those crying fits occurred when my wife was leaving for the evening after visiting, but not always. I was confused to say the least.

It was not until I had started reflecting back on my time in the hospital and taking note of my losses that I began to understand. The grief process had begun without me, and I was oblivious to it. As I looked back, I began to see the losses that I was subconsciously feeling even back then, though consciously I was still in denial. I think the counselors would refer to that as grief suppression.

The first thing I became aware of once I gained consciousness and was cognizant of my surroundings was being helpless. Not just a little, but totally. I could not move anything below my waist and had very limited function between my waist and neck. I could move my arms some but had no use of my left hand an extremely limited use of my right hand. I could not eat or drink through my mouth nor could I even go to the bathroom to take care of business. I could not get out of bed and walk to the bathroom, and worse, either, as initially, I had to evacuate in the bed and then be cleaned up or, later, as I progressed, someone had to take me to the bathroom and prepare me for business. Everything had to be done to and for me or by some alternate means. I am sure this would bother almost anyone, or maybe for some it would not really be a problem, but it was huge for me. All my adult life I had been in control. My parents had raised me to be self-sufficient and not to need or more importantly not to depend on anyone. I had taken that lesson to heart at a young age and had not let anyone have any control in any aspect of my life unless I granted them some access. Even then, what I granted was limited. I would not let others do me favors because I did not want to feel obligated to them. I even kept those I considered my closest friends at a safe distance. Now, suddenly, I needed to depend on everyone for everything. This dependency was not just isolated to friends and family but complete strangers also. This was a very difficult transition for me to handle, and it felt very humiliating.

Although this was occurring, I still did not recognize it as a loss because I had not resolved myself to the situation. I still felt this was a short-term inconvenience albeit an extended one because I felt I would get better and would once again be independent and self-reliant again. Regardless, it was disturbing to me, and it was very difficult to accept. In tow with this helplessness was the sense of being out of control and *fear*. Being a police officer, I looked at everything and everyone with a suspicious eye because I saw the underbelly of society in even those regarded as "respectable." Because I saw so many negative aspects of society as a whole, I was already a little paranoid and very guarded, but now the paranoia seemed to run amok on its own without even a slight leash. Where before my injury my suspicious mind was tempered with a balance of reality, now I seemed to have no balance. Mentally I was still very guarded and eyed any stranger, even hospital staff, with suspicion, but I had nothing balancing my paranoia. Because of my injury and the way in which it occurred, I was possibly suffering from some type of psychosis. Everyone was suspicious and a threat, but in my condition, I could not protect myself. Even worse, I had always, probably like most men, considered myself the protector of my family. Suddenly I could not only not protect myself, but I could not protect them either, and as they did something simple like leave the hospital to go home, I would have a tremendous sense of fear and worry. I would be questioning if they would get home safely, if Susan would be hurt at work next or some other paranoid concoctions that brought tremendous uneasiness and feelings of fear.

At night I would not be able to sleep and, especially after a bad day in rehab, I would be thinking about the wife and kids and questioning my self-worth. I would question if in a sense I would have been better off dead for my family's sake. I questioned if I could be a husband with regard to all that entails or if I could truly be a father to my kids. Could I teach them or interact with them due to my physical limitations? What was my future? How could I be a provider? It seemed there was no end to the questions of what and how. All those questions basically led to my concern of how I could be anything other than a burden to those I loved.

I knew of course that I was not better off dead because if I had died, I would have had a lot of explaining to do to God for my behavior and not much to show with regards to good works (Ephesians 2:10). God had mercy on me by not calling in my life and giving me an opportunity to repent and to start doing right, but I did seriously question my self-worth and value to my family. But it was not until I had been out of the hospital for a year or so that I began to get a sense of what were in some ways my more substantial and real losses rather than my imaginary ones.

Up to this point, my main focus had been on recovery; and during this time, I was reading the Bible to learn about the God I had forgotten, and in fact, the one I had never really known or understood. But after about two years, my recovery appeared to have peaked and I began to see where I would likely remain for the next several years until old age, and other things would start to creep in to cause further decline. It was at this time that I truly began to experience what I had lost and the grief associated with it.

Though I was experiencing grief, as I said, I did not recognize it as grief at the time. I was getting short-tempered and was experiencing fits of anger over some minor issues. I would seem calm over things most people would get excited about but would fire off in a tantrum over something little. It was insane. I was moody and irritable, but I did not fully understand why. Often I related some of it to the constant pain I was in. The pain was not so severe that it was intolerable or ceased my general ability to function in what I had regained, but it was always present, constant and irritating. The pain would even grow worse the longer I had to sit in the chair without some type of stretching. Eventually the irritation from the pain would spill over to my family with my exhibiting a terse and unpleasant attitude. But that attitude would surface at other times even unrelated to pain. There was something more that was bothering me, and it crept in slowly and quietly.

On a general level, I had noticed things that were occurring even in the hospital. When I was with other able-bodied adults, someone would walk up and begin asking questions *about* me to other able-bodied people rather than *to* me, like, "How is he doing? How is his therapy?" and other questions, while I was right there in front of them. They would talk like I was not there and often not even look at me. Eventually my wife caught on to the same thing, and after talking, we would half-heartedly laugh about it. She finally had to tell people to talk to me because I was right there.

Just like it seemed I was being ignored in the hospital, I noticed the same thing occurred in society. For example, normally when a family goes out to a restaurant, toward the end of the meal, the wait-staff would bring the check and generally place it by the man or give it directly to him. I know things are changing some, but it was always that way when I was able-bodied. Now when we go to restaurants, they give it to my wife nine times out of ten or place it in the middle on the table at best. It seemed to me I had lost my place in society just by being crippled. For some reason, people seem to have the impression if you are physically handicap, then you must be mentally also. At retail stores or other public places where a crowd was located, I would roll up to the counter to order something only to have the employee acknowledge other people around or behind me and act as if they did not even see me. They would not even acknowledge my presence initially. I have come to suspect that society as a general rule is somewhat uncomfortable with the disabled because it is not itself familiar with disability. Able-bodied people, it would seem, somehow feel those whose handicap can be seen are not "normal," or they think they might somehow catch a disability germ. It was very bewildering and slightly humorous at times, but it was also subtly irritating, and though I am sure it was unintentional, I felt it as somewhat demeaning. The public response to my disability was bothersome, but I attributed it simply to people's fear of the unknown and discomfort around that unknown.

In the meantime, though, for a short time, prior to my downturn, I had returned to work. I was proud of being a police officer, and it was the only thing I had really ever wanted to be. One of my biggest ambitions in working toward recovery was actually to return to duty. But what I had failed to remember was I had always been a street officer even during my years as a homicide detective and other investigative assignments. As a detective I would still spend as much time in the streets investigating leads as I would in the office. When I promoted out of Homicide and went back to patrol as a sergeant, I loved being back on the street with my troops and would often go out and bring in as much activity as they did. I felt my role was to lead by example, and I never once asked my troops to do something I would not do. Eventually I promoted again to lieutenant, and I continued in that style of leadership. Hence, how I managed to be in the position to be shot on a warrant. Not that it mattered; if God was going to get my attention, He was going to get it one way or another. But this was His way, He had foreseen the shooting event and had made the necessary arrangements for when it happened.

Upon returning to work, I was placed as a supervisor over an investigative assignment at the South Central Property Crimes Unit, which handled burglary and theft cases among other things. Though I liked investigations, I unfortunately found I could not get out on the street. I had to sit back and watch others do the work while I just read reports and supervised their activity. I would get my mandatory supervisory work done within a couple of hours and then be bored out of my mind. I had to attend meetings, which were difficult for me due to my hearing limitations, and I also discovered there were other communication issues. At my rank, a big part of my job was communication. Because communication was so important, it was not long before I did not feel I could give the assignment the attention and service it needed. I felt I had become a weak link in the chain. I also found that my heart was only consoled through my reading the Bible and meditating on scripture. Police work, though still a job I loved and desired, no longer held the importance it did, especially since I could not go on the street and actually be hands-on. That being the case, I elected to retire only a few months after I had returned to work so some other able-bodied sergeant could make rank and his career could move forward in my place.

Though I elected to retire because I could not be on the street anymore, I still loved being a police officer. As I said, part of what motivated me while in the hospital was my goal was to get back to work, but I just did not realize how the job would change for me. Nor did I realize the effect retirement would have. A large part of my identity was being a cop, and when I left, I felt I was leaving a part of myself behind. Part of my identity, so to speak, was gone. My career had ended prematurely and was going to be sorely missed. There are still times I miss the job and wished I had taken a voluntary demotion and maybe worked on leads for other homicide detectives or something else where there were no mandatory meetings or other communication issues, just good old crime fighting. But that was just fantasy thinking; the reality between my desire and my limitations regarding my ability was that I could simply no longer do the job. Yes, I could have done some investigative work making links between leads, but unfortunately because of physical limitations and needs, I would have had to have the assistance of an aide throughout the day, and that was not realistic. I still miss the job, and this was one of my first noticeable losses that I considered big.

Another loss that snuck up on me was the subtle shift in my family role. At least it was a perception I felt. I was still a husband and father, but it appeared I was no longer the "leader" of my family, and I felt that many decisions were being made without regard for my input. For a while I had accepted my role change due to the injury and necessary recovery time. I had accepted stepping back for a while because recovery was my focus, but unfortunately the shift in my family role, instead of being temporary, seemingly became permanent. Eventually, though still with my limitations, I was ready to step back into the role as "man of the house" and family leader. I felt instead, however, that at least certain aspects of that role had subtly disappeared. I had been dependent too long, and my wife had been handling the household responsibilities for that whole extended period of time. The restoration of the old roles as I perceived they should be was not going to happen, at least not easily. I was also looking at the way I thought things should be in my mind under the old course of how things used to be, and I was not looking at the present-day reality of my new circumstances. That is, there were certain things at least physically that I just could not do. It was also understandable that even if I could do everything, the shift would not come quickly or easily without testing the waters so to speak. The reinstatement of my role would have to come slowly as we tested what I could and could not reliably and consistently do. Part of this reinstatement was not just based on the evaluation of my abilities, but was also based upon Susan's need for comfort and security, her safe zone so to speak. Most of us go through life thinking bad things will not happen to us, and Susan and I pretty much had that mindset. Bad things might happen, but they would not be major. Because of this, when I got shot, Susan had been blindsided; but in the midst of all the turmoil at the initial time of the shooting, she had finally gotten everything under control. Police officers I think in particular feel a need to be in control. That is how we are trained, and for a while, things had become very awry and out of sorts for her. She had finally managed to gain the upper hand of the hugely encompassing mess, and she was now not comfortable with releasing it. Prior to my shooting, we had not made wills, consolidated bills or checking accounts, or kept each other informed about any other important paperwork. As a result, her hands were full with not only my situation at the hospital with filling out all the necessary forms that allowed her to legally make medical decisions for me but also trying to locate and consolidate everything financially in our private lives in order to pay bills in addition to caring for the children.

This loss of family role was not just mine, it was hers too. She had to take charge of both our responsibilities for over two years, and that itself took considerable time and effort, which literally stole her personal time. Though she had managed to get everything situated and felt safe having control, that additional role added stress to her life. But to gain control and then to voluntarily give it up, especially when you could find yourself personally affected, is a hard thing to do. Having that control and the responsibilities that come with it thus placed her in the role of family leader whether she wanted it or not. Her role she took as a supportive spouse allowing me to pursue my career and being a mother to our children as well as other dimensions were all changed—and in several ways negatively.

One way she was negatively affected was that she had to sacrifice a lot herself. She now had to put her career on hold again in order to take care of me as well as the children. Not only did potential future promotional opportunities have to be put on hold but desired transfers to other assignments as well. Promotion and transfers would most likely require evening or night hours or callback responsibilities. Upon giving up those opportunities as well as assuming additional responsibilities on the home front, Susan's life took a hard twist. It was a turn however that she was forced to accept, and now after finally accepting it and gaining the upper hand on it, to just relinquish it would be a very difficult process. She was affected in many ways probably as much as I was.

Along with my perceived loss in what I considered my primary role within the family and my identity as an officer, I also suffered additional losses or inconvenience of a mostly unobservable physical nature. Due to the type of injury I sustained, my body does less than just "not walk." A spinal cord injury affects the nerves below the point of injury. Muscles and potentially organs fail to work, or if they do get some nerve intervention, the muscles and organs do not work at fully functional levels. Muscles need the nerve messages to keep them stimulated and maintain mass. When these nerve signals get disrupted, the muscles typically lose the stimulation and sink into an atrophic state, not only losing function but also mass. Organs and organ functions are also affected, and that is why many spinal cord injury patients have to use respirators or other helps. Additionally, depending on how and which nerves are affected, the muscles and skin area lose sensation to touch and temperature. Functioning around hot and cold items can be hazardous to people with spinal cord injuries because they may not realize they have scalded themselves or frozen to some object until it is too late. Since the limbs do not have sensation of touch, unexpected drops, bumps or other such accidents can result in injuries that one might be totally unaware of until it manifests in some other way. One arm may be good, and strength and muscle mass are returning, but the other is skinny and weak, and the whole system is thrown off-balance. The legs, torso, etc. are all affected and begin to take physical changes. There are many behind-the-scene problems that develop that most people who see you are completely unaware of. I lost my chest and gained a belly; I lost function in my legs and torso as well as a good percentage of the left arm, all my left hand, and a percentage of my right. There are many physical aspects that are affected with these type injuries that most people never see and are even mostly unaware of, they just see a person in a chair. The fact is, if just being confined to a chair was the biggest issue, I could handle it with no problem, but I consider the related and not necessarily seen issues to be the real problem.

Sadly, as I said before, from my experiences, I perceive a person with a visibility disability seems to lose at least some degree of status and is no longer considered "normal." Because of their disability they are often overlooked or counted out by the able-bodied because people just assume you are unable to help or participate in almost any manner. With regard to people in particular who do not know you, they may appear to acknowledge your presence, but they also seem to look quickly away or even past you, not wanting to make eye contact. It is almost as if they are thinking, "Don't look. If they see us looking at them, they may try to talk to us." The truth is however that disability of all types does exist, and though it might be a smaller portion of the population, disability is a normal, it is just a normal many cannot fully comprehend or easily accept.

On a more personal level with people, family or friends or someone they knew pre-injury, the emotional feelings may still exist, and they look at you and speak to you in the same way they did before, and maybe even with a more caring attitude since you were almost lost to them, but often there can still be a variance from the normal of the pre-injury relationship. Because of that variance combined with the general lack of public interaction or bad reactions, you begin to question your own self-image. This was lightly addressed in the true story of Bethany Hamilton in the movie *Soul Surfer*. When Bethany had lost an arm to a shark attack, initially she was treated differently and with concern and caution by the public, as well as her own her own family members. She also began to develop a low self-esteem and wonder who could be truly accepting of her with only one arm or who would be open to accepting her as an equal for her natural abilities though visibly hampered. She refused to be catered to or treated differently and finally gained acceptance on her own accord. For single people who have sustained some sort of substantial and visible disability, it could be a daunting task to find close personal relationships due to the general public attitude which wants to reject what is perceived as not "normal". For me, already being married, I had my wife and knew she loved me, but I also knew there would be a new normal for us. The attractive, physically strong, fit, and interesting person I was before (I would like to think of myself as having been so anyway) no longer existed. Now I was broken and basically nonfunctional for many things. The variance in interaction occurring between my old self to my new self is understandable, and I believe somewhat natural and realistic, considering my new normal, but it was still bothersome to my ego, especially since I was still remembering and thinking from an able-bodied mindset. But the reality was that though I was remembering and desirous of the way things existed pre-injury, I simply could not physically do the things I once could and adjustments would be mandatory, and I think in many ways actually for the better. It is hard to explain exactly how it was for the better, but I will say that in one way it was for the better was that it reshaped and matured Susan's and my marital relationship, or at least my perception of it at the time, and placed it on a higher level, and I see that our love, and especially Susan's love for me, was not only tested, but it was proven.

As I said, my wife still loves me, and I know it. Her love is revealed because she is not only very protective of me but also very defensive of me. For example when I park in a van-accessible parking spot and go to a show or something and then return to find someone has parked in or severely encroached the block-out area of the handicap parking spot so I cannot lower my ramp and access my van (and it happens more often than you would think), she becomes infuriated. In addition, she constantly looks for options that would protect or benefit me and tries to keep my comfort in mind when making plans to attend events or take vacations. My welfare is always on her mind to the point I worry about her stress level and if she will really even be able to enjoy our vacations.

The subject of marital relations came up one day while talking with a knowledgeable friend of mine regarding another couple. We discussed men's mentality versus women's and how their priorities are typically different. The conversation in some ways hit an area I had been struggling with. The fact is, pre-jury, I considered the physical part of the relationship to be quite important and close and spontaneous intimacy was a huge loss for me as a man, I guess it boosted my ego or self-esteem and made me feel loved and accepted. That is a messed up way of thinking about it but it was part of my fallen nature. I think the fallen nature is the reason many men often tend to equate physical intimacy closely with love and acceptance, but that is our mistake. The reality of a good marital relationship encompasses many aspects that are spouse first oriented. The physical aspect, though nice, is usually self-oriented and though it may enhance the marital bond, it is not a necessarily essential part of a truly loving relationship. Unfortunately, most men tend to focus on the physical. After this conversation I began to understand my error and that things are somewhat different for a woman. I understood that though some women might fall into the same "needy" mindset, and others may enjoy physical intimacy, most studies seem to show it is not necessarily as high of a priority to them like it is for most men. Not having understood this initially, and because I was missing what once was without accepting it could no longer be as it was, it did not take long before I subconsciously began to question her continuing love for me because, since my injury, she was always too busy with other things and I was selfishly feeling neglected. Being too busy was a new fact of the relationship, one of those things that was involuntarily forced on her, and I did recognize that because there were things that needed to be done that I could no longer help to do. Regardless of my awareness to this fact, some mild depression set in, or more so, it kindled a negative attitude. Whether it was true or not, I was feeling overlooked or even ignored, but that once again was because I was thinking of myself and my wants rather than looking at the whole picture and putting her first and thinking of her needs. Because I pitied myself, some strange type of resentment developed in my subconscious. I eventually noticed myself being overly critical all the time, and my critical attitude was justifiably causing issues. Imagine you were the able-bodied person living with a disabled person. Though they suffered some physical changes incurred from an injury or illness, emotionally you still love them because of who they were and are, but then the person you love, because of their own physical and emotional struggles with their disability, begins to treat you unjustly and respond to you negatively when you are trying your best. Eventually it begins to grind on you, and your tolerance starts to fade. You then begin responding or reacting defensively because you are always feeling attacked, and that opens the door to conflict or worse issues. The avoidance of such unnecessary and mistaken conflict is why I recommend open and honest communication with people, if they are willing, and most importantly with your spouse. It may sometimes hurt to hear some things, but I believe getting them out in the open in order to be resolved is much better than holding them in and letting them fester. If left unaddressed, eventually the issues will explode or, at the very least, seep out and expose themselves in undesirable ways and at unexpected times. I knew I was being too critical, and I had to take active and purposeful measures to change.

The conversation with my friend eased my mind considerably and helped me realize the errors in my thinking. The fact is that my injury has had tolls beyond just being in a wheelchair. It seems to me, in my experience, that the heavier tolls might be the larger emotional and self-esteem issues than the physical. Mentally I still picture myself as I was before, but when I look at myself in the mirror, I become aghast at the changes. Regardless, everyone has a need for intimacy of some type and I was hurting with the memory of the physical relationship I had with my wife prior to the shooting even though I knew it was no longer possible. My desire in my "able-bodied mindset" was for the past I remembered though I knew my level of disability made that part of my life—for all realistic intents and purposes—obsolete. I now needed to adjust to the more honest emotional intimacy, but the desire of my old mindset was messing with me psychologically and at times making me feel unloved. That feeling was a lie Satan was promoting for his own interests. The truth was I knew she did love me, I knew. The fact that she stayed with me after this event occurred speaks volumes in itself. I also saw that she took great pains to see that I was accommodated in any situation. She had her priorities right, I was the messed-up one. When I kept listening to my feelings and the lies of Satan instead of concentrating on the truth, I began to feel unloved and just tolerated.

Eventually, like I said earlier, communication was the key, and I just had to know for sure. All I could do was ask my wife, and also relate my feelings, however erroneous they might be. My wife was open to the conversation and basically confirmed what my friend had said and what I knew outside my emotional feelings by what I could actually see by observing how she cared for me. My wife loved me, but intimacy as I gauged it was not on her top three priorities like it is with most men, not even in the top ten. The fact was that she stayed very busy between her job, the farm work and the home front and all it entails, and by the time she completed everything she just did not have the time and was practically exhausted from the day's activity. My wife loved me but priorities and necessities took precedence over exorbitant wants. She was right, and our relationship, I think especially for me, has actually grown and matured beyond where it once had been.

Because of all these losses, as well as others, I had to leave my comfort zone and begin to adapt to new roles and a new identity. My old life and roles were forever changed. I definitely was not the person I was before whether physically, emotionally, or spiritually. Though I could not do many of the things I once did, I had to look for ways I could help out at home and look for the things I could do instead of focusing on what I could not do. I had to alter my pre-conceived ideas of what my role was in order to take on new "father and husband" roles in a way I probably would not have taken before. A way that I think is in fact better for my family. These new role changes would be another blessing that would eventually reveal itself as a result of this event. Where my career would have taken a huge part of my focus and time, and as such my relationship with my wife and kids would suffer, now I did not have a career to get in the way. I had a much stronger focus on God, and not only could I spend time looking for and drawing toward Him, but I could set a better example for my family by seeking Him and relying on Him. I could show my family how to lean on God during adversity and how He could change the inner man and provide peace even during the hard times and trials of life.

As I look at the losses I recognize I have suffered but also give consideration to my restored relationship with God and my actually improved relationship with my family, I know I have come out far ahead in the bargain. I would even go as far as to call it an undeserved blessing that God by His mercies bestowed. I deserved much worse, but God in His great compassion and in His mercy and loving-kindness saw fit not to destroy me. But besides not cashing in my chips, He also saw fit to grace me with the abilities I still have. He additionally has opened my heart and mind and eyes to a new way and a better way to live my life both in communion with Him and also in interaction with my family, and others. As a result, I am now quite at peace with my circumstances. I will admit I still sometimes get aggravated, but when I do, it is because I am focusing on myself and my wants. When I get agitated, once I get my eyes centered back on

God and remember what He has done and still is doing for me and how He has actually improved my life through and as a result of my situation, then peace and even happiness abound.

To readers who might be struggling with their own disabilities, I want to encourage you to look beyond your disabilities and look toward your abilities. Do not look at what you can no longer do, but at what you can still do and how to use those abilities you still have. There is life beyond disability. Sure, some things are gone forever, and other things that might have been easy are now a challenge, but they can be done even if by alternate means. But other things are open, maybe new things that had not been open before or that you had never thought of doing before. God controls all things, and if you are still alive, then God still has plans for you. It is up to you to overcome or to adapt to your challenges and look for those openings and opportunities God has in store for you. Look at the silver lining in the midst of the storm cloud and see the things you can do, even new things you have never done before and normally would not have considered. Look to and see the mercies God has extended and the blessings that exist. They are there, and so is the new normal that God has planned for you, a new and better normal.

Have We Met?

ONCE I HAD BEEN RELEASED to go home, I began reading the Bible again. I had read the New Testament before as well as some of the Old Testament, but it had been years. I had a new zeal for God, and as I read the Bible, it seemed like a book I had never read before. I was being reminded of things I had forgotten, seeing things I had not seen in the past, but most of all I was seeing God in a way I had never seen Him or even remember hearing of Him.

As I read some of the things I had known, I realized my neglect or rather my ignoring of certain commandments and instructions and how I had allowed my thinking to be twisted by Satan's lies. I had justified my way around the commandments and excused my actions in order to pursue the wants of my corrupted nature. I had failed to be decisive in my commitment of obedience to my Lord. I was, to say the least, a poor representation of a Christian. Frankly it would have been hard to distinguish between myself as a believer and that of a nonbeliever if you observed us side by side just by our deeds and conduct.

But the Bible was opening up much more, and as I read it, not only was I further convicted upon those areas of sin I had been aware of but ignored, but I also realized to a greater extent just how sinful my life had gotten. I saw sins I was committing not just willingly, but also those that I was rather ignorantly committing but certainly should have recognized if I had been living by proper moral standards. As I read these things and became more aware, I realized just how much mercy God was extending to me, and it brought me to an even more humbling mind-set.

I began a routine immediately of reading the Bible every day. Upon reflecting on my fall away from God and into sin, I recognized that a large percentage of that fall was due to lack of frequent communion with God and other believers. Once I had graduated high school and moved from my Christian-support groups, I failed to reestablish those support groups at college. I also was not at that time in the habit reading the Bible or spending regular time in prayer or study and meditation on scripture. I told myself that I was okay and could handle life by my own fruition. Actually it was Satan who was planting that lie, and I bit off on it. At the time I felt I had a strong mind and manner toward God, but little did I realize just how immature my relationship was. I then went on my way and subsequently fell flat on my face. I believe that is a hazard for many young Christians as well as older, to assume their relationship with Christ is solid and mature, but unless they are reading the Bible daily and studying it, spending time in prayer and applying what they are learning, they will eventually realize by some means in the future just how immature and weak their relationship really was. God warns us to stay humble and dependent upon Him and we should realize we will never be fully mature until the day of His return. Since we will never be fully mature while in this life, we need to continuously grow and mature and never allow ourselves to become complacent by thinking we are good enough. We are fully sanctified by our position in Christ, but while in this life, we must continually grow in our sanctification in order to conform to the image of Christ, and pride can quickly overtake us if we are not careful, and stunt that growth.

As I continued to do my daily reading, I continued to draw closer to God; and as I did so, I saw Him as the God I had never met before. I saw traits He possessed that I had never even heard spoken of when I was going to church and that now, twenty-five-plus years later, are still not talked about or certainly not with any intensity. I had heard of old fire and brimstone preaching of the past but had never really experienced it, but what I was reading certainly would justify it. These unspoken traits were such things as His anger, wrath, and jealousy. Besides these, I also saw a very intimate and involved God who had His hand heavily entwined in our lives in very intricate ways. I saw a God who by providences, both good and bad, interlaced with our lives daily. His desire is to lead us in the right directions and decisions, but He also, by His sovereignty, created us with free will to make choices related to those providential occurrences and to reap the fruits of those choices, either good or bad. Our choices made in relation to those providential occurrences and the outcomes or repercussions related to those choices can be understood by reviewing similar choices given to mankind throughout history in the Bible. Some examples readily identifiable are Adam and Eve, the nation of Israel and their various kings, Abraham, Noah, Moses, the apostles and many others, and even Jesus Himself. It operates the same even today.

I now saw God for who He is, a more complete picture of who He is and what He expects. I see not only the loving, full-of-grace, and merciful God who is forgiving, all of which are true and constant, and this was God as I initially knew Him, but now I also see another side of God. I now see a very holy, righteous, and just God who possesses traits of wrath, anger, and jealousy and who takes actions for the sake of His holy name upon those who would profane it, especially those calling themselves His children.

I should definitely make it clear that those traits we might consider negative such as wrath and anger should *not* be considered the same as we might think of them from our modern definition and experience through a fallen nature. All of God's traits are centered in His most noteworthy and distinctive attribute of love and extend through that love. God's traits of anger and wrath are fully righteous in their function and are extensions of His attributes of being holy, righteous and just in His dealings with a fallen and sinful creation. It is possible that because of the misunderstanding of these so-called negative traits, that is the reason they are not spoken of much at all, if any, in most modern teaching and preaching. If they are spoken of, it is usually in a mild and somewhat truthful but slanted presentation, and it is why I now see and understand Him in a whole new light.

I think over the centuries there has been a lie and delusion instigated and promoted by Satan to try and pacify God and make Him our "friend" instead of our God. He is our friend sure, but He is also more than that, He is also our God and Master to whom we should be fully submissive. Being our God, He is not the type of "friend" who can be bargained with in regards to sinful conduct. He is our friend because He loves us and leads us in the right path and will never forsake us even though we fail. He is a true friend who is not afraid to and will in fact faithfully confront us with wrong, but being God, He fully expects us to submit to what He reveals to us in the matter. As a result of much of mainstream Christianity gradually swallowing that lie, and pacifying Him down to a friend instead of God, modern civilization has lost an understanding of God and who God is. By making Him our friend instead of our God, we have tried to bring Him down to our human level and standards. We have tried to bring Him down, make Him pliable, and mold Him into conforming to our wants and desires instead of dying to ourselves and rising to His standards and expectations. As such, it is imperative that we, as a "modern" culture, having lost the understanding of God, really begin to reevaluate ourselves and our understanding. Our God is a sovereign and self-existing being who is ever-present, all-powerful, and infinitely wise and He never changes nor can He be formed to the mold we would desire to bring Him down to fit into. Hopefully by fully reflecting on and understanding who God is, we will amend ourselves and will give Him the honor, devotion, and obedience He deserves and, more to the point, *demands*. There simply needs to be an accurate understanding of who God is by those who profess Him.

Certainly God is loving and merciful, and these are the attributes most people in present-day society focus on. Many people want a feel-good God and want the benefits of "being a Christian," without having to adhere to God's expectancy of our love and obedience to Him. That is a shortcoming of our fallen nature. However, among the many other attributes ascribed to Him, I believe one of the most important, yet often misunderstood, is His holiness. What I mean by that is the full scope of what His holiness is. Most people know that holiness means to be set apart from and that by being Christians we are God's children and we are "set apart" from the world. Yet holiness as it pertains to God reveals not only that He is set apart, but that He is set apart because He is unique and there is nothing that can be compared to Him. Additionally, God being holy also means He is a perfect being and is spiritually pure. In His holiness, God cannot overlook or allow sin in any measure, and He will address the sins of the sinner whether they are believers or not. He will turn His back on or His face away from the sinner, even if it is a professing sinful believer, not abandoning them entirely, but letting the consequences of sin befall them, because that sin is their choice. God is faithful in His holiness, and in righteous holiness He will fulfill His promises for good or bad and the consequences we often face as a result of our sin choices are manifestations of that curse and are supposed to instruct us. As the Puritan writer John Owen pointed out in his book *The Mortification of Sin*,[1] "God will justify us from every sin, but He will not justify the least sin in us." Do you understand that statement? Do you believe it? I do. God is holy and will not abide sin in any form. Jesus Christ Himself, the perfect and sinless Son of God, was, as a man, also rejected temporarily when He became sin. As I reflect on the crucifixion, I saw, as Jesus was dying on the cross as the perfect sacrifice for our sins in order to pay the penalty of our sin, He took all the sins of mankind upon Himself, thus becoming sin. As a result of Jesus "being sin," God the Father had to turn away. For a brief period of time, but one that might have felt endless, the human nature of Jesus was rejected by His Father, and He experienced *all* man would suffer by separation from God. Please understand Jesus was God manifested in the flesh, and He could not stop being part of the triune God, but He was also fully man simultaneously, and His man aspect had to suffer *everything* normal man would experience if reconciliation were not made by Christ's sacrifice upon the cross. When I say He experienced everything mankind would have to suffer, I mean everything and that includes experiencing hell itself. The Bible documents that Jesus even went to Hades during that time between His crucifixion and resurrection (1 Peter 3:18, Ephesians 4:8–10, Matthew 12:38–41), and I dare say it was to experience the separation from God. Matthew 27:46 states, "About the ninth hour Jesus cried out with a loud voice saying, 'ELI, ELI, LAMA SABACHTHANI?' that is, 'MY GOD, MY GOD, WHY HAVE YOU FORSAKEN ME?'" God is righteous and holy and wants nothing to do with sin. When we sin against Him and most particularly when we choose to sin against Him purposefully and habitually, we will reap the repercussions of that choice and that sin. When we sin, we separate ourselves from God, and though He is faithful to His children and will never abandon us totally, He will turn His face from us for a time, our communion with Him will be interrupted, and we will face separation and chastisement in some form or another until we cry for Him in repentance. This disruption in communion with God and facing the consequences of our sin choices are part of His sanctifying work and are a small sampling of a holy, righteous, yet loving God.

I would like to share my understanding of these traits that are perceived in a negative connotation, and show how these traits are not negative at all but are rather positive and loving and extend through His holiness and righteousness in conjunction with His attribute of love. I would also like to reveal just how involved, loving, and merciful He is in our lives every day even when He chastises and that He is not just staying aloof and watching. Although we do not have the prophets today as those we read about in the Bible, and we do not see the obvious miracles we read about in biblical times, in truth we can still see God's hand in our lives if we will look and perceive with an eye toward more than just coincidence. There are many things related in the Bible that one could equate to coincidence, fate, or bad luck; but it is clarified that these things occurred to fulfill the word of the Lord, which He had given earlier. In my opinion, though Christ died and paid the penalty for sin, we still, in this temporal life, face the justice of God by several types of afflictions, consequences, and other events that are to act as warnings to us. We can also see God's power displayed through various ways including blessed providence and specific prayers answered precisely, which should get our attention. We are even blessed when we face everything from car wrecks and other accidents, where survival was negligible at best but survival yet occurred. We face high-risk surgeries that were successful and see cured illnesses and other events that realistically should not happen. But sadly and traditionally these blessed events rarely gain our focus and it is almost always the consequences and afflictions that get our fullest attention. Though often these afflictions can be very intense both physically and emotionally, if viewed and received properly, they can bring our most life-changing and beneficial results and so are actually hidden blessings in disguise themselves. Our faith, if it is real, may be tested, but it eventually is strengthened; and we can draw closer to God through our afflictions. These trials can also be viewed as a display of God's love for us, as taught in Hebrews 12:5–6 in that He would subject us to such measures for our betterment spiritually. God's presence and power can be seen if only we would open our eyes to recognize them. Many benefits can be obtained, even during times of chastisement, if only we would accept those benefits and grasp them through the continuous mercies and providential opportunities He gives us. I hope the story of my life and this incident as I have related it, and the occurrences within it, will show how God is still very active in our lives today, and is in fact just as active today as compared to God's active hand in the lives of those shown in the Bible.

THE PRELUDE

ALTHOUGH WHEN I STARTED READING the Bible again and I was seeing much more than I had seen when I read it as a teenager, it was not until I had read through it several times that the deeper revelations of God and His attributes and the more complete picture of His purposes began to strongly appear. As the Bible says, "Draw near to God and He will draw near to you" (James 4:8). I realized as I began to grow spiritually and have a greater understanding of God, that when I was first baptized and the first few years of being a Christian, I was only a baby in Christ, and I was only in the very basics of understanding God and His expectations of me as I entered into the covenant with Him of salvation through faith in Christ. I remember while in high school I would go for runs and, while doing so, just carry on conversations with God about all sorts of stuff; but as much as I had a friendly relationship with God, I was still just a very immature Christian.

I did realize as a teenager that God's commands were important in living a good life and for not having undesired complications as a result of sinful actions, but in a way I saw any actions I may be involved in, that is those things I justified for myself, to be based on my own common sense and judgment with God's command-ments as a rather flexible guideline rather than a hard and fast rule. I had the errant attitude of Him as my friend rather than my awe-some God. He was and is my friend, but He is also God and should be highly respected and also resolutely obeyed. Being an immature Christian, though at the time I did not have that sense of myself as being immature, when I had left for college, and I lost my Christian support bases, and because I was not firmly founded in any type of prayer or devotion time, Satan seized the opportunity. The Bible says, "Bad company corrupts good morals" (1 Corinthians 15:33), and how true that is. When I had gotten to college, I knew nobody, and so I just started associating with everyone. That is not to say they were bad people as the world might rate them, no, they were pretty decent, most of them, and many would probably even classify themselves as Christians also; but much like myself, they had varying levels of moral behavior, at least some of which were not consistent with proper Christian thought and practice. I dare say some had no Christian beliefs and just lived by their own moral code but were still decent people as we might perceive them. Still, for me while in college, there was a definite break in my communion with God and I had many shortcomings which existed. Because of those weak areas it was not long before I began to fall into sinful activity using Satan's traps of justification such as, "It's not hurting anyone," "Everybody does it, it's natural," "Nobody will know," and the worst and most deceptive justification and one in which many Christians fall susceptible to is "God will forgive you anyway, I mean, that's what Christ died for, right?" I bought in to the justifications, and my relationship and communion with God began to suffer in a spiral of sinful behavior.

Now, skipping forward twenty-five years later, here I was reading God's word and finding out just how immature I was and how I had brought many things upon myself due to my own free will choices. The Bible talks a lot about free will. God, in Deuteronomy 28 when talking to Israel just before entering Canaan, lays out the blessings for obedience and the curse if they choose to be disobedient. It was plainly laid out again in Deuteronomy 30:15–19, where it says,

> "See, I have set before you today life and prosperity, and death and adversity; in that I command

you today to love the LORD your God, to walk in His ways and to keep His commandments and His statutes and His judgments, that you may live and multiply, and that the LORD your God may bless you in the land where you are entering to possess it."

"But if your heart turns away and you will not obey, but are drawn away and worship other gods and serve them, I declare to you today that you shall surely perish. You will not prolong *your* days in the land where you are crossing the Jordan to enter and possess it. "I call heaven and earth to witness against you today, that I have set before you life and death, the blessing and the curse. So choose life in order that you may live."

Our free will choice is laid out again in Ezekiel 3:17–27, when God tells Ezekiel to warn Israel about their sins and then says, "He who hears, let him hear; and he who will refuse, let him refuse; for they are a rebellious house."

There are many other verses that display our free will to choose and decide in both the Old and New Testaments, and I really had no problem with this, but what truly struck me were some of the verses that related to the repercussions of those choices we make. God clearly reveals that through many of our choices, we bring our own trouble upon ourselves. Often we classify things as consequences that might "just happen" to occur as the result of an action, but that is not so; God may prevent those consequences initially, or not, but He will certainly allow them to fall upon you if you persist in sin activity, at which time we might see God's hand and the error of our way or we may continue in blindness and say, "Oops"; but there were other events we might face that are unequivocally the direct action of God by His providential hand which may occur as a result of a choice we make. God poses the question in Ezekiel 8:17, regarding Israel's sin, which I equate to the Christians engaging in willful sin. He asks, "Is it too light a thing for the house of Judah to commit the abominations that they commit here, that they should fill the land with violence and provoke me still further to anger?" In the several books of the prophets, Israel was facing temporal punishments or chastisements as a result of their sinful activity, but it provides the scenario for the modern professing Christian believer: Are we apathetic about any type of sinful behavior we might pursue? When we sin, are we unfazed by it? Are we remorseful? I dare ask, if we are not offended by our sins, how can we be repentant of them? If we are not repentant of them, do we not expect to face God's sanctifying chastisement and the consequences for our choices?

God revealed to me that many of the problems and issues of my life, I had actually brought upon myself—up to and including even my shooting. Jeremiah 2:17 states, "*Have you not brought this upon yourself by your forsaking the LORD your God* when He led you in the way?" Jeremiah 5:25 says, "Your iniquities have turned these away, and *your sins have kept good from you.*" The book of Ezekiel also reveals this very strongly. Though God gives us free will to choose, the freedom He gives us in Christ Jesus is the freedom from the bonds of sin so that we can choose to reject sin and to do what is good and right just as Jesus set the example for us. What I failed to grasp at that time in my life and even till my awakening was that the freedom to choose did not absolve me from the consequences I might face as a result of my choice. Those consequences could vary from little complications or feelings of guilt and interrupted communion with God to more intense problems up to and including direct actions by God Himself. My freedom through Christ and eternal security does not mean I can do whatever and not suffer consequences if it violates God's laws, even if it is legal or acceptable in the secular world.

While in college and engaged in drunken behavior through frat parties and other activities and engaging in activities I should not have rather than paying attention to my studies, I found myself in a situation that caused me to have to drop out of school and go to work for a living. Even though this occurred, I still did not place two and two together, and my situation was placed in that "sometimes these things happen category."

The fact is that God had blessed me with many talents and abilities. I should have recognized His gifts to me and used them accordingly for His glory and service. However, since I grew up with those abilities and felt I had honed them to the level they were at, and because nobody had educated me to understand that God gave me those talents, I somehow thought I owned them and was responsible for creating them. I, just like Eve in the Garden of Eden who ate the apple for her own wants, then turned my talents toward use for myself rather than for God and started placating my own wants and comforts instead of serving Him. Because of this, I faced the consequences of those decisions and choices.

God's Hand

I HAD ALWAYS FELT A calling to be a police officer ever since my youth, even though both my parents (though my dad reluctantly) had tried to get me to pursue other professions. While in college, I had decided to pursue physical therapy and to work within a sports therapy field, but upon having to leave that behind me and having no other real means of a trade or decent income, the original desire that had been smoldering to pursue law enforcement reignited. I applied to two separate departments, and both accepted me, but Dallas was first, and to Dallas I went.

Even as I moved to Dallas and began my career, and my dad was actually very proud about that decision, I did not realize God's hand was involved. The Bible speaks about the providences of God and how by His grace we have the skills and abilities we have and we find our place in life. It is by His providence we are rich or poor, boss or employee, one nationality or another; and whatever station in life we may find ourselves, that is the station in which He placed us and in which we should serve Him in. Though He desires us to be content in our station of life, He does not necessarily demand we stay in our circumstances or in whatever station we are in; if He gives us the ability to move forward and upward, and we choose to pursue it, then so let it be, but it is still even He who actually allows that, and He is watching to see what we do with it. Will we use it for Him or for ourselves?

The book of Esther somewhat addresses God's providential hand at work. The Jews had been dominated by Babylon and were carried away to captivity and were now under Persian rule. During this time, the king of Persia had a falling out with his queen and was looking for a new queen. As God's providence would incline, Esther, a Jewish captive, would be selected as the new queen. Later a plot to annihilate the Jews would come to the awareness of her uncle Mordecai, and he imposed upon her to make the plot known to the king. She was afraid to go before him because to do so without him first summoning her could be the cause of being killed for violating the king's law. But Mordecai tells her in Esther 4:14, "For if you remain silent at this time, relief and deliverance will arise for the Jews from another place and you and your father's house will perish. And who knows whether you have not attained royalty for such a time as this?" She decides to go to the king, the plot is uncovered and overturned, and the instigator of the plot is hanged. This brief story is an exhibition of God's providential workings, but I think if we will reflect on lives and circumstances around us and give consideration to them, we can recognize His hand involved in many of today's circumstances.

Once I had finally pursued my calling to be a police officer, I found myself in my dream profession. I loved being an officer and going out on the streets to do some good and try to protect people and change lives hopefully for the better. Each and every day was different, and for the most part, it could be as exciting or uneventful as one wanted it to be. Because I loved the job, I chose to have it exciting, and I worked hard at addressing crime problems. Because of my attitude and work ethic, it was not long before I developed a reputation, among some anyway, as a hard working officer and go-getter. I was very fortunate to have good partners who were likewise work oriented and after a few years of seasoning and experience we became unofficial mentors as it were to younger officers coming on the department. I knew several officers who never made official rank but were counselors and leaders in their own right. These officers were mentors and advisers who could provide advice and instruction due to their seasoned experience. I had several who were such for me and I'm only glad I could do so in turn for others.

As I reflected back on my career, especially in patrol, and I remember all the fights, car chases, armed confrontations, and other situations, I realize now that God had been closely watching over me during my career both on duty and off. I remember being involved in several situations or having near-misses under certain circumstances in which realistically I never should have walked away from, much less walked away unharmed. As I reconsidered those situations, I now realize it was not as a result of anything I truly did, but it was by God's grace, His unmerited favor, alone. By His grace, not only did I walk away, but I walked away unscathed or barely bruised and scraped.

I remember hearing my daughter Jessica singing "Amazing Grace" in a school production along with her classmates a few years after my shooting. I had heard that song a thousand times and, at one time in the past, had often played it for my grandmother on the violin because it was her favorite hymn. But as my daughter sang it that evening, I heard the words like I had never heard them before and finally understood their meaning. I heard the words, "'Tis grace hath brought me safe thus far and grace will lead me home." It suddenly struck me as I heard these words that God had been immensely patient and protective of me. As I reflected on all my disobedience over the years and I recognized all those situations I should never have walked away from, I saw it was only because of God's grace in protecting and delivering me. In those situations where I had been put under extreme trial in an attempt to awaken me, it was God working. Then finally my shooting through which God confronted me directly and I finally did awaken spiritually, all this was by God's doing. All these circumstances were actions by God as He continually extended His grace and displayed His forbearance while working to turn me from my path of sin. God was being extremely patient with me and was protecting me while doing so. Through all my activities, risks and foolishness, both on duty and off, it was by God's grace I survived, and it was by His grace—even in the form of an affliction—I would eventually have my eyes opened. "I once was lost but now am found, was blind but now I see."

After about five years in patrol, I transferred into the investigative unit of Internal Affairs. Although I was now investigating complaints on other officers, I held myself to a high ethical standard. I wish the same could have been said about my spiritual life. It was in Internal Affairs (IAD) I learned who my true friends were. Several officers who I thought were my friends stopped talking to me while others remained friendly and open. I could understand it to some degree because IAD had a tarnished reputation depending on who the chief of the department was at the time. On years past, a complaint would roll in; and as the complaint itself went, the officer would be cleared of wrongdoing, but then the investigators would find some small infraction like failing to "mark out" or "code 6" (arrived at the scene), and they would hammer the officers for that. I am glad it was not that way during my time.

Even though officers were not getting hammered for minor infractions (though they were being identified and addressed), there was still the involvement of politics, which could create problems where none should be. I had no problem with investigating a complaint and calling foul if something was identified, but at the same time, I had no room for politics and damaging an officer's career over politics, especially if the officer was not in the wrong. I watched a few cases come in and get mismanaged, and I quietly shook my head as investigators were forced to make decisions the command staff desired because of political issues.

I had been there just about a year when I landed a case that was a political hot potato. My case was just shortly after a storm in another department. We had a new chief from that department, and there were allegations against two officers about an issue of a similar nature. I initially thought the complaint might hold water, but as I investigated further and further, I discovered and was able to prove the officers did nothing wrong as the allegations were expressed, or at least there was nothing—and I mean nothing—to indicate they did. On the other side, I also developed proof that the complainant was lying and was just trying to get money out of the city by filing a bogus lawsuit. As all this developed, I informed my supervisor of the information and that I was going to clear the officers of wrong-doing. The information was welcomed by my first-line supervisor, and the information went up, but then the answer came back down from commanders that I would find something against the officers. I stood my ground and refused to shade my investigation even after a few shouting matches with my division chief. I watched as several improper things occurred due to the politics, and after it was done, I requested a transfer out of the division. I had signed up for a two-year stint, but I was not going to be part of anything like that again—and said so. I was allowed to transfer without any backlash. I think those persons in the command staff, though they were following orders from their bosses, that is, the politicians, respected my integrity to stand firm and thus allowed me to move without repercussions. I then transferred to the Homicide division.

My ethics and integrity in IAD promoted my reputation among commanders and line officers even further as both recognized my integrity and fairness. Eventually I saw a supervisory need and decided to promote to sergeant after five and a half years as a homicide detective. Upon promotion I returned to patrol, but this time as an actual supervisor and leader by rank. As I said, I loved patrol work, and so I spent as much time on the streets as I could with my troops. I would answer calls and make arrests and write my own reports just like I expected them to do. Eventually I was asked to form an evening deployment unit for crime issues to be addressed, which I did. The unit received two Unit Certificate of Merit awards during my time there, though I still tend to believe it was because of the officers who were inclined to work for me and not necessarily my leadership in itself per se. Because of my investigative experience I was able to teach the officers how to research and develop criminal intelligence which made the unit productive, but I think the essential key was those officers, who were go-getters themselves, chose to work for me because of my reputation.

It was while I was supervising the deployment unit that while I was off-duty, I was kicked in the head by a horse. In 2004, I was off-duty and training a saddle-broke but very green horse. I had him in the round pen and was teaching him to "give to the bit," that is, to let me control his movements and direction with a long thin mouthpiece connected to reins I was holding in my hands. I should have done this from ground level, but I was making a mistake by rushing the training. Along with trying to train him to the bit, I was at the same time also continuing to get him used to carrying a rider.

I had been on him for about fifteen minutes and was literally just thirty seconds from getting off. There was a tree branch that stuck out over the round pen, and the horse had been quite receptive in giving to the bit even though it was new to him. I then made my second mistake when, instead of remaining vigilant, I relaxed and become inattentive. I allowed myself to become a passenger on a green-broke horse instead of a rider. As we were walking under the tree branch, which stretched over the round pen, I unthinkingly pushed it aside. The sound of the branch whooshing through the air upon my release of it scared the horse, and he started running and bucking. I naturally responded by pulling back on the bit, but a tad too hard, which caused him pain. Because he was unfamiliar with it, already being scared by the branch and then adding pain through the bit, I scared him even more. The next thing I knew, I was in a full-blown rodeo and was bucked off. On the way down, I got kicked in the face.

I landed on the ground in a sitting position and never lost consciousness, but my nose was bleeding profusely. I had broken my nose a couple of times in the past, and so I knew my nose was broken by the way it was bleeding; but because I had broken it before, I was not real concerned. This would be the third time I had broken it, so I knew I would survive, and it did not hurt like you think it would. I quickly decided I was going to get back on the horse for just a second then get off and unsaddle him. Supposedly remounting the horse after a negative incident would help me psychologically as a rider and also the horse by showing him who was in control. Also, when training a horse, or anything else for that matter, you should try to end the training session on a positive note. However, as I stood up and reached to pick up my hat, my teeth and the roof of my mouth moved. I knew then that something was not right, and I was hurt worse than I thought.

I called my wife right off to tell her I had been kicked by the horse, was hurt, and I probably needed to go to the hospital. I guess I was slurring my speech due to the injury because she had a hard time understanding me. She had just left the courthouse and was on her way home. She must have assumed since I was calling her that I was not too bad, but she had gathered enough from my statements to ask me if I had called 9-1-1 and requested an ambulance. When I told her I had not, she replied, "Well, stupid, call 9-1-1." I responded in the affirmative and told her I would see her soon and then dialed 9-1-1 after hanging up with her.

I live in the county area just outside of three cities. The call contacted the nearest city, and upon telling them my location, I was put on hold while they transferred me to another agency. After a bit of a hold, I spoke with another operator and told them what happened and I needed an ambulance. I was put on hold again, and then the operator got back on the line and told me an ambulance was en route and would arrive in about fifteen minutes. I responded in the affirmative and hung up the phone. A few seconds later, my phone rang again, and it was the 9-1-1 operator. She told me I should lie down, but I told her I felt fine. (I truly did.) Apparently the endorphins must have kicked in quickly because I never did feel any real pain other than the initial kick, which was like a strong punch, and I was not weak or dizzy. In fact, while I was talking to her, I was unsaddling my horse and taking the bridle off. She must have suspected something because she asked me what I was doing. When I told her, she gasped and yelled, "Don't do that! Lie down." I assured her again that I was all right and that I could not leave the saddle on my horse because I did not know when I would return home, and I was afraid he would roll on the saddle and break it. I do not recall, but I must have kept hanging up or otherwise getting disconnected because she kept calling me back. After I got the saddle off my horse, I walked to the house to get a towel because my nose was still bleeding rather profusely. After I got the towel, I waited outside on my truck tailgate for the ambulance to arrive. I also called my dad and told him I was going to the hospital. I assured him I was fine but asked him if he could come to the hospital to be with Susan. After a few more minutes, Susan pulled in, and right behind her was the ambulance.

I greeted them both by standing up, and Susan went inside while the ambulance attendees put me on the stretcher and had me explain what happened again. For some reason, I could not lay my head back without considerable discomfort, so they propped my head up with a pillow, and I continued to feel fine. As they wheeled me across my gravel driveway to put me in the ambulance, it hurt from the constant bumping over the rocks, but once they put me in the ambulance, I was good again.

Susan came back out with a camera about that time and was steadily taking pictures. The attendees were taking my blood pressure and asking medical questions and such and then turned to my wife and told her, "CareFlite will be here in a few minutes." At this statement, she stopped taking pictures for a few seconds, and her face turned pale. In our line of work, CareFlite was only called in serious cases where someone was hurt so bad that death was an imminent threat. They saw her face drain and quickly backtracked and started explaining that they were only taking precautions being concerned that I might have suffered a skull fracture that could cause brain swelling. They adamantly reexplained it was only a precaution because I was not exhibiting any signs. After this statement, seeing my confidence and my reassuring her I was all right, she relaxed some (and I mean some) and began taking pictures again. After a few minutes, the helicopter arrived and landed in the front pasture.

At this point, they took me out of the ambulance and began to wheel me across the pasture. Pain hit me again from the jolting as we went to the helicopter. I wish they would have just let me get up and walk.

Once I was on the helicopter, it took off, and I was headed to Baylor Hospital in Dallas. I had never been in a helicopter before, and I was quite disappointed because I was not allowed to sit up to look out the windows. As we arrived at the hospital, I was preparing for a jolt of pain, expecting a nice bump as the chopper landed. As I braced myself for the bump, suddenly the attendees opened the door. We had landed, and I had never felt a thing. I think it was the smoothest landing of any kind I had ever experienced. I gave a big sigh of relief as they whisked me out, only to be surprised with pain again because the hospital had tile floors, and the gurney going across the grout lines of the tiles was quite bumpy.

Once I had arrived in the emergency room and the bumping stopped, things were comfortable again. My dad had arrived at the hospital parking lot just before Susan. He saw her arrive and get out of the truck and knew she was really under stress because as she got out, she had a phone in one hand and a cigarette in the other; and as she closed the truck door to quickly start toward the hospital entrance, she threw the phone to the ground instead of the cigarette. She then stopped and looked at what she did, threw the cigarette down, and picked up the phone.

In the emergency room I explained to several doctors what occurred, and they continued to ask me if I wanted any pain medicine. To their surprise, I continued to tell them no because I was not in pain. I joked with my wife and dad and was then told I would have a CAT scan. My dad and I had joked about them waving cats over me for the "CAT" scan, and the doctor looked at us weird and thought we were serious. Eventually when the scan started, I cried out, "Here, kitty, kitty," and he finally realized we were joking, and he and the technician started laughing. After a while, I began to feel a headache coming, so I finally asked for some pain medicine. I do not remember what they gave me, but boy it was good stuff! Eventually that evening I would undergo reconstructive surgery. Susan and I then joked about them making me look like Mel Gibson or Harrison Ford or somewhere in between. I must have already been "somewhere in between" because I came out looking just the same except for the swelling.

It is not just everyone who gets to see a helicopter land in their front yard. It turns out the kick broke not only my nose, but also both cheekbones and the maxilla, the upper jaw, from my cranium, which is why the teeth moved, and it also fractured the right condyle joint of the lower jaw. Fortunately there was no skull fracture or risk of brain swelling. Up to that point, this was probably the worst injury of my life. I was laid up for about thirteen weeks before I could return to work, and even then, I had to take it easy for a few more weeks on light duty.

God is very patient in His work to get us to repent and walk the right path. He speaks to us in many ways, sometimes using the threat of danger, sometimes through a friend or stranger, sometimes through answered prayers, through afflictions or other means, and sometimes by all of them. If we take the nation of Israel as an example, again we can see that they were first blessed with release from Egyptian captivity, observed firsthand the powers of God, they were given the commandments, then guided to Canaan, but upon lack of faith they were forced to wander the wilderness for forty years. They were blessed and cursed throughout their wilderness excursion as God tried to lead them and guide them. Each act of continued disobedience caused them to face more tribulation and afflictions of some type, but these incidents of tribulation along with His continued care and blessings were all geared toward gaining their repentance, their spiritual revival, their full trust and reliance, and to display Himself as a loving and merciful yet also a just and holy God.

God was doing the same thing with me. He was blessing me, giving me grace, moving me through His works of providence, as well as exposing me to the consequences of my sins and placing me in tough situations in order to show me the frailty of life. He did these over and over again, but I had become so hard-hearted I was not listening or heeding.

> "And now, because you have done all these things," declares the LORD, "and I spoke to you, rising up early and speaking, but you did not hear, and I called you but you did not answer." (Jeremiah 7:13)

> "For I am with you declares the Lord, 'to save you';...I will not destroy you completely. But I will chasten you justly and will by no means leave you unpunished." (Jeremiah 30:11 NASB)

As a result of my not listening, my consequences and afflictions were getting worse, but I was still too hardheaded to pay attention and learn. I kept on living my life my way, still refusing to recognize the signs.

In 2005, my son Joseph was born six weeks premature. His lungs were not fully developed, and he was placed into the NICU at the hospital. In my mind, having my infant son in such distress and its life in possible jeopardy was a much worse circumstance than being kicked by the horse and distressed me greatly. Although the doctors and nurses had some concerns, they did not really seem too worried. I guess for them this was relatively common, but for me, it was the first time I could remember being scared because of worry for my son and feeling totally helpless. I was not bothered by the broken face from the horse kick. The kick and following surgery did not scare me in the least, and I was far from helpless. I just couldn't eat solid food. I could still walk and talk, though my speech was a bit impeded. Back then I was on a liquid diet and had some pain to deal with for a while, but so what? This time was different. This time I was unable to control anything, I was helpless. I could do nothing physically to help my son, and for the first time I could remember in years, I knelt down and prayed to God. For the first time in a long time, I felt I truly needed Him and His help. I could do nothing for my son but pray.

A week later, our son had improved, and we got to take him home. He was small, weighing only six pounds five ounces, but his lungs had developed, and he was fully healthy otherwise. Although I knew that week I had prayed daily, even multiple times daily for my son's well-being, when God blessed me by answering, I forgot to thank God for watching over my son and bringing him into good health. The scare was now over, and in my typical fashion, I accepted it as almost routine. That is how hard-hearted I was. I was grateful to have my son, but somehow it never dawned on me that it was God blessing me in response to my prayer, and He was trying to show me that He was the right direction. The blessing did not awaken me, and it never even struck me to thank God for listening to and answering my prayers.

Over the next few weeks, I was on family medical leave, and I thoroughly enjoyed my new family while I was off, but then once I returned to work, I was back into my old routines. My distress over my son was gone, everything was fine, and God got put on the back burner again.

As my career continued, so did my reputation through how I related to citizens, officers, and commanders; and eventually I promoted to lieutenant. I moved quickly through several assignments as a lieutenant because the chief wanted to give all of his potential future commanders a wide experience to draw from. Eventually I moved to the Gang Unit, where I thought I would be for a while. Once I had gotten there, I became involved in a federal grant procurement that I felt would help not just the unit or the city, but the entire DFW Metroplex. There were rumors lieutenants would be moved around again, but I was sure I would not be one of those.

But my thoughts are not as high as God's thoughts. As it turns out, by God's providential hand, He would incline the command staff to move me to SWAT (Special Weapons and Tactics). It was on November 2, 2006, a little less than three months prior to my daughter's birth, that I had been transferred to SWAT. It surprised me that I would find SWAT as the best assignment of my career. I had enjoyed a terrific career and had been in several great assignments throughout my time in the department, and several of those assignments would contend for that ranking, but there was something about SWAT that took the top spot. I absolutely loved it. The focus on an operation, trying to account for each detail or possible occurrence in advance so as to be prepared, the professional skills of being able to adapt or alter a plan quickly when something unexpected did occur, and the tenacity to see the job done and then even the willingness to rehash each operation and identify the good and bad in order to improve themselves as much as possible to perfection. Nothing was "good enough." This was my kind of team, and I loved being part of it.

Truthfully, prior to going there, throughout my career, I did not have a great opinion of SWAT. My father had been there and enjoyed it, but I had never gotten the bug to go there myself. But upon being placed in this assignment and actually seeing the work firsthand, I know if I had known what it was like before, I would have tried to go there years ago. Once I arrived and found the professionalism for what it was, I would have been satisfied to have remained there until retirement. I absolutely loved it and had gained a great respect for the team members and their work.

As it was, I tried to quickly develop a hands-on working knowledge of each operator's assignment so I would have not only a working knowledge of their job from a supervisory standpoint but also be able to perform those duties where, when, and if needed. Alas, I was the unit commander of SWAT's E-Unit, and as such, my job was to supervise and not be an operator unless necessary. On the date of my incident, we were running a federal search and arrest warrant for the Internal Revenue Service. Because of my supervisory role, I had no major role in any warrant. In fact, if I wanted to, all I had to do was stand back to watch and supervise the service of the warrant. But in my entire career, I had never been a stay-in-the-office or stand-and-watch type of supervisor. I loved police work, and though I was making rank, I had never lost my love of the streets or the job, and so I enjoyed participating in the action with my troops. I would never ask my officers to do anything I was not willing to do, and my supervision style was to lead from the front and "do as I do." My troops, through previous assignments, often voiced their respect for me because of my being fully involved; and as a result, they were more willing to do even the unpleasant work. It was the same in SWAT. They gave me respect because of my rank, but more sincere respect because of my desire to be part of the team and involved.

An added bonus to being involved was that my troops could not really complain because they knew I would be willing to be there with them even if I could not, and I would never ask them to do something I would not do myself. The more distasteful an assignment, the more involved I became because I knew it was distasteful and most supervisors would bow out of them. They in turn exerted more effort and raised the bar just for me.

Unfortunately, supervision does have its drawbacks. Along with mounds of paperwork and various meetings, which took my time away from the streets where I wanted to be, I also had to keep myself available to supervise. As such, on this particular warrant, I gratefully took a simple containment position on the outside so a team member could be more effectively utilized elsewhere. As soon as the warrant was over, I was going home to start a three-week vacation. I was staying home for my vacation; there was a lot of work on my little wannabe ranch to be done, and I was going to catch up. I just wanted to run this warrant before I took off. When I left the house at three o'clock that morning, I told my wife I would be home in just a few hours. What I thought would be just a "few hours" turned out to be eight and a half months later.

PREPARATIONS MADE

AS IT TURNS OUT, BY God's providence, just three years earlier, the SWAT Docs Program (officially called City of Dallas Tactical Medical Support Team) had been initiated. God's arrangements for my future shooting had started years ago by putting it into the mind of Dr. Alex Eastman to develop the SWAT Doctors Program and having it come to fruition in Dallas just three years prior. Some examples of God's providence in the Bible are such scriptures as Nehemiah 2:12, "What my God had put into my heart," Nehemiah 7:5, "God put it into my heart," and Ezra 1:1 and 5, "The Lord stirred up the spirit of" and "everyone whose spirit God stirred up." These verses and many more are found throughout the Bible. Whether Alex realized his brainstorm to develop this program was initiated by God Himself, inclining his heart, I am unsure. I am not even sure about his own beliefs because we never discussed them, though I think he has faith. But regardless of if a particular person has belief or not, God has and can still use them if He so desires. An example would be the Gentile pagan Cyrus, the king of Persia who was inclined by God to allow Israel to go back to Jerusalem to rebuild the temple (Ezra 1:1–3; Isaiah 44:28; 45:1, 13). It is in my opinion that God was using Alex and, as such, influenced Him by some means to start this program. This providential action also extended to inclining the command staff to put me into SWAT where I would subsequently be shot and where the doctors of the program would be present in order to give me immediate medical attention at the scene.

It was by His hand I had been placed as a commander over SWAT even though I had no military or special training that would qualify me for such a position. Other than just for experience sake, if anything qualified me in the department leadership's mind, it might have been simply my work ethic throughout the years, which was also grace given by God Himself. He geared me that way. Through the preceding years of intermittent prayer, I had relied on God to fix or to restore me to my previous relationship with Him, but I had done nothing on my own initiative to facilitate this change except to occasionally pray. God had been patient with me and had been giving me opportunity after opportunity to take the initiative, grab the reins, and turn my life around. When I failed to properly do so and was apparently not going to, God being omniscient and already knowing I would be unresponsive, began to orchestrate the events that would lead up to this occasion where I was transferred to SWAT and where the doctors were assigned. God knew what I would and would not do, but He had other reasons and purposes behind presenting the preceding opportunities that likely had ripple effects which I may never fully understand. Though the doctors had done some medical work with other team members during those three years, I was only the second substantial medical emergency they had taken under their belt, and they performed that action superbly. I have been told that according to departmental records, I am the highest-ranking officer to be shot in the line of duty in departmental history. I don't know if that is actually true or not, and if it is, I do not mind necessarily being written down in departmental history as it were, but this sure was a hard way to get there.

God had been listening to my prayers and had even tried to bring them to fruition through more subtle means since it was apparently in my heart because of my praying in the first place. But though it was my desire to change, I was so heavily ensnared in my sins and had become so hard-hearted I failed to change under God's more subtle urgings. We must remember that sin and Satan have already been defeated by Christ's sacrifice and we are no longer enslaved to sin. Since we are no longer enslaved, we have free will to choose if we engage in sin or not, the choice is ours, but so are the repercussions. Even though God knew I would not choose the right path at that time, He had other reasons and purposes behind all that He was doing. Though I was not responding, God was still patiently working, and as the Bible points out, His way and plans are much higher than ours. Lamentations 3:33 states, "He does not afflict willingly" (NKJV), but I have found when He does afflict, that affliction—that chastising, is done out of His love for us and a desire to produce improvements. I can only say I am blessed that God loves me so much that He would chastise me over my choices to sin and that His plan in chastising me would not only be for my spiritual benefit (1 Corinthians 11:32) but it was doubtlessly for the benefit of my children as well. God's plans and His advanced preparations were not limited to just me. They were for my children and any uncounted number of others.

God knew this shooting would not stop me from turning back to Him; in fact it would be under this distress that I would, instead of relying upon myself, turn to Him and lean upon Him. Satan did not know the outcome of his action. You see, Satan is not omniscient; he is only a created being himself, and as such, he does not know everything, and thus is a bit of a gambler. He plays the odds and thinks he knows what the outcome will be. He is a master gambler, and he tries to manipulate us by telling us various lies and using information he has accumulated on our weaknesses, which are his statistical odds, in order to deceive us and cause us to fall. But God, being omniscient, knows all things, and He allows things to happen for His purpose, and that purpose will "work together for good" for His children, even those less than obedient. He allowed my tribulation knowing I would endure it and become more focused on Him than ever.

God was answering my prayers in a means totally unexpected, and my move to SWAT and the subsequent shooting were all part of that plan, not only to answer my prayers, as shortsighted as they were, but to answer them far beyond what I was asking by bringing my relationship with Him much further than that which I had in high school. In a similar manner, the apostle Paul had prayed to see the Christians in Rome, stating in Romans 1:9–10, "For God is my witness, whom I serve with my spirit in the gospel of His Son, that without ceasing I make mention of you always in my prayers, making request *if, by some means, now at last I may find a way in the will of God to come to you*" (NKJV, emphasis added). Little did Paul realize that while he was in Jerusalem, the Jewish Pharisees, jealous and prideful, were going to have him arrested for his preaching of the gospel message. Paul would see the Roman Christians, but as a prisoner of Rome, appealing his arrest to Caesar—and not as a missionary as he had planned.

The Pharisees were stirred up by Satan, and Satan used them to cause Paul to be arrested thinking it would stop Paul from spreading the gospel. God allowed this arrest to happen even though Paul was doing his obedient missionary service. I again refer to Romans 8:28, in that "God uses *all things*." While under arrest in Rome, Paul wrote his letters to the Philippians and stated, "But I want you to know, brethren, *that the things which happened to me have actually turned out for the furtherance of the gospel*, so that it has become evident to the whole palace guard, and to all the rest, that my chains are in Christ; and most of the brethren in the Lord, having become confident by my chains, are much more bold to speak the word without fear" (Philippians 1:12–14, NKJV, emphasis added).

Though Satan tried to stop Paul by having him arrested, God used this to His advantage in the spreading of the gospel and thereby most likely saved many other souls. God's ways are higher, and He can use all things; and in this instance, He made a fool of Satan by causing Satan's scheme to backfire. Because of his arrest, instead of stopping Paul's teaching, it made Paul's ability to spread the gospel even stronger because his arrest for preaching the gospel gained the attention of those who would probably not have listened to Paul as a missionary in the first place under normal circumstances. This is the hand of God at work, and His hand is in all our lives in even the minutest details. His hand is working in ways and for reasons we can hardly begin to fathom or explain. For me, God's answer to my prayers was in a totally unexpected manner, and it would have ripple effects far beyond me to the benefit of others.

It was while I was finally quiet and motionless that God confronted me and my sins, and He had finally gotten my attention. I had wandered off from God to pursue my sins, and He had allowed me to, although it was through His great displeasure. Because of my wandering away, He had been subtly and quietly working behind the scenes and getting everything arranged—all the players in position—in order to take what was possibly His last act of mercy on me.

Does that sound strange that I would call my shooting an act of mercy? Remember what I said about free will? It was my decision to be involved in sin, and it was my choices that brought my affliction on me. God's previous light urgings did not awaken me, the horse kick did not, nor my son's premature birth. My heart had gotten so hard I simply was not listening and out of mercy He was still trying to awaken me to repentance before my time in this life would end and I had to face Him in judgment.

The truth is that God loves me, and my shooting, which He used to awaken me, is proof of that love. In chastising the church of Laodicea in Revelation 3:14–19, Jesus tells them the reason for His threat of chastisement and harsh words and why He was going to do it. He then tells them it is out of love for them that He will do it, "Those whom I love I reprove and discipline," and He tells them to "be zealous and repent," as should be the proper response to His chastisement. Throughout biblical history, God has afflicted, tried, chastised, and disciplined those He loves for their own good. I told you earlier that one of God's traits is wrath, but His wrath is out of love. His wrath is love for us but hate against our sin, and it is the sin that He is invoking His wrath against and not us ourselves. Sin is the object of His wrath but our benefit and sanctification is His focus, and if we will listen and learn from it, we are the beneficiaries for it. If God did not love us, He would just ignore us and let us continue to wallow and harden ourselves in sin until it resulted in our eternal ruin, but instead He loves us and disciplines us in order to cause our repentance and to further perfect and sanctify us.

People often talk about the Judgment Day, or God's judgment, as relating to that final day. But as I understand the Bible, God's judgment comes in two areas. One is of course the final judgment on

Judgment Day, which will be an eternal judgment. In this judgment, persons who have truly accepted Christ into their lives will be saved due to their positional sanctification in Christ and His righteousness being imputed, that is, attributed, ascribed, or credited to those persons. They then will be presented as pure and righteous before God, and salvation will be theirs.

The second judgment however is a temporal judgment, a judgment that occurs in our current time. The Bible, particularly the Old Testament, lists numerous visitations from God among us on earth in which He addresses our iniquities. Examples are Exodus 32:34–35, Leviticus 18:25, and Amos 5:17–18; and there are many more that reveal God visiting His justice among us during our temporal lives. We often see these as consequences incurred by doing something wrong; however, this judgment goes much further than just consequences, they are for our sanctification. Those things we may perceive as consequences are there to show us the error in our actions or manner of thinking, and to turn us from sinful behavior. For the believer, those consequences are a disciplinary judgment or chastisement from God, a rebuking in our time for sins—all sins, but most particularly the unrepented, purposeful, willful sin. This rebuking and chastising is part of what is referred to as progressive sanctification. Our progressive sanctification actually comes in many forms from blessing both great and small to tests of various kinds, and even God's chastisement against sin, depending on how we react to the lesser occurrences. In Matthew Henry's Bible commentary,[2] he described these incidents:

> Sin, long continued in, will kindle the divine wrath, and make it flame out against sinners.

> God keeps an exact account of the time that people go on in sinning against him, and grieving him by their sins; but at length if they by their sins continue to grieve the Spirit of God, their sins shall be made grevious to their own spirits, either in a way of judgment or mercy.

> Though God grieves long, and bears long,
> when pressed with the weight of general and pre-
> vailing wickedness, yet he will at length ease him-
> self of public offenders by public judgment.

It is the wrath of a just and righteous God who cannot allow even the smallest obstinate sins. A verse in the New Testament seems to address the consequences that might occur for continuing willful sin of the Christian and those consequences come in the form of chastisements that are described as "a terrifying expectation of judgment and the fury of a fire". The verse is Hebrews 10:26–27 and says, *"For if we go on sinning willfully after receiving the knowledge of the truth, there no longer remains a sacrifice for sins, but a terrifying expectation of judgment and the fury of a fire which will consume the adversaries."* And this entwines with Hebrews 12:4-5 and Revelation 3:19. Now before we just bite off on this verse and run with it, I think it is important that we understand the context in which this verse was written. This portion of the letter to the Hebrews was addressing some Jewish converts who were in danger of falling away from their faith in Christ's sacrifice by thinking His sacrifice was not sufficient. That is, Jews, who had heard the gospel message and had converted but were in danger of sliding back into Jewish religious practices, fearing faith in Christ's sacrifice was not enough on its own to warrant salvation and they had to earn it through religious works, in other words, they were in danger of committing apostasy, which is the falling away from or forsaking what one has believed. The writer was warning and rebuking the Jewish converts of falling into such a practice or mindset and telling them that Jesus sacrifice was the last and final sacrifice for sin, which he had explained in Hebrews 10:10, 12 and 14, "And by that will we have been sanctified through the offering of the body of Jesus Christ *once for all*", "But when Christ had offered for all time *a single sacrifice for sins*, he sat down at the right hand of God", "For *by a single offering he has perfected for all time* those who are being sanctified" (Emphasis added) and if they did not accept Christ's sacrifice as sufficient, that "there no longer remains a sacrifice for sins." Many Christians get quite nervous about this verse and want to limit it to the context of Hebrew apostasy and not accept that any such judgment or fire could be pending against them for any reason. It is certainly correct to view and accept scripture in the context in which it is written, but I think we should not necessarily limit it to only the context. Although the context of the scripture is written to those who were verging on apostasy to the faith, or were thinking of reverting back to or incorporating certain traditions of Judaism for the wrong reasons, I personally cannot help but feel it can also be fully applied to the disciplinary action of God in order to correct grievously errant Christians and draw them back to a righteous state in mind and spirit. The two portions of this verse that specifically drew my attention were "sinning willfully after receiving the knowledge of the truth" and "the expectation of judgment" and I feel the verse when considered alone is consistent with the entire theme of the both the Old and New Testaments of the Bible with regards to God's purpose in chastisements against sin. Hebrews 12:5–6 describes the chastisements of the Lord to correct and discipline His errant children and examples of those chastisements are seen throughout the Old Testament which was to be an example to us for our discernment under the new covenant of grace in the New Testament. God does not and has not changed and He abhors sin of any kind, especially willful sin. Christ's sacrifice on the cross can cover any and all sin, but sin in God's children will still not be tolerated and it will be addressed. God is faithful to His children and His holiness. Just because a person professes to be a Christian does not exclude them from His judgment and this is certainly true for those Christians who might be hypocritical in their conduct and presumptuous about the forgiveness of sins under "the law of liberty". The conscience will testify against sin even if the person tries to disregard their conscience and the sinner will still feel guilt and disrupted communion and the "terrifying expectation of judgment" because they know they are wrong even if they may have justified it to themselves in order to quell their conscience. When God's sanctifying judgment against their sin does come, it comes as a "fury of fire" that awakens the sinner and causes them to search out the sin that is the cause of their judgment and turn away from it.

In support of this view, King David says in Psalms 94:12, "Blessed is the man whom You chasten, O LORD, and whom You teach out of Your law." Possibly one of his best and clearest statements that identifies the corruption of man and the love of God and His effort to sanctify man is Psalms 119:67 and 71, "Before I was afflicted I went astray, but now I keep Your word." "It is good for me that I was afflicted, that I may learn Your statutes." God—in His holiness, His hatred of sin, His just righteousness, and in His great love for us—causes affliction and distress for His children in order to chastise us for our sin and further sanctify us. We are called to be holy just as He is holy, and when we violate that calling by willful and persistent sin or a presumptuous attitude about sin, He will take action to exhibit His holiness both to us as well as others and to keep us from profaning His holy name. As I reflected on Hebrews 10:27, which states, "But a fearful expectation of judgment, and a fury of fire that will consume the adversaries," I considered that although this verse certainly addresses actual persons who reject Christ, I could not help but also consider the "fury of fire that will consume the adversaries" to possibly be related to God's stern and intense chastisement, which will destroy the idols and purge or purify like fire the wayward Christians' heart in order to bring them to repentance and obedience. After all, this letter to the Hebrews was written to those who were professing believers who had professed Christ but were sliding back to parts of their old life, which many of us tend to do still today, letting parts of our old life wander into our new life and becoming complacent of sin in our lives and its effects and erroneously thinking it no longer matters.

We can even see this chastising action through some of the great biblical heroes. Moses and Arron were not allowed into Canaan because Moses had tapped the rock instead of speaking to it, and they also took glory from God.

> So Moses took the rod from before the LORD,
> just as He had commanded him; and Moses and
> Aaron gathered the assembly before the rock.
> And he said to them, "Listen now, you rebels;

shall we bring forth water for you out of this rock?" Then Moses lifted up his hand and struck the rock twice with his rod; and water came forth abundantly, and the congregation and their beasts drank. But the LORD said to Moses and Aaron, "Because you have not believed Me, to treat Me as holy in the sight of the sons of Israel, therefore you shall not bring this assembly into the land which I have given them." Those *were* the waters of Meribah, because the sons of Israel contended with the LORD, and He proved Himself holy among them. (Numbers 20:9–13 NASB)

I initially thought the sin was striking the rock rather than speaking to it, which was of course wrong of Moses, but a friend of mine named Emily Crenshaw pointed out that Moses said "shall we," and it appears he meant himself, Aaron, and God inclusively; and he thereby took glory from God, who was providing water from a rock. Before this point, Moses was always talking about God's power; suddenly he was including himself and Aaron. What he should have said was, "must God bring forth water." Neither Moses nor Arron could do that, only God could. The way I understand it, it is not only by still mercifully bringing water out of the rock because Moses failed to follow His instruction, but also by His disciplining Moses and Aaron because they took credit and glory from Him and failed to treat Him as the only and most holy God, that by chastising them "He proved Himself holy among them."

Moses, who had with God's help gotten them released from slavery; Moses, who talked to God "face-to-face"; Moses, who led them for forty years in the wilderness, even he was not allowed to escape with that sin. He could not be allowed because God is holy and cannot allow sin to be unaddressed. This was a sanctifying lesson for Moses and he accepted it without complaint.

In a similar manner, King David, who slew Goliath in faith, who refused to kill Saul because he felt Saul was God's anointed, David the king of Judea; this same David was not allowed his adultery with

Bathsheba or to get away with the death of Uriah the Hittite, her husband. He was told that because of his sin the first child he had with her as a result of the adultery would die, and he would have adversity in his house the remainder of his life (2 Samuel 11 and 12).

There are numerous accounts of Israel as a nation as well as individual kings such as Asa, Hezekiah, and others who were chastised as a result of their sin. If these examples and great men close to God and others cannot escape God's temporal justice and judgment against their sin, why should we believe we can? I realize we are under a new covenant of faith in Christ, and He paid the propitiatory sacrifice for our sins, but in my view, God does not and has not changed. The God of the Old Testament is the same God as in the New Testament and He still even today disciplines and chastises us in our temporal lives for our sins and rebellious nature and He does it out of love in order to progressively sanctify us and judges our sin now in this life so we will not be condemned in the next life (1 Corinthians 11:32).

Christ's blood covers our sins, and we will not be found guilty on judgment day, our salvation is secure. But that is the *final* judgment day. For there to be a final judgment, there has to be preceding judgments, and those preceding judgments are God's chastising actions against our sins in this temporal time. We will face and deal with the consequences of our sins in this life. Just as God disciplined Moses and David and others temporally for their sins, so will He judge and chastise us for ours, especially blatant and willful sin by God's professing children which profane His name. "Her priests have done violence to My law and have profaned My holy things; they have made no distinction between the holy and the profane, and they have not taught the difference between the unclean and the clean; and they hide their eyes from My sabbaths, and *I am profaned among them*" (Ezekiel 22:26). Then the word of the LORD came to me saying, "Son of man, when the house of Israel was living in their own land, *they defiled it by their ways and their deeds; their way before Me was like the uncleanness of a woman in her impurity.* "Therefore I poured out My wrath on them* for the blood which they had shed on the land, because they had defiled it with their idols. *Also I scattered them among the nations and they were dispersed throughout the lands.*

According to their ways and their deeds I judged them. "When they came to the nations where they went, they profaned My holy name, because it was said of them, 'These are the people of the LORD; yet they have come out of His land.' But I had concern for *My holy name, which the house of Israel had profaned* among the nations where they went" "Therefore say to the house of Israel, 'Thus says the Lord GOD, "It is not for your sake, O house of Israel, that I am about to act, but for My holy name, which you have profaned among the nations where you went. *I will vindicate the holiness of My great name which has been profaned among the nations, which you have profaned in their midst. Then the nations will know that I am the LORD,"* declares the Lord GOD, *"when I prove Myself holy among you in their sight.* (Ezekiel 36:16–23 NASB). Though in these last two verses He was going to invoke His wrath upon the nations that He used to discipline Israel for their sinfulness, and He did so by having the Persian nation overthrow the Babylonians and then also caused the Persian king Cyrus to allow Israel to return to Jerusalem in order to rebuild the temple just as prophesied, notice that He did so in order to *"prove Myself holy among you in their sight"*. God will not allow His name to be profaned especially by His chosen. Though the physical church in some ways seems to be conforming to society at large and thus causes some of its membership to fall into the same worldly mindset, and those members maybe not even realize they are mistaken because they have been raised in that church and it has become acceptable in their church, God will still correct His errant children for their benefit and His glory. He is holy, and sin is no part of His.

Many people want to quote the verse of Romans 8:1, "There is therefore now no condemnation for those who are in Christ Jesus." Though I agree there is no "condemnation," that does not impede temporal and sanctifying judgments now or a future accounting in the Final Judgment Day. I believe according to 2 Corinthians 5:10, the parable of the guests in Luke 14:7–11 and similar related verses that on Judgment Day, there still will be a judgment, accounting or evaluation made in which we will be brought forth and we will make an account, rewards will be given or lost, and we will find our eternal placement in heaven. Our salvation is assured assuming our confession of faith was sincere in the first place, but though we will not be condemned, that does not preclude or omit judgment, and our deeds—good or bad—will affect our "crowns" in heaven eternally. I also believe, as I stated earlier, that there will be ongoing judgments exacted for our sin now in our temporal time whether they are seen by us simply as consequences of our actions or something more direct. Going back to the story between Nathan and David regarding Bathsheba and Uriah the Hittite, it should be noted that though David had told Nathan that the person who had committed the wrongful act in a story Nathan had just told "deserves to die," that after Nathan confronted him and told David that he himself was the sinner deserving to die, he also stated, in 2 Samuel 12:13, "The LORD also has taken away your sin; you shall not die." Which concurs with Romans 8:1, "There is now no condemnation for those who are in Christ Jesus." David would yet be disciplined for his sins, but he would not be condemned to eternal death.

A second thing that struck me about the verse of Romans 8:1 is the word *in*. There is no condemnation *in* Christ when we walk *in* His light and when we are humble and repentant of any sins we commit. But when we willfully and intentionally sin, how can we be repentant? Are we walking *in* Christ if we are not obedient or, worse, resistant and unrepentant? We also have to consider the passage in which this verse is contained, which reveals those walking *in* Christ are walking in the Holy Spirit and not in the flesh. This is confirmed by Galatians 5:13, 16 and 25 which say, "For you were called to freedom, brothers. Only do not use your freedom as an opportunity for the flesh", "But I say, walk by the Spirit, and you will not carry out the desire of the flesh" and "If we live by the Spirit, let us also keep in step with the Spirit." 1 John 3:6 and 24 also supports what it is to walk "in" Christ. They state, "No one who abides in Him keeps on sinning" and "Whoever keeps His commandments abides in Him, and He in them. And by this we know that He abides in us, by the Spirit whom He has given us." Remember Hebrews 10:26–27, "For if we go on sinning willfully after receiving the knowledge of the truth, there no longer remains a sacrifice for sins, but a terrifying expectation of judgment and the fury of a fire which will consume the adversaries." This verse I believe goes much deeper than the initial context in which it was written. I think it may also address Christian believers who have strayed from the righteous path by being deceived by Satan and letting their old life interfere with their new life and are becoming apathetic toward sin and are even engaging in it willfully. I am not saying in any way that salvation could be lost, assuming you were saved in the first place. What I am saying is this: There is "no condemnation" for those in Christ, but God, out of His love for them, will still exact a chastising judgment against His children in the here and now, both for their benefit and to prove Himself holy.

The apostle Paul in Romans 6:1–7 states that if we have died in Christ, then we are dead to sin, and we are not to live in sin. He asks if we should continue to sin so grace may abound, and then replies, "May it never be!" The apostle Peter says in 1 Peter 4:17, "For *it is* time for judgment to begin with the household of God; and if *it begins* with us, what *will be* the outcome for those who do not obey the gospel of God?" It is also my opinion that "judgment to begin with the household of God" and "begins with us first" is a reference to temporal judgments by God against sin by His professing children. According to Hebrews 12:6 all of us who are children of God will face chastisement of some nature, but I think it will come for those especially who willfully profane His name and His chastisement even of His children proves His holiness to both us as well as others, and the fiery trial that Peter talks about in the preceding verses is not, in my opinion, just limited to persecution for being a Christian. Those fiery trials could be a reference to God's chastisement of sin as well as testing of faith. God in His love for me and His righteous hate of sin could not and would not allow my unrepentant sin to continue. Though there certainly is "no condemnation for those *in* Christ Jesus," the point is, all while I was purposefully ignoring God and intentionally committing sin, I was not "*in* Christ." I was not living in the Spirit of Christ and being obedient to Him; rather, I was living in my sinful flesh, and for that, there *is* a reason for righteous judgment to chastise me for my sin. That chastisement would not lead to my condemnation because I am secured in Christ, but likewise, just like king David, my sins would not be allowed to continue unaddressed.

God in the Garden of Eden told Adam and Eve not to eat from the tree of the knowledge of good and evil and if they did they would die. God was speaking mainly of spiritual death due to their separation from God, but it also began their physical death which would occur in the future. Here in the Romans 8:1–8 passage we are told that the mind, even the professing Christian's mind, set on the flesh "is death," that is, that by pursuing fleshly desires to sin instead of walking in the power of the Spirit to reject sin, we are in spiritual death by having separated ourselves from communion with God by our choice. I often wonder however if by pursuing the sins of the flesh, if we are not also facilitating or escalating our physical death? I have heard preachers speak about the wages of sin being death and infer how each sin, especially willful sin, takes a toll upon our bodies and brings us closer to death then we would have been otherwise. We have already shown how sin can interfere with our communion with God, and I feel it can also make our given life span more miserable than it has to be, and as such, it can cause us to very well shorten our life by our own choice. That is, we are destroying our quality of life and some actions may actually bring us closer to death. I do not really know this for a fact, but it sounds reasonable especially as modern science has discovered that certain actions can create unhealthy chemical reactions in our brain and body and also shown the various ill effects of stress. Though the Bible teaches that God has numbered the days of our life span on earth, we must realize God has also given us free will to choose, just as He did with Adam and Eve when He told them if they ate from the tree of the knowledge of good and evil "you shall surely die." Adam and Eve were immortal until they chose to sin which began their death process. God has given us a life span, our days are known, but by our choices, if we choose sin, do we shorten our life from what was originally provided? God provided Israel the options of life or death by their choices and that option of life or death by our choice is still in effect for us today. Some other verses to contemplate while considering this are Hebrews 12:9 and 1 Corinthians 11:30; 15:56. This is something to think about. Though we could certainly debate this issue, and I do not think anything can necessarily alter our given time span, barring sin itself whether our own or others, I do know that willful and intentional sin against God does create a rift in our communion with Him until such time as we sincerely repent, because not only does the Bible teach it, but I have experienced it firsthand. God being holy and righteous had to respond both for His sake so people would recognize His holiness and righteousness and, for my sake, in order to progressively sanctify my spirit and correct my corrupted flesh. 1 Thessalonians 4:3 tells us that our sanctification is the will of God and unfortunately much of that process comes through chastisement for sins we commit. "For God has not called us for impurity but in holiness." (1 Thessalonians 4:7).

Condemnation is defined by *Webster's New World Dictionary*[3] as "to pass judicial sentence on" or "to doom." That I was not condemned is accurate in that sense. If you believe one cannot fall from grace and in "once saved, always saved," then this judgment was not a question of my salvation itself. My salvation was secured when I was baptized at sixteen, just as King David's was secure. However, although my salvation is secure, it does not mean my obstinate and willful sins would not have any negative effects or consequences. There are scriptures that state all sins will be forgotten, "as far as east is from the west," but that does not mean we will not face judgment, either here temporally or even a later eternal judgment, or that sin—though not held against us because of Christ's sacrifice as a substitute in payment for our sin—will not have an eternal effect on rewards at Christ's judgment seat. There are too many verses regarding judgment for each and every person, and all those letters that contain those verses were written by the apostles to believing Christian churches warning the Christians about the potential consequences of their actions, and cautioning them to be attentive to how they walk in Christ's instruction and example, and they were not written to the unbelieving masses. I looked at and studied and read at least twenty-two verses on judgment, but there are several more. Judgment for Christians regarding how we conduct ourselves in this life is real, and Christians today should not ignore this. I interestingly noticed there are verses in the Old Testament that talk about sacrifice for sins committed on accident and in ignorance but never was a sacrifice provided or described for purposeful and unrepentant sin. Think about that for a minute. Nowhere in the Old Testament sacrifices did God provide a sacrifice for intentional sin. Intentional sin is obstinate to God and He will not accept that. If anything, He will determine to break the sinner until any sin is no longer intentional, and all recognized sin will be confessed and repented of. I feel under the new covenant in Christ, the same will occur. A verse that caught my eye was Hebrews 8:12 that states, "For I will be merciful toward their iniquities, and I will remember their sins no more." Note that He will be merciful to our iniquities and will remember our sins no more. I asked myself, "What is the difference between sin and iniquity?" Though most people would lump them together, I researched it and discovered sin is basically failing in one's purpose in life or straying from one's purpose, while iniquity was committing moral wrongness, basically by intentional choice. One might define it as accident verses purposeful, and this distinction can make a difference. Our "sins," accidental shortcomings, are forgotten, but our iniquities may not be forgotten though they will still be treated with mercy. This may be exactly what the verse of 2 Corinthians 5:10 addresses. Think about it. Unrepentant sin, and wrongful choices in conduct and decisions, though not leading to loss of salvation, can still have eternal consequences, and they most certainly have temporal ones, and this is one reason Satan continues to attack us even after our baptism and profession of faith. While watching the Christian channel TBN I heard Dr. Robert Jeffress, the pastor for First Baptist Church in Dallas, make a statement to the effect that Christians under the new covenant of grace were actually held to a higher standard than the old covenant under the law. Not actually hearing the sermon itself (It was forthcoming to air on a future episode), I thought about this for a few seconds and realized he was absolutely correct. The "law of liberty" through grace does not give us a right to a free-for-all. In fact, more is expected of us. For example, under the old law you could hate your enemies and it had that "eye for an eye" mentality, but under the new law of grace we are to love our enemies, forgive them of their wrongs and do good to them. Our law under the new covenant is the law of the Spirit of Christ written on our hearts. We are not to hate a brother or look on a person with lust in our heart because doing so was committing murder or adultery in our heart whether we actually physically committed the acts or not (Matthew 5:17-20; 5:221-22; 5:28, 1 John 3:15; 1 John 1:6; 2:9; 4:20; 5:3). That is just a small area of comparison I thought about. We as Christians led by the Spirit of God are actually held to a higher standard. We may be saved and in the Kingdom of God, but as Matthew 5:19 reveals, if we become apathetic about sin and teach others to be also, we "will be called the least in the kingdom of heaven." As 2 Corinthians 3:6 explains, we are ministers of a new covenant of the Spirit of God whose laws are written on our hearts. Satan wants us to become apathetic toward sin, and he wants to affect our eternal standing.

I think Hebrews 12:4–7 supports my opinion of temporal judgments when it says,

> You have not yet resisted to the point of shedding blood in your striving against sin; and you have forgotten the exhortation which is addressed to you as sons, "My son, do not regard lightly the discipline of the Lord, nor faint when you are reproved by Him; For those whom the Lord loves He disciplines, and He scourges every son whom He receives." It is for discipline that you endure; God deals with you as with sons; for what son is there whom *his* father does not discipline? (NASB)

Not only are we to "resist to the point of shedding blood" and "strive against sin," but as Peter, James, and Paul all point out, we should rejoice in our sufferings, especially if those sufferings are for Christ, but also rejoice in any disciplinary action the Lord God exacts upon us in order to purify and sanctify us. David says it well in Psalms 90:15, "Make us glad according to the days You have afflicted us, *and* the years we have seen evil" (NASB). This tied in with similar verses such as Psalms 119:71 as noted earlier reveal the reasons in rejoicing in our afflictions. He says make us glad in our affliction because it is in our distress and affliction that we call and turn to the Lord and seek Him and align spiritually with Him, that is, that through our affliction we are progressively sanctified and improved and we gain a better understanding of God. "O LORD, they sought You in distress; They could only whisper a prayer, Your chastening was upon them" (Isaiah 26:16). "I have surely heard Ephraim grieving, You have chastised me, and I was chastised, like an untrained calf; Bring me back that I may be restored, for You are the LORD my God. 'For after I turned back, I repented; and after I was instructed, I smote on *my* thigh; I was ashamed and also humiliated because I bore the reproach of my youth" (Jeremiah 31:18). Hosea 6:1 also exhibits a merciful God seeking repentance in His afflicting, "Come, let us return to the LORD for He has torn *us,* but He will heal us; He has wounded *us,* but He will bandage us" (NASB).

First Corinthians 11:27–32 also reveals the presence of temporal judgments most specifically made by God. In this passage God was exacting judgment on those who take the Lord's Supper in an unworthy manner, but it still reveals that temporal judgments do exist and exist for a purpose. I refer again to the highly respected Bible commentator Matthew Henry, who had this to say about that section of scripture,[4] and his commentary supports the temporal judgments I have described and the purpose behind them.

> The Corinthians came to the Lord's table as to a common feast, *not discerning the Lord's body*— not making a difference or distinction between that and common food, but setting both on a level: nay, they used much more indecency at this sacred feast than they would have done at a civil one. This was very sinful in them, and very displeasing to God, and brought down his judgments on them: *For this cause many are weak and sickly among you, and many sleep.* Some were pun-

ished with sickness, and some with death. Note, A careless and irreverent receiving of the Lord's supper may bring temporal punishments. Yet the connection seems to imply that even those who were thus punished were in a state of favour with God, at least many of them: *They were chastened of the Lord, that they should not be condemned with the world,* v. 32. Now divine chastening is a sign of divine love: *Whom the Lord loveth he chasteneth* (Heb. 12:6), especially with so merciful a purpose, to prevent their final condemnation. In the midst of judgment, God remembers mercy: he frequently punishes those whom he tenderly loves. It is kindness to use the rod to prevent the child's ruin. He will visit such iniquity as this under consideration with stripes, and yet make those stripes the evidence of his lovingkindness. Those were in the favour of God who yet so highly offended him in this instance, and brought down judgments on themselves; at least many of them were; for they were punished by him out of fatherly good-will, punished now that they might not perish forever. Note, It is better to bear trouble in this world than to be miserable to eternity. And God punishes his people now, to prevent their eternal woe.

After my awakening in the hospital upon God's revelation and my sobbing fit of repentance, I could not be angry at God for my condition. There are times I am frustrated by my situation or lack of ability, sure, but I have never been angry at God because I realized from His revelation in the hospital that I brought my situation upon myself. If I should be angry at anyone, I should rightfully be angry at myself. But the fact is that upon seeing God's chastising hand, I actually can even rejoice because I see what His chastisement has done for me. It is proof that I am a child of God. It has brought me back to God much further than in high school, and it has given me a new heart and mind for Christ, which not only is for my good, my eternal good, but also for my children's good and maybe others. My faith is now stronger even in the midst of my affliction because I know He is stronger than my affliction, and I have had exceeding growth spiritually. I'm not perfect, I make mistakes, even more often than I care to admit, but I am now fully trusting and reliant upon God, and there is no better way to be.

In the revelation in the hospital, God never said, "I did this to you because," but as Romans 8:28 says, "And we know that God causes all things to work together for good to those who love God, to those who are called according to *His* purpose" (NASB); and after reading and studying the Bible, I see His hand and at least some of His purposes. I also know that ultimately all things come from God in one way or another. He may cause them, allow them, or even do them in some manner; all things—both people and nature—are at His bidding and are used to fulfill His purpose. Lamentations 3:37–38 says, "Who is there who speaks and it comes to pass, unless the Lord has commanded *it? Is it* not from the mouth of the Most High that both good and ill go forth?" "Shall we indeed accept good from God and not accept adversity?" (Job 2:10). "The One forming light and creating darkness, causing well-being and creating calamity; I am the LORD who does all these" (Isaiah 45:7 NASB).

Jeremiah, Job, Isaiah; and now I realize the sovereignty of the Lord, and He does nothing without plan and purpose. In fact, Ezekiel 14:23 says in regard to all the discipline Israel was undergoing, "For you will know that I have not done in vain whatever I did to it, declares the Lord GOD" (NASB). When He commands it, it will be done; and when He decides to exact His disciplining judgment in order to save His prodigal child or if it is to manifest His glory and holiness, it will be carried out until it succeeds. And after it is all said and done, when we turn back to Him, we can be grateful. "The fierce anger of the LORD will not turn back until He has performed and until He has accomplished the intent of His heart; In the latter days you will understand this" (Jeremiah 30:24 NASB). God has a purpose in His afflicting anger, and once it is completed, we will have an understanding. I now have an understanding. It may not be complete in all aspects, but it is sure in one: God loves me and afflicted me, that is, chastised and disciplined me through affliction, for my good as well as for the welfare of my kids. It is this humbling knowledge that has enabled me to accept almost any kind of adversity. It is not that I enjoy my current physical state by any means, but I now know God has not only allowed it but is using it for not only my improvement but that of others as well in some form or fashion.

It seems when things are good and running smoothly, we rarely grow spiritually; in fact, when things are good and running smoothly, that is usually when we tend to stray. That straying, when things are good, is part of the fallen human nature and is revealed in the passage of Deuteronomy 31:20–21, "For when I have brought them into the land flowing with milk and honey, which I swore to give to their fathers, and they have eaten and are full and grown fat, they will turn to other gods and serve them, and despise me and break my covenant. And when many evils and troubles have come upon them, this song shall confront them as a witness (for it will live unforgotten in the mouths of their offspring). For I know what they are inclined to do even today, before I have brought them into the land that I swore to give." Alternatively it is during our hard times, our tribulations and afflictions that we tend to grow. It is during our distress that we turn to God and begin to depend on Him and eventually come to know He is the one and only way. I know that was the case for me. Though I believed in God and had accepted Christ Jesus into my life, it was almost always during times of distress of some type that I called on Him and grew some spiritually even if it was a minute growth. When I was not in distress, I rarely gave God much thought because I thought I was in control, and so my growth was miniscule if not nonexistent or, worse, was even backsliding.

> [10]The LORD spoke to Manasseh and his people, but they paid no attention. [11]Therefore the LORD brought the commanders of the army of the king of Assyria against them, and they captured Manasseh with hooks, bound him with

bronze *chains* and took him to Babylon. [12] *When he was in distress*, he entreated the LORD his God and humbled himself greatly before the God of his fathers. When he prayed to Him, He was moved by his entreaty and heard his supplication, and brought him again to Jerusalem to his kingdom. *Then Manasseh knew that the LORD was God.* (2 Chronicles 33:10–13 NASB)

"We will…cry out to You *in our affliction*, and You will hear and deliver." (2 Chronicles 20:9, emphasis added)

Even for nonbelievers, when going through tribulation, they will often call to God in whom they may not profess to believe in but still somehow sense the presence of. They may not be atheists per se, but they have just never given God serious consideration. Though they may not give God much consideration within their daily lives, most, honestly, still have a sense of a greater power beyond themselves. The same can be said for many who claim to be atheists and rely on modern science for their answers. Yet the awesomeness of God simply cannot be denied, and even many scientists, as they delve further and further into their fields and see the intricacies of creation, often realize and claim that Deity must be involved in creation. For many, whether believing or not, their tribulation is often tied to some questionable behavior. Even if that is not the case, tribulation is very often God's initial way of calling them, of showing them the futility of their lives, the futility of power, money, fame, health, or anything else. If they will recognize that futility and, in response, turn to God, then they will benefit from their tribulation.

I often wonder where I would be today if I had not repented, if I had remained hard-hearted or became angry with God rather than repentant. Would I be alive? Would I be alive but in worse shape? Once my shooting occurred and I survived because God's hand had put the SWAT Doctors Program in place and they were there to intervene and save my life, I had two possible ways to respond: I could consider this a fluke and just a part of life and too bad for me in a similar manner as I had responded to being kicked by the horse, or I could recognize the hand of God. He left the door open to respond either way and was awaiting my response. As in 1 Chronicles 29:17, "Since I know, O my God, that *You try the heart* and delight in uprightness." God rewards an upright heart, and He sees us when we humble ourselves and hears us when we call upon Him in our distress. Remember Jeremiah 10:18? "I will…cause them *such distress* that they may be found" (NASB). The horse kick did not affect me at all whereas my son in NICU certainly was enough to stir me, but not enough to awaken me because I still fell back into old practices. In this shooting event, if I did not respond properly, then I may have faced further discipline, such as not having nearly the recovery I have had or maybe additional tribulations making my current situation even worse, making me go even further toward hitting rock bottom so the only direction to look is *up*. Some passages which reveal this probability are 2 Chronicles 32:24–26, "In those days Hezekiah became mortally ill; and he prayed to the LORD, and the LORD spoke to him and gave him a sign. *But Hezekiah gave no return for the benefit he received, because his heart was proud; therefore wrath was looming over him* and on Judah and Jerusalem. *However, Hezekiah humbled the pride of his heart,* both he and the inhabitants of Jerusalem, *so* that the wrath of the LORD did not come on them in the days of Hezekiah." And later, 2 Chronicles 32:31, "God left him *alone only* to test him, that He might know *all that was in his heart*", and finally, Isaiah 28:21–22, "For the LORD will rise up as at Mount Perazim, He will be stirred up as in the valley of Gibeon, to do His task, His unusual task, and to work His work, His extraordinary work. And now *do not carry on as scoffers, or your fetters will be made stronger* (Some translations use harder or heavier); For I have heard from the Lord GOD of hosts Of decisive destruction on all the earth." (NASB).

After revealing to me how I had strayed from Him and had abused the gifts, the grace, and the mercies He had given me throughout my life, such as my abilities—physical, mental, and emotional— and my using them for my desires instead of for Him, God stepped away from me to allow me to endure my affliction. Upon being confronted, my affliction was not the spinal cord injury because as I said before I was not even fully aware of my total situation, but my affliction was rather the realization of how sinful I had become and how severely I had abused His grace. After confronting me, God stepped away to see my heart and my response. If I remained prideful and hard-hearted, I would face further hardship from the wrath of God. If I admitted my failings and humbled myself, repented of my sins, and submitted myself to Him, then I would be benefitted. That benefit might not be immediate, and certainly I would still have to deal with the hardship I was in as a result of my sin, but grace and mercies can be extended even in hardship. For example, the hardship might not be as severe as it could be. The purpose for facing the hardship even upon submission and repentance would be to serve justice for my sinfulness as well as to verify my actions were sincere and I was not just looking for a quick fix, and also because of God's wrath against the sin itself as well as proof of His holiness. My response in the hospital, not even knowing about these and similar passages of Scripture at the time, would, I believe, dictate my future.

The fact is God was very, very merciful to me even in my affliction. The injury was duty related, so I was able to retire under disability pension and under Texas Worker's Comp Law. For the most part, I will be financially stable, and my health issues and needs related to my injury will be mostly handled. He has allowed me to recover some reasonable use of my right arm and hand, so I can do certain things by myself or with minimum assistance. He did not have to do that, but He did. In addition, He secured for me the *Extreme Makeover: Home Edition*, which substantially assisted me and my family in our living condition, and He has done all this in a time of my life where I could stay home to be involved with and help raise my children. I find it interesting that even though the *Extreme Makeover* show was quite popular for many seasons, it cancelled the season after my home was built. Many families were blessed by that show over the preceding years, but in a way, I cannot help but feel it more than coincidental that it did not cancel until the season after my home was built and that it had been put in place years before by the providence of God to eventually bless me, as well as the other families, in response to my repentance and return. I am sure the show was not just for me, but I am also certain it was there for me to receive a blessing. I sometimes wonder, like in the passage of Hezekiah, if I would recognize the benefit He provided? I did, and I do, but I wonder how many benefits and blessings I fail to recognize and be thankful for? God's providing these graces to me is sort of like the story of the prodigal son in Luke 15 when the son returned poor and hungry. Upon the son returning to the father, the father gave him "the best robe," a ring, sandals and fed him the fattened calf. God the Father was doing the same for me, there are more blessings being given and in the making than I can count, and they all started many years before.

Possibly one of the largest blessings and where His providence was in force again was with regard to my wife. According to statistics, over 70 percent of police marriages will end in divorce. Also, over 70 percent of marriages that experience life-altering situations will suffer divorce. But God had me covered. I do not even pretend to know why, but when my wife was ten years old, her mother suffered a stroke that left her wheelchair bound. My wife grew up with a disabled mother, but one who was in a strong, stable and committed marriage, regardless of affliction. In my mind, God was actively and providentially working for mine and my families benefit by preparing Susan to be able to handle and deal with my disability so when it happened, she would be strong enough to stay with me. By preparing her as she lived through her mother's disability, God was not only preparing her for what she would face, and building her strength, but by doing so He was also protecting both me and my family as a whole. Thank You, God, for all Your loving mercy and acts of providence.

FAITH IDENTIFIED

AS I BEGAN TO TRULY mature in my walk with Christ and to understand the workings of God, it was not long before I began to realize my definition of faith as I had initially understood it was actually insufficient. That is, the faith I had from the time of my youth when I was baptized was rather shallow in understanding and application as compared to what it was supposed to be. No one had ever instructed me in the full context of what it meant to have true faith. I thought initially this misunderstanding was my own, but as I again became more involved in church, and looked around me and heard others speaking of faith, it became apparent that the definition of faith as many understood it and how it was apparently being propagated or instructed on by many churches was also insufficient. At the very least, it appears the more in-depth understanding of faith was not being developed, and the shallow understanding was being allowed to pass as sufficient enough. It seemed that over generations, the definition of faith in mainstream thought and practice had slowly been watered down. Faith, as the biblical authors understood and spoke of faith, had a much deeper meaning than faith as I was seeing it being taught and defined by many churches.

In the English language, faith is synonymous with the word believe. In fact, due to translation issues, the English word "believe" had to be used in certain verses because the English language, being a rather flat language in comparison to Greek, had no equivalent to certain Greek verb forms of faith. Though in the English language faith and belief are synonymous in Christian thought, I feel the problem that exists is in the modern definition of believe as our modern culture defines it. Though the official definition of believe is to accept or have confidence that something as true or real, the actual application of the definition falters because the modern or worldly definition of believe as compared to faith is diluted to just accepting historical facts or information as true but then taking that acceptance no further. There seems to be no application with our belief of the historical facts other than having a head knowledge of them and believing they are true. Faith goes much deeper. That being said, it appears that many churches may have conformed to this generally held world definition by allowing faith to be diluted to just believing in a head knowledge of certain information. That is, a person may "believe" Jesus died on the cross for the sins of the world, but his belief stops at that point of historical knowledge and goes no further, yet this head knowledge only belief is equated by many as having "faith". The concern I have however, is that if the "believer" fails to ascend and act on his belief which results in a changed life, I fear that limited level of belief may in fact be worthless. James 2:19 says, "You believe that God is one. You do well; *the demons also believe, and shudder.*"

Based upon what scripture has revealed to me, it is my opinion that this level of only having head knowledge "belief" does not entail the complete essence of what it means to have faith. Because of the lack of fully understanding the meaning of faith and unfortunately, the apparent failure of many of today's churches to convey the complete aspects of what faith truly entails, the modern, normal definition of faith carried by many professing Christians falls short of what was intended, and it is my fear that many persons may be confidently walking around with a false sense of security, or at best, a shallow faith that can be easily manipulated. When I talk about "duties", I want it understood that I am not implying there is anything more than faith in Christ's sacrifice that must be done. There are no works or anything else that must be performed in order to gain salvation. What I am saying however is that the meaning and principles of faith itself entails duties of belief that are more than just a historical knowledge. It entails actions of heart that are consistent with faith which will be discussed below.

My faith was shallow in my immaturity as a Christian because I was not taught nor did I understand what true faith entailed, and as a result I easily fell to the schemes of Satan who "prowls around like a roaring lion, seeking someone to devour" (1 Pet. 5:8). Had I understood faith properly and the duties I had to God, I would like to think I would have been more stable and resistant to the devil's schemes. I would not claim perfection by any means, but I would hope I would at least have had more perseverance to be able to overcome when tempted and therefore saved myself a lot of grief. Jesus taught that we were to be like children with regard to our relationship with God and if we were not, we would not enter the kingdom of heaven (Matt. 18:3). In one context the kingdom of heaven is applicable to our lives in the here and now. If we are not like children, our trust in God would falter, we would not be at peace with ourselves and others, and our usefulness to the service of God might be ineffective. If our faith was strong and active and we believed in God and trusted His providential workings, the kingdom of God would be manifest to us and we would be at peace no matter what was occurring in our lives. Paul, Peter, Stephen and other disciples were able to rejoice even while being beaten, imprisoned, and executed because of their faith. In Luke 22 the disciples, while following Jesus during His ministry, being prideful, had debated among themselves who was the greatest. That same prideful thinking caused Satan and his angels to be cast from God's kingdom. Jesus warned about prideful thinking and even threatened that prideful thinking would cause them to not enter the kingdom of God, not only now, but if their faith was on their works and not solely upon God, possibly in the future. Pride and ambition ruin the Christian walk and spirit, so we need to maintain a humble mindset of trusting only in God and not ourselves. How are we to be like children? How does a toddler act? I see children as being fully trusting of the parents and loving them and because of that, believing everything they are told by them. It is a result of that love and trust that they are obedient. Children depend on the parents to feed, clothe and to provide for them, and are receptive to their teaching them about life. Sometimes, just like Adam and Eve, they are curious about what they were told and might touch that hot stove after being told not to, but once they burn their fingers they learn their lesson and know their parents told them correctly. Our relationship with God must be the same. We have to trust Him and rely on Him in everything including all His providential workings and we must strive to be as obedient to His commands and instructions as possible. If we do this, if we submit to Him in humility and trust Him in everything, we will be like His children, we will be at peace with ourselves and with God because we will have a clear conscience. We may mess up and burn ourselves after being warned, but once we do, and we realize He is right and told us the truth, we will turn from our wrong and become even more reliant, obedient, and trusting.

An example that appears to reveal that the definition of faith goes much deeper than just believing some historical facts can be found in such passages as Mark 1:21-27. In this passage Jesus was confronted by a demon possessed man and the demon not only believed, but actually knew Jesus was the Christ. He stated to Jesus, "What business do we have with each other, Jesus of Nazareth? Have You come to destroy us? *I know who You are*—the Holy One of God!" In another passage in the same chapter, Jesus is continuing to go around healing and casting out demons, but "He was not permitting the demons to speak, because *they knew who He was*." (Mark 1:34). Again in Mark 5:6-9 the demons knew Jesus was the Son of God as well as Luke 4:41. The point is that the demons factually knew who Jesus was, but even though they knew Him, because they did not rise to and function accordingly to their knowledge of Him, they failed to reach the level of belief. Because the demons did not yield to their knowledge and subsequently submit to God's will and way because of that knowledge, they were still damned and they will still find themselves in hell.

To help define the true essence of faith or belief, let us consider a paraphrased analogy my friend Fred related to me. We might see a chair and we "believe" it will hold us up, but though we believe it would hold us, for some reason, though we are tired of standing, we decline to sit in it because it might not. Since we decline to sit in it for whatever reason, we have failed to take actions in accordance with our belief that the chair would hold us and so our belief becomes useless because we did not apply it. In other words, we failed to act in accordance to our beliefs by submitting to and applying actions to those beliefs, and as a result we fail to derive the benefits of it. If, on the other hand, we believe it will hold us and we accordingly sit in the chair because of our belief, we prove what our belief is; we display our faith in the integrity of the chair because we actually yielded to or concurred with our belief by taking action consistent with it. In the same way, if we believe in Christ Jesus, in His sacrifice, and in His instructions, we will act in accordance with our belief and obediently submit to Him and His way which incidentally leads to a changed life.

I heard another story that seems to fit along this line of thinking. A tightrope walker had decided to walk a tightrope across a large local waterfall and advertised his intent to do so. On the day of the event there was a large crowd gathered to watch. At first the crowd was silent as he made his first crossing, having doubts he could do it, but cheered wildly as he crossed and then walked back across. He did this a few more times and then stated he would cross with a wheelbarrow loaded with weight. He asked if the crowd they thought he could do it. They cheered that they believed he could. Once again he went across and came back with the loaded wheelbarrow. The crowd was ecstatic and cheered him loudly. He asked again if they thought he could cross while carrying one of them on his back. They cheered and said they believed he could. He then asked for a volunteer from the crowd and even offered to pay them, but he had no takers, not one. The crowd claimed to believe, but they would not put their belief into action. In the same way, I am convinced faith, true lifesaving faith, requires more than just a shallow belief; it requires actions in accordance with that belief and those actions not only prove our faith but result in a reward.

In the earlier paragraph regarding the recognition of Jesus by the demons, it should be noted that the demons were "cast" out of those they were afflicting. The demons knew for a fact that Jesus was the Son of God; they factually knew which actually equates to something stronger than belief because belief is the acceptance, trust, or confidence that something is true. In other words, we may still believe in something even though we may not have a firsthand factual knowledge. In this case, though the demons knew factually that He was Lord, they did not in fact rise to the level of "belief", because *they did not willingly submit themselves* to His lordship. Although the demons were forced to leave when Jesus told them, we can notice that they resisted leaving by either throwing their victims into convulsions prior to leaving or otherwise pleading against being cast out beforehand. The demons had to comply with Jesus command to leave because, after all, Jesus is still Lord whether they willing submitted to His lordship or not. But because they did not submit to their knowledge of Him as being Lord and apply that knowledge appropriately for themselves, they failed to rise to the attainment of belief, and thereby derived no benefits for their knowledge. If we do the same, if we fail to submit to His Lordship and accordingly rise to and apply His teachings to our lives, we would likely fare no better than the demons. After all, Jesus said, "Not everyone who says to me, 'Lord, Lord,' will enter the kingdom of heaven, but only the one *who does* the will of my Father who is in heaven." (Matthew 7:21, Emphasis added) We thereby see that faith means rising to, submitting to, and applying ones belief, but we will find more.

When I had become a believer at the age of sixteen, I was taught to "believe" historical facts as put forth in the gospels, that Jesus was the Son of God, actually God among us and the Word. I was to believe that He died a propitiatory, substituting, sacrifice for our sins, that He was resurrected to life and therefore defeated death and then ascended into heaven to be at the right hand of God the Father where He would be our advocate and mediator. Whoever believed these facts and accepted Christ into their life would be saved. The belief in these facts without further instruction being clearly taught was the modern definition of *faith* as I understood it and was what constituted my "faith." In reality I did have a deep appreciation for the work of Christ on the cross and for God's mercy, and I did believe the historical facts as they were presented, but now I was seeing having faith meant so much more than just believing some historical facts. This head knowledge belief as I described above was missing one important factor and that is the Lordship of Christ. We might ask Christ into our lives in order to receive the benefits of His sacrifice, but if we are not willing to accept and submit to Him as our Lord and give Him our whole lives, at best we will miss many benefits of the kingdom of God and our life's journey will be filled with undesirable and unnecessary strife that will hopefully bring us to faith and His Lordship. At worst, if we only accepted Him into our lives for desired "benefits" but nothing further, we might be like the demons and never saved at all. To honestly ask Him into our lives is to ask Him to be our Lord. It has become largely propagated by some churches that Jesus could be accepted into our lives as Savior without the necessity of Him being also our Lord, Master and Ruler. I believe this theory comes primarily from the misapplication of a couple of verses taken out of context. If you believe the Bible is inerrant and does not conflict with itself, and I do, then these scriptures must be taken in relation to the scriptures and theme of the entire Bible and that theme is Jesus as Lord, Master, Ruler and King. Jesus as King and Ruler is one of the major points emphasized throughout the Bible along with the prophecies of His sacrificial and redemptive work on the cross. If we do not accept Jesus as Lord, then we have not truly accepted Jesus. If you understand the Triune God properly you will understand that Jesus the Messiah is actually the eternal God Himself taking on a human body in order to communicate directly with us in bodily form and to set a visual example for us. Jesus of the New Testament, though in human form, is still the same Lord God and creator of the universe as in the Old Testament (Col. 1:15-16, Hebrews 1:2), and just as it was necessary for believers to submit to the LORD God of the Old Testament, it is also necessary for today's believers to submit to Jesus as Lord because they are one in the same God. Not to submit to Jesus as Lord over all creation is to not submit to God. In my opinion the churches which are propagating the theology that Jesus can be Savior without being Lord, are seriously mistaken and this erroneous thinking has created a huge chiasm between what is commonly called "belief", that is, just accepting certain historical information as true but going no further, and true belief which is submitting to Jesus as our Lord and rising to our beliefs by implementing and applying our thoughts and actions in accordance with Christ's instructions. This shallow understanding of what faith truly means has created a huge breach between a shallowly defined belief and true faith and that chasm has in my opinion opened the door to bad teaching and bad theology which can facilitate sinful conduct by allowing loose standards of behavior and promote apathy regarding sin, all of which is offensive to God and will reap consequences accordingly.

My friend Fred related information from one of his seminary professors and once told me that English was rather a flat language as compared with other foreign languages, and especially the ancient Greek language. He told me English had six verb tenses whereas Greek had I believe he said twenty-six with all the tenses, voices, moods and such combined. He explained reading the Bible in English was like watching the television in black-and-white; you see the show and get the idea of the story. But he stated reading it in the original language was like watching television in high-definition color because all the depth and color of the story was revealed. He was right because as I began to try to study the meaning of certain words and their verb tense and their meanings in the original Greek, I got a taste of their depth and the true meaning they conveyed, and I am just a novice in the understanding of Greek, much less a full-blown linguist.

One thing that probably struck me the most in my understanding of faith was that I perceived to have authentic faith was to have a true love of God, and to love God was to be obedient to Him. As a result, I determined for myself that faith, in short, included obedience to God and obedience to God equaled love of God. First John 5:3 states, "For this is the love of God, that we keep His commandments." That true love of God is not God's love for us but our love for Him, and in John 14:15, Jesus is speaking and says, "If you love Me, you will keep My commandments." These verses in themselves do not say faith equals obedience, but when we review other verses, we see that obedience is a product of faith, or rather a pillar of faith so to speak. Some examples that reveal this are Abraham leaving Ur at God's command not knowing where he was going, or later being willing to offer Isaac, his son of the promise, as a sacrifice when commanded. Abraham's obedience was a product of his faith and completed or perfected his faith just as James 2:21–23 reveals when it states Abraham's faith was completed by his works. There are many examples of such throughout the Bible, and so it does seem to apply. I encourage you to review Hebrews 11 and see how faith and obedience are related. Conversely we can also see in other sections that being disobedient to God were acts of "faithlessness." Such as Numbers 14:33 in which the people of Israel refused to go into Canaan at God's command for fear of the fortified cities and the people, even though God had freed them from Egypt by His power and performed many signs and wonders during their travels there. The verse says of their disobedience and lack of trust, "Your sons shall be shepherds for forty years in the wilderness, and they will suffer *for* your *unfaithfulness*, until your corpses lie in the wilderness." Throughout the Bible, God reveals Himself to be in a relationship to His people, first Israel and then the Christian. In fact, the Christian believer, the church, He relates as a marriage; and any disobedience, especially willful or presumptuous sin, which takes the believer away from God as idolatry and equates it to adultery or, as it might be called, unfaithfulness. In a human marriage comparison, though a spouse might claim to love their partner, their love was not real or strong enough to keep them faithful, and eventually they commit adultery. God equates willful disobedience and a love of sin as adultery and unfaithfulness in our relationship with Him. Hosea 6:6–7 in the ESV translation seemed to me to emphasize this point. It states, "For I desire steadfast love and not sacrifice, the knowledge of God rather than burnt offerings. But like Adam they transgressed the covenant; there they *dealt faithlessly* with me." I believe the word *love* is proper here. In other translations, it might be called loyalty or mercy, but I feel love is a more accurate term because God is love, and His first and foremost commandment is for us to love Him. His second greatest commandment is for us to love each other, so love is the ultimate theme and core attribute of God (Matthew 22:36–40). But when we look at the verse in relation to an obedient faith, we see in verse 7 that by disobedience, the Jewish people "dealt faithlessly" with God—that is, in my opinion, they did not love Him with the steadfast love that they should have so they violated the covenant and were disobedient toward His commandments. This verse in Hosea is also referenced in Matthew 9:13 when Jesus is eating with tax collectors and sinners and being criticized for it by the Pharisees. In the New Testament verse, the word *love* is translated *compassion* or *mercy* depending on the translation; but here Jesus, God in the flesh, loved us so much He came to earth in the body of a man in order to lead sinners to salvation and subsequently die on the cross for their sins in order to give them salvation through faith in Him and the propitiation made through that sacrifice. Jesus, the Son of God, in His humanity, completed this task in obedience to the Father with regard to the salvation plan out of love both for Him and for us and in doing so set an example of just how obedient we should be, even to the point of shedding our own blood, if necessary, in our strivings against sin (Hebrews 12:4).

In response to that unfaithfulness referenced in Hosea 6 above, God punished or chastised unfaithful Israel. The chastisement for sin can be seen both nationally and individually throughout the Old Testament and is a witness to God's holiness and justice. I found it interesting that in Leviticus 4, God made laws of sacrifice for "unintentional sins" and sins of ignorance in which a person later comes to recognize as sin. Numbers 15:22–28 does the same, but notice in neither does He mention any sacrifice for intentional sin. In fact, nowhere have I found in the Bible is a there specifically a sacrifice given for intentional and unrepentant sin. Nowhere does the Bible condone sinful behavior and say "it's okay, it doesn't matter." Numbers 15:30–31 rather states the opposite, "But the person who does anything with a high hand, whether he is native or a sojourner, reviles the Lord, and that person shall be cut off from among his people. Because he has despised the word of the Lord and has broken his commandment, that person shall be utterly cut off; his iniquity shall be on him." Now I am not saying that our salvation can necessarily be lost because of our purposeful sins, but it should be a soul-searching concern for us. Christ Jesus died for our sins and paid the price for them, and even believers may sometimes go astray for a while, but hopefully, we will eventually come to repentance. What I am saying is that our sins, especially willful sin, displays unfaithfulness to God and a lack of love for Him. Our sins lead us from God and are acts of unfaithfulness, and this is especially true when our sins are blatantly willful and intentional because then we are being obstinate by justifying our sins and making excuses for them. When we choose to sin intentionally, our sins have become our idols, our other god, and we are committing adultery by willfully engaging in them. Correspondingly, because of our willful sin, we display a lack of knowledge of God and His holiness and exhibit a failure to faithfully love God. If we knew Him, we would not commit our intentional sins. "By this we know that we have come to know Him, if we keep His commandments. The one who says, 'I have come to know Him,' and does not keep His commandments, is a liar, and the truth is not in him" (1 John 2:3–4).

If our sins are intentional and willful, we have justified them to ourselves; and because we have justified them, we cannot truly be repentant of them, unless we have had a change of heart, which usually comes through a humbling experience caused by God in His continued patience and mercy. I am not saying we will not slip into sin upon occasion, but we should not willingly and habitually allow ourselves to practice sinful behavior. We will slip; we cannot be perfect in this life, but a slip is usually followed by a confessing and repentant heart. But often, because we have justified them, our pride and corrupted nature will not let us repent of them because we do not want to admit being wrong and guilty. We would rather justify our sins and try to not even acknowledge they are sins because we know if we confront them, our doing so will reveal our guilt and God's righteousness. As a result, God—in His faithfulness to us— must intervene by chastising us until our pride is broken and we are humbled. At that point, we can truly acknowledge our guilt, be repentant, and make our return to God. This is shown in Hosea 6:1 with a cross reference to Hosea 5:14–15. "Come, let us return to the LORD. For *He has torn us, but He will heal us*; He has wounded *us,* but He will bandage us" (Hosea 6:1). "For I *will be* like a lion to Ephraim and like a young lion to the house of Judah. *I, even I, will tear to pieces and go away*, I will carry away, and there will be none to deliver. I will go away *and* return to My place *until they acknowledge their guilt* and seek My face; *in their affliction they will earnestly seek Me*" (Hosea 5:14–15, emphasis added). Note that God has torn and afflicted "until" we acknowledge our guilt and return to Him. I had sinned for many years in willfulness, and God had tried many times to get my attention to return, but my heart had been too hardened in my sin. Even though at one time I had as a youth recognized my sin and sought salvation, now my heart was hard, and I was not listening. I had not listened due to the horse kick, not through Joe's premature birth, or any of the preceding events before those. It was not until I had been shot and was unable to do anything but listen, and He confronted me with my sinful conduct, that I became humbled and finally repented. How sad for me that it took such an intense episode as that to break my hard heart and renew it to a heart desiring God.

A belief in the historical facts of Jesus is certainly an important part of faith, but as I understand it, a belief in the historical facts is only a small percentage of what true faith entails. As I carefully studied what faith meant, the Bible revealed more than just historical belief. It was also the belief and acceptance that God's commands, His statutes and guidance and providential workings for our lives were totally and completely what was best for our lives and our eternal souls, even if we do not understand them. Faith entailed not only the acceptance of that belief, but it then equated to adherence to those commands and directions and an acceptance of His providential workings, in other words, obedience *to* them, the application *of* them and trust *in* them. These are the duties of the Christian, to be totally reliant and trusting of God no matter the circumstances and obeying and applying His truth to our lives. Though we can do things that will help strengthen these duties, such as regular Bible study and so forth that enhance our faith and knowledge of God, those actions will supplement and strengthen but not replace total trust. Just as Abraham obeyed by faith, so did Noah, Moses, Gideon and the prophets and many others even though the tasks they were given seemed difficult or impossible. Though they had no firm knowledge how events would occur, they obeyed and trusted God to empower them to perform their tasks and in His power to see it completed. As a result of their faithfulness they were blessed and rewarded. If we do the same, we will be also. Like those in the parable of the talents in Matthew 25:14–29, if we trust and obey, we will face our Lord and Master and He will say, "Well done, good and faithful slave. *You were faithful with a few things*, I will put you in charge of many things; enter into the joy of your master" (emphasis added). I now realized I was to obey and conform to the standards God set for me, and accept His providential workings and follow His leadings by His Spirit, even if it did not seem easy, or it did not always seem enjoyable, favorable, or doable in relation to my own fallen and corrupted flesh and limited perspective.

My submission to God's will and obedience to His direction even if—and especially if—it was not easy would not only equate to fully trusting and relying upon Him but also to placing full confidence in Him for providing me with the abilities to conduct and complete whatever task and direction He might give me. I know now that God will provide me with the tools and abilities to do whatever He assigns. This obedience, trust, and reliance on God reveals a love of God and His ways. By that I mean our love for God is proven as we faithfully obey and trust in Him. Remember 1 John 5:3, "For this is the love of God, that we keep His commandments"? Hosea 4:1 echoes 1 John 5:3 in that it instructs Israel to "listen to the word of the Lord." *Listen* does not just mean "hear," it means "to hear, accept, apply, and to do," and He had taken issue with Israel because there is "no faithfulness…or knowledge of God."

When I first accepted Christ into my life at sixteen, I had an appreciation for the mercy of God and for having been done a huge undeserved favor, yet I cannot say at the time I had a true and appropriate love for God because I did not recognize just how corrupt my human nature was and, as a result, what an immense favor He actually did for me. Because of this, it was easy to fall susceptible to Satan's lies and slip off into sinful conduct, which my flesh craved, without my having too much grief over my sin. I should have had deep regrets and remorse over my sinful nature. What did Jesus say in the Sermon on the Mount? "Bless those who mourn" (Matthew

5:4). That mourning was not for hard times that might have befallen us but was for our sinful nature as well as the sinfulness of the world which can draw us away from God. My willful slip into sin when I justified that slip was just enough to give Satan a toehold in my life. Once Satan had a grip, since both Satan and sin are never satisfied, they wanted to take me even deeper into sin. As I did delve into more sin by continuing to justify more sins, I drifted further from God, my heart grew harder, and my love, however much there was, also grew colder. This is the corrupting nature of sin.

The wonderful and blessed thing about being under the new covenant with Jesus Christ is He is the "Faithful and True" (Revelation 19:11), and though I would forsake my covenant with Christ, though I would break faith by my intentional disobedience, Christ would not abandon me. He is the faithful and true. In John 6:37, 39 and 10:27–29, Christ states,

> All that the Father gives Me will come to Me, and the one who comes to Me I will certainly not cast out.

> And this is the will of him who sent me, that I should lose nothing of all that he has given me, but raise it up on the last day.

> My sheep hear My voice, and I know them, and they follow Me. I give them eternal life, and they will never perish, and no one will snatch them out of my hand.

> My Father, who has given them to me, is greater than all, and no one is able to snatch them out of the Father's hand.

Christ, in His love for us, even when our love for Him appears to fail, is fully and completely faithful to us and will not let us be taken away. It may mean that for a while He might withdraw His communion (Isaiah 59:2) and let us see the emptiness of our sins, and eventually He might also, actually will, chastise us in order to discipline us, maybe even severely, because of our sin (Hebrews 12:6), but He will never leave us. That is much of what I believe occurred to me. I had strayed from the covenant path and had finally reached a point where I was seeing the emptiness and futility of sin and was asking God to restore me to my initial relationship with Him after my baptism. I was even praying for help for my children because I knew the mire I was trapped in, and I wanted much better for them. Eventually God would answer those prayers in a quite unexpected way through my shooting, which I believe was not only a chastising action for my constantly willful sins but also for my benefit to break the bonds of that sin in which I was ensnared. God is faithful even when we are not.

Faith is in effect a belief in God and what He has done on the cross through His Son Christ Jesus. But faith also includes an adherence to His commands as well as a full and complete reliance upon Him in everything, a trust in all His providential workings whether they appear good or bad. Those providential workings can come in many forms. These workings might be a presented opportunity to action or a blessing to be grateful for or injury or illness or maybe even something small like a flat tire on the way to work which presented an opportunity or prevented an event that that would have been bad, but all God's workings are for a purpose and for our benefit in some way. It is through this knowledge that we can trust Him and have faith because "God causes all things to work together for good to those who love God, to those who are called according to *His* purpose" (Romans 8:28).

Because God causes all things to work for the believer's good, by faith we can fully trust and rely on Him even when we do not understand why we are going through something. We live in a fallen and cursed world and there are many people of every age, gender or any other variation who go through tragic or traumatic experiences of all sorts. Many of these experiences are hard to grasp regarding what benefit could be derived from them. We shake our head and ask, "How can this be used for good?" I cannot stand to see a child suffer and I cannot wrap myself around why a child would have to suffer or would even die at a young age. What good can come from that? But in my limited knowledge and not knowing what the future holds or the ripple effects of each event, I have to trust in God's workings though I am grieved and do not understand. Although I may question certain things, what I do know is that God is in full control and He will cause it to be used for good. One thing I have noticed about children suffering is that they seem to handle their suffering quite a bit better than most adults do and though I hate their hurting, I personally am inspired by them and am in awe. I obviously do not think that is why they suffer, but for me, inspiration can be one byproduct of their tribulation. Again, not understanding why any particular person may suffer, I have to reflect upon the positive results of my shooting and also refer to the list of reasons provided by the authors of "WHY, O GOD? Suffering and Disability in the Bible and Church," by Larry J. Waters and Roy B. Zuck found in the next chapter.

Though God is in control of all things, including a person's suffering, we can and should pray for the healing of those who are suffering. God has instructed us to and if the prayers we lift up are in God's will, He will answer them. That answer may not be what or how we expected, but it will be done and it will be done with the most beneficial results. I have done it and I have seen prayers answered with miraculous results. Many times our prayers, though not intentionally, might be out of selfish motives. Our prayers might be for our own needs or the needs of others and are prayed sincerely, but unfortunately they have some type of self-seeking motive and may thereby fall short of God's will and are not answered or at least not to the degree we would have liked. For example, the apostle Paul prayed three times for the thorn in his flesh to be removed, but God would not remove it because God's power is perfected in weakness and Paul's testimony and God's power would in fact be more effective as Paul continued to work and give praise even in his weakness. Though God did not answer Paul's prayer as he wished, He still answered and gave Paul the reason for not removing his particular affliction. He then used that weakness for good. God will do the same for us if we will train ourselves to listen and not just ask. Alternatively, I had prayed several times for God to help me restore my relationship with Him from which I had fallen in my youth. That prayer was in the will of God even if it was a bit short-sighted. God answered that prayer in a most extraordinary way through my shooting and simultaneously answered the prayers of the mass of people who were praying for me afterwards, and the benefits derived by His actions were far better than I ever could have expected. God hears our prayers and He actively works through them in one way or another. Faith, along with being fully trusting, is not just the belief that God can do something in relation to our requests, but it is the belief that He is in fact actively doing something in response to our prayers even if sometimes it does not seem like it from our limited point of view.

Though I have identified many facets of what authentic faith is, and I have asserted that faith entails obedience to God because by our obedience we reveal our love of God, I want to make it clear that I am not trying to argue that we can and will be sinless if we so choose to be. The truth is, because of our corrupted and fallen nature we will sin at least occasionally and probably in some way even daily. These sins will occur daily whether by accident, or ignorance, either by omission or commission, and realistically most will be likely, in some way, intentional because honestly most sins, due to our corrupted nature are intentional even if we are not consciously aware of those intentions, but I think the difference is whether we habitually practice sin (1 John 3:4 and 9; Romans 1:32; 6:1–2, 11–12); or whether it is an occasional slip, and then we subsequently regret it and repent of it. Regardless of the circumstances, God is very merciful and patient; and when we recognize our sins, repent of them, and seek forgiveness, He is faithful to forgive us. He will even forgive us upon our repentance for those sins we committed when we may backslide and subsequently fall into a pattern of willfully engaging in sin for a period of time. Even though I am not arguing perfection in this life, and I have related God's faithfulness to forgive upon repentance, I also believe, because of God's righteous and just holiness, we may still face certain consequences for our sins even though they have been forgiven. Those consequences may be lost blessings and disrupted communion in this life or lost eternal rewards or some other circumstances in which God enacts justice. For me, I can certainly say that though I am grateful for the benefits derived from my situation, I certainly do not like being a quadriplegic. But being a quadriplegic was the chastising consequence necessary to finally get my attention and break the bonds of sin that I was bound by. Though I repented, being a quadriplegic was the consequence necessary to get my attention and, as a result, is now the circumstances where I am at, and considering the whole scope of things, I consider it more than just and even merciful though not enjoyable. It is because of God's justice against my sin in order to break the bond of sin that I awoke and now desire to serve God in the best way I can in my current situation. I have to suffer those consequences as a "thorn in the flesh" as they remind me of the cause and keep me humble. That being said, that consequences for sins might still be necessary in order to break the bonds of those sins, I am pointing out that there must be cautious consideration about the matters of God and the repercussions we may bring upon ourselves as a result of our sin and God's holy justice. We should be fearful about our own corrupted nature and though while having confidence in Christ, we need to remain humble and cautious regarding ourselves and our faith, always testing ourselves about whether we even truly believed (2 Corinthians 13:5, Galatians 6:3-5), because there is a fine line between being a prodigal but a saved believer and being a professing believer but one who never was saved in the first place.

Eventually after much patience and subtle but building efforts to nudge me awake, God saw fit to discipline me harshly so I would finally awaken and cry out to Him in my discipline. It is sort of like finally having a bucket of ice water poured on you during your sleep in order to wake you up because you keep hitting the snooze button. After being confronted with my sins, I was terrified of what I had done. God had confronted me with my sin and broken me—that is, He broke and humbled my heart in order to regain my heart and cause me to repent. This event of God's action was somewhat described in Ezekiel 14:4–5, 7(b) (paraphrased), "Any man who sets up idols in his heart...I the Lord will be brought to give him an answer, to answer him in My own person, in the matter in view of the multitude of his idols, in order to lay hold of the hearts...of those who are estranged from Me through all their idols." Honestly it was not being bedbound and suffering the spinal cord injury that distressed me. At that time I actually had no real understanding of how badly I had been injured even though I had been told. In my mind I had been injured before and recovered, and with hard work, I would again. What distressed me was when confronted with the sins I had committed in such a willful and knowing manner, and I knew I had no justification for them and could make no excuses to God. I had tried to justify my actions and to bring God down to my standards rather than making myself rise to meet His standards. I tried to place upon Him "human" conditions that fit my needs and desires and tried to place limitations on Him rather than recognizing God for who He is—the all-powerful, sovereign deity with no limitations, needs, or wants. He is the Almighty God. He is completely content and sovereign, and no conditions or bargains of any type can be placed on Him. By failing to understand Him and trying to place my own limitations and conditions on Him, I tried to live and control life by my own power instead of humbling and submitting myself to adherence and submission to His commands. I in effect was trying to control God and was unknowingly committing idolatry because I was placing myself and my wants above God. I was not only sorry but terrified because I had no reasonable explanation to give and no justification that would hold water. My bucket of justifications was leakier than a sieve with gaping holes in it. I had no recourse to save myself except to fall on His mercy. I had truly awakened to God in the hospital, my sins had been exposed, and I recognized there was nothing God did not know. During that moment, I felt God's presence and heard His voice as I never had before. Jeremiah 30:7 says, "Alas! for that day is great, there is none like it; And it is the time of Jacob's distress, but he will be saved from it." Or rather I interpret it in the context of Jeremiah 30:14-15, 24, "he will be saved as a result of it." My distress over my sin and God's presence awakened me, and

I cried out to Him for forgiveness and drew closer to Him than I ever had been, even closer than shortly after my baptism.

The fact is that God knows how to prevent sin, how to keep His lost children from further sinning, and to rescue His strayed. If I had continued on my path before the shooting, I would have continued in many types of sin, which would have affected me as well as others, but God in His providential workings, as I spoke about earlier, will rescue and prevent. I reflected back on Genesis 20 where Abimelech innocently took Abraham's wife for his own, but God in a dream made him aware of his potential sin if he violated Sarah. He said in verse 6, "Then God said to him in the dream, 'Yes, I know that you have done this in the integrity of your heart, and *it was I who kept you from sinning against me.* Therefore I did not let you touch her.'" Another passage could be the rescue of Lot from Sodom and Gomorrah. Though Lot was essentially righteous, upon living around the depravity of those cities, his moral compass had fallen a bit. Lot had received and was protecting the strangers (angels) but was willing to give his daughters up for abuse, but God took them out. In yet another passage, 1 Samuel 25, David was angry and planning to kill Nabal and all his men for his insolence, but Nabal's wife, Abigail, went out and met him with gifts of food and humbly apologized. David calmed, and his response was in verses 32–34: "Blessed be the Lord, the *God of Israel, who sent you this day to meet me!* Blessed be your discretion, and blessed be you, who have kept me this day from bloodguilt and from avenging myself with my own hand!" (Emphasis added). The Bible has several more examples of God's preventive providence. For me, God was not only causing my return through my shooting but He was also preventing me from escalating in certain sins and rescuing me from continuing in the cycle of sin in which I was so deeply ensnared. This prevention not only stopped me from those sins against God but likely protected others from the emotional and spiritual harm my sins might have subsequently caused.

My afflictions and the subsequent distress derived as a result of them as well as the blessings later received is reflective of the parables of the Lost Sheep, the Lost Coin, and the Lost Son in Luke 15; in each story, the lost items represented sinners who were being searched for by the owners who represented God. In each case, the owners, similes of God, searched for each item. In other words, God loves us and searches for our return when we wander off and become lost. In the Lost Coin parable, I interpreted the term "swept" to represented tribulation or other stormy events that occur until the item (sinner) would either recognize their need for Him, such as the Prodigal Son, or would otherwise be "found." In each case, upon being "found," that is as a result of our circumstances we lose our pride and humble ourselves, and return to Him asking forgiveness, God would not only accept us and forgive us but would rejoice and even bless us. This action of God seeking us is also described in Ezekiel 34:11-12 and 16 and was fulfilled in the birth of Christ. "For thus says the Lord God: Behold, I, I myself will search for my sheep and will seek them out. As a shepherd seeks out his flock when he is among his sheep that have been scattered, so will I seek out my sheep, and I will res-cue them from all places where they have been scattered on a day of clouds and thick darkness." "I will seek the lost, and I will bring back the strayed, and I will bind up the injured, and I will strengthen the weak."

My faith in my youth at the beginning of my Christian walk was weak and ill-defined, but God, in His love for me, patiently tolerated me and my immaturity and worked to awaken and mature me for many years. He sought me out, exacted the fatherly discipline that was necessary and lovingly but sternly confronted me with my sinfulness and unfaithfulness in order to bring me to the mature and solid faith I hold today. I'm sure a more solid teaching and instruc-tion of the true meaning of faith in my beginning walk with Christ would have assisted me in walking better and thereby saved me from a lot of grief, and I encourage church leaders to develop and teach their congregations, and especially new converts, the true meaning and understanding of what faith is. But I also now realize God, the Great Shepherd, will take all the necessary actions needed to bring even the weakest in faith into a strong faith and a true love and trust in Him. God loves us that much.

Trials Are Our Friend

I WOULD EVENTUALLY DISCOVER THAT upon honestly and sincerely accepting Christ into my life, I was sanctified. Being sanctified essentially means being set apart or being made and presented as holy to God. But I also discovered there are two stages of sanctification. The first stage was that upon truly accepting Jesus Christ into my life, I then and there had what is termed Positional Sanctification, that is, I was at that point and forevermore positioned as a child of God in heaven. Though I might stray for a while, that position as a child of God through faith in Christ would never be lost. The prodigal son, though he strayed from the father and lived an immoral life for a while, did not stop being his father's son. As an earthly perspective, I may declare my parents are not my parents but my declaring it does not abolish the truth, that they are and always will be no matter what and DNA tests will prove it. It cannot be changed. As mentioned before, our conduct could cause some of our inheritance to be impacted, it could undergo some eternal alterations with regard to rewards, and it appears that is one thing that Satan strives at, but the position itself as a child of God could not be lost.

There is however a second stage of sanctification that exists while I am still living in the body of flesh, and being in my still-corrupted body, affects my current existence. That second stage is theologically called Progressive Sanctification. Progressive Sanctification in essence means that though I had Positional Sanctification, because

I also continued to exist in a corrupted and fallen body, I was still very imperfect and apt to sinful behavior. Due to the body's fleshly nature, I was inclined to being drawn away from God; but by the work of God through His Holy Spirit, I would slowly and *progressively* be transformed into the image of Christ. I would slowly improve so as to become less sinful and self-centered and more faithfully trusting and obedient; my love of God would grow stronger and simultaneously, as my love of God expanded and deepened, I would also become more loving and others-oriented and would in time glorify God by my conduct and bearing in Christ. The apostle Paul talked strongly about the struggle between the Spirit and the flesh in Romans 7:14–24 and our sanctification in Christ from Romans 7:25 to Romans 8. Jesus also mentioned this struggle in Matthew 26:41 but ensures us of our security in John 10:28–29 and the Holy Spirit's help in assisting us into becoming the image of Christ in John 14:26.

It was not long until I found that the progressive sanctification process involved many things at various levels. It involved the blessings of God in many ways as well as His providential hand presenting certain opportunities or events and at the same time preventing certain opportunities and events. But what I found that seemed most applicable to me in my particular case was that God works very strongly and quite frequently through trial and affliction. God's efforts through blessings to me reciprocated no grateful effect or gratitude, and I did not take notice of His providential efforts, but then God allowed my shooting and confronted me directly in the hospital through that event and revealed to me my willful sinfulness and how I had strayed like a lost sheep from His righteous path. Once I had awakened to God as a result of that, I then saw others who were going through trials of their own and observed how they were also drawing closer to God as a result of their circumstances. I likewise observed a very similar pattern for persons of the Bible. If we look again at the prodigal son parable as an analogy, we see the son was blessed under his father's guidance while home and we see the father again bless his son with the early portion of his inheritance. The son was unappreciative of what he had at home and left and subsequently squandered his inheritance on sinful living. During this time, he sustained many hardships that caused him to become very appreciative of his father and what he had under his father's care, and thus he returned. If we will observe in many instances in the Bible, the Holy Spirit led persons in a manner and into circumstances that tried them and tested their faith, and these trials they faced were for the purpose of their progressive sanctification. He also rebukes us as we pursue our fleshly cravings and reminds us of the truth of God. We often go through similar phases as we are progressively sanctified by being cleansed and transformed from our fleshly nature as we see the emptiness of fleshly behavior and the holy and righteous nature of Christ.

As I read through the Bible many times, and particularly the Old Testament, I saw God is heavily involved in our temporal lives. He allows many things to occur, prevents others, but actually, in many cases, causes things to happen in response to our behavior either one way or another, but always out of His righteousness and His love for His creation and intent for our good. It quickly became obvious that faith itself is not fully grown or perfected when we first believe. It takes time and exercise of faith to make it grow and strengthen, as can be observed even with the apostles and other biblical forefathers. We can see that even though the founding fathers and the apostles had faith to be obedient in many ways, they also had many failures for various reasons, most of which were centered around thinking based upon human experience, pride, and worries. Though they would have failings, God worked things in such a way that they eventually returned ever stronger in faith as they obtained a greater understanding of God and His way. (2 Peter 3:18; Ephesians 4:13; 1 Timothy 4:6–7; Romans 11:33; Mark 8:17; Hosea 4:1). Faith begins small, even smaller than a mustard seed, but though it is small in itself, it is still strong enough to believe in Christ and accept Him as Lord and Savior. But faith needs to grow, and the only way it grows is to be exercised through acts of trust and reliance on God and a growing knowledge of Him through not only the good times but also the bad. It should be easy to be faithful when things are good and everything is comfortable and going well. I said it "should be" easy, but it is during these comfortable times we most often actually become complacent in many ways and begin to fail Him and even digress. Whether we backslide or not, it is still my opinion that during these good times, faith does not grow much mainly because we fail to recognize and be grateful for the blessings we have been given or even acknowledge where they are from. Our blessings are meant for the building of our faith and awareness and knowledge of God, but because of our corrupt and greedy nature, they rarely are; and in fact, we become rather apathetic toward our blessings and begin to take them for granted. Instead, it is during our hard times while undergoing trials and afflictions of various natures and we turn to God for support that our faith and knowledge of God really begin to grow. Just as our love needs to grow beyond infatuation, our faith needs to grow from smaller than a mustard seed into a giant tree.

In the progressive sanctification process, when we first become Christians, we are immature in our Christianity, and are as the apostle Paul labeled us, as "babes in Christ," but over time, through God's trial and testing, His blessings and chastisements, His graces and mercies, we progressively mature and become more transformed into the image of Christ. We will never be perfect while in this life, but we will always be improving. As a result of our continued growth in Christ, as we continue to transform, our faith also grows; and as our faith grows, our love of God and Christ grows. When I became a Christian at a young age, I think my love for God was more of an infatuation and in some ways like the beginning of a marriage. At the first of a marriage, everything is new and exciting, and the couple still tries to avoid things that might be unsightly or undesirable to the spouse. But as time wears on and the newness of the marriage fades and the couple becomes more settled and comfortable, some of the less desirable attributes begin to appear, but, in my opinion, that is when love and marriage truly begin to grow. Once the flaws appear and the couple becomes more accepting of each other's flaws, then they can truly become more comfortable with each other and accept each other, and when they do, their love grows stronger. God has no flaws, but unfortunately, I had many, and I failed to nurture my relationship with God as well as I should have; and because of my fallen nature, I was not as accepting of some of the restraints of His commandments as I should have been. God Himself loved me even while stained with sin and was willing to send His Son to die for me in order to redeem me and restore my relationship to Him, but sadly my love for Him in return was not nearly as perfect so I strayed.

I think many, if not all, Christians experience a time of great joy and have little perceived conflict with Satan during this initial time of salvation. There are temptations, sure, but their power over the new Christian is minimal if even nonexistent. Possibly this is also a gift of God to allow us to enjoy this time of freedom before the progressive sanctification is to begin. But Satan is aware of your salvation decision, and though he may not be able to stop it, he will do everything in his power while here on earth to impact it and prevent you from displaying the glory of God by your conforming to the image of Christ. Satan bides his time during this initial period and waits for the elation to cool, and then he starts attacking. His attacks may be subtle at first or sometimes come at a full assault or anywhere in between, but rest assured he has not forgotten.

In a way it seems strange because it often appears many unbelievers seem to have many things going for them. For many, their life seems hassle free, and they often excel while many believers seem to have a hard time and are struggling with one thing after another. This really should not be surprising though because Satan really is not worried about the unbeliever. If they are caught up in worldly pursuits and pleasures and not giving God or Christ or their eternal future much thought, then that is just fine with him because he still has their soul. Satan is the temporary ruler of this earth and just as he offered Jesus all the treasures on earth if He would worship him, he will do the same with us. If Satan can distract a person with wealth, power, and comfort in order to keep their focus off Jesus he will. So nonbelievers will often seem to prosper while believers seem to struggle. That is not to say there are not prosperous Christians, there are, but I dare say wealth and ease can be a prickly situation and the financially prosperous Christian has an additional area in their lives they must deal with. The prosperous Christian must continuously be on guard because being financially prosperous adds a new dynamic and opens opportunities others would not face. What did Christ say? "Truly, I say to you, only with difficulty will a rich person enter the kingdom of heaven. Again I tell you, it is easier for a camel to go through the eye of a needle than for a rich person to enter the kingdom of God." (Matthew 19:23–24). Regardless of the circumstances, it is the believer that makes Satan angry. Though he will still harass the unbeliever in many ways, it is the believer he specifically targets and gives a hard time. If the believer keeps their focus on Christ, they can overcome, but the struggle and striving against Satan's schemes can feel quite intense.

Though Satan's attacks were going to happen regardless, I had opened myself up for his assaults even further when I failed to keep my communion with and obedience to God active through church fellowship, Bible study, and regular prayer time. In fact, shortly after entering college, my communion with God had all but ceased on my end. This in actuality was even a subtle attack by Satan himself as he tapped into my pride and planted thoughts in my head, making me think I could maintain my Christian principles on my own. When I bit off on that lie because it was difficult for me, or rather I was too lazy, to get to a church without a relatively long walk, then Satan really put forth his efforts to draw me into sin. Those efforts still began slowly and subtly, but he consistently and persistently began to wear me down as he wove his web of temptations, lies, and deceit.

Due to my lack of communal time with God and fellowship with other Christians and also because of my corrupted nature, it was not long before I began making excuses to sin and, as a result, became apathetic toward my sin. By becoming apathetic toward my sin, I was actually making a trifle of Christ's sacrifice on the cross. I had lost the sting of sin and failed to recognize just how much God hated it and what it cost in the way of Christ's redemptive payment for my sin.

I see many Christians who are happy about the gospel message and well should we be, but I also see many professing Christians who, like I had once been, are taking sin lightly. They do not feel grief or guilt for their ongoing and even possibly willful sin because they have lost their sense of the cost of it. They have lost worry over it because it is in their eyes not costing them anything since they think it will not be held against them due to Christ's sacrifice on the cross. In addition, because they have become complacent with their own sin, they have also become apathetic about the sins of others, and so the line has been crossed and the spiral of sin increases. There are even some preachers who tell them not to worry about their sin and they can be guilt free, all the while tickling their ears but severely impacting their eternal life. Many Christians are happy Christ died for them and happy it was God's redemptive plan preordained from the beginning of time. Though we should be happy for Christ's sacrifice, what we should be doing is mourning and being sorrowful for our sins as well as the world's sinfulness (Matthew 5:4, James 4:9). Why should we not be sad and grieve because of our sins and feel guilt knowing it is for our sins that Christ had to die on the cross? God is so holy it took that extent to redeem us, why should we not be conscience-sticken at the cost? I am humbled and greatly remorseful when I consider Christ had to die on the cross for me. I am even further saddened that after hearing and accepting the gospel, I would subsequently justify my sins and take the cross so lightly. How sad to have become so callus.

Where once I was callus and apathetic about my sin, now upon my awakening, I grieve how sinful I had become. I still feel remorse about how sinful I can still perceive myself to be. I loathe even being faced with temptation when I realize the reason I am facing that temptation is primarily because of the internal lusts of my own corrupted nature (James 1:14). Often when I pray, I thank God for willingly sending His Son, and I thank Jesus for willingly coming and dying for us, but then I also apologize and ask for forgiveness because He had to die for me due to my nature being so corrupted that no other sacrifice would suffice to restore me. Would any one of us readily and willingly die for a total stranger, especially one who was mean and evil and unappreciative? Would any of us even more willingly let our child die for that stranger? I doubt any of us would, but God loves us so much that He did.

Can you see now how much God hates sin and how harmful and disruptive our sin is? Can you realize this and truly be remorseful and grieve? That is, I believe, what God is wanting. He wants us to hate sin as much as He does and to grieve over it as much as He grieves over our sinfulness. Our freedom from guilt is not supposed to be freedom from feeling guilty about our committing sin, it is instead, freedom in Christ from being bound by the power of sin to commit any sin, and ultimately it is the freedom from being found guilty—that is, it is freedom from being condemned on the great Judgment Day. Paul in 2 Timothy 3:18 said, "The Lord will rescue me from every evil deed and bring me safely into his heavenly kingdom." Though Paul was facing persecution and death and the Lord can rescue us from that, what Paul was more specifically referring to was that, by faith in Christ, no matter what we may face or endure, even death itself, Christ Jesus, by His blood sacrifice, will rescue us from any evil by Satan and give us eternal life. Christ the Judge has broken the bonds and the power of sin and has set us free from our sins, and we will not be condemned. But though Paul confirms for us that Christ can rescue us from all the evil attempts of Satan and we will have eternal life, he also warns us our sin can carry eternal consequences, so we must still fight against sin and be ever grievous and remorseful over our sin while in this life.

I would later come to realize that though I had strayed from God's path and was not in any regular communication with Him, He had not stopped watching over me. I discovered my temptations and the trials I would undergo as a result of decisions I made regarding those temptations were all part of the progressive sanctification process, but I also came to realize that even as I experienced those situations, that God was still watching over me as the good shepherd and was still in full control by having set limits with regard to each situation I would face. None of my temptations were to such a degree that I could not resist them. God does not allow us to be tempted beyond what we are able to resist. (1 Cor. 10:13). The problem is, in our fallen human nature, we choose to allow those temptations to enter our minds and dwell on them until they are out of control rather than kicking them out as soon as we are approached by them (James 1:14–15). Once we have accepted Christ, since He has broken the bonds of sin, any sins we chose to commit are just that, our choice. These temptations are not by God, they are by Satan and our own corrupt nature, but God allows them for the purpose of allowing the choice to see what we will choose. When I say "to see what we will choose", I am not saying God does not already know, He does, He is omniscient and knows everything, but what I mean is that He will reveal to us, by our choice, our lack of strength and corruptive nature. He allows them for the maturing of our faith, the improvement in our growth as a Christian as we come to realize we made a wrong choice when we sin, and showing us our need for Him, all in order to progressively sanctify us. I still had free will to obey or not or to do or not, and these tests of my faith and the myriad of failures in passing these tests would eventually show me I could not succeed on my own. My failures in particular would cause me to cry out for help, eventually bring me to repentance and recognize my need for God's power, grace, and mercy through Christ Jesus. These trials were to mature and grow my faith into obedience and a true love of God. They would eventually give me stronger self-control and perseverance, not only perseverance against my temptations themselves, but also for persistence in my strength of faith by recognizing God's way is best. It is because of the effects of these trials and temptations in growing my faith and maturing me that I discovered I should in fact rejoice in going through them, though they were, and are, often very difficult. To be honest, it is hard for me to rejoice facing and battling my temptations. It is hard because I know how corrupted and weak I am, and facing my temptations and striving against them really feels like suffering to me. I can handle being in a wheelchair and many of the things related to that, but fighting against my sinful nature is rough. But because I now know the purpose for these temptations and that they are in fact allowed, though they are never allowed to the degree that I could not overcome, I can in fact rejoice, or rather find a reason to joy in my temptation, especially when I am able to overcome them and I see His perfecting work making progress. James 1:2–4 says, "Consider it all joy, my brethren, when you encounter various trials, knowing that the testing of your faith produces steadfastness. And let steadfastness have *its* full effect, so that you may be perfect and complete, lacking in nothing." This is echoed by Peter in 1 Peter 4:12–13 and by Paul in Romans 5:3–4.

The apostle Paul stated in 2 Corinthians 4:8, "We are afflicted in *every* way," but then follows that with verse 17, which states, "For momentary, light affliction is producing for us an eternal weight of glory far beyond all comparison." There are many reasons besides our willful sins for which we must endure various kinds of tribulations. Jesus tells us temptations not only will come, but even that they are necessary (Luke 17:1; Matt. 18:7). All the trials and temptations and testing we face, all of these are certainly part of God's work as He makes us more disciplined and further sanctifies us for our ultimate good as well as the good of others. Paul reveals two other purposes of our trials other than for our rewards and sanctification as mentioned in verse 17: He tells us they also occur so that we will be able to comfort those who are in any affliction with the comfort with which we ourselves are comforted by God in our affliction (2 Corinthians 1:4), and that we would rely on God and not ourselves and our power (2 Corinthians 1:8–9). Though in this passage Paul points these purposes out, we will find there are more.

As I read through the Bible, I noticed many of the great men of the Bible suffered various chastisements and disciplines by the hand of God. These temporal chastisements or discipline building events were either consequences or tests or other life-shaping events God used to build discipline in one form or another and/or to correct errant behavior and erroneous thinking in His children, all in order to create a higher level of righteousness and a greater awareness and understanding of God Himself. These events occurred on national levels such as is noticeably observed with Israel, but they also happened individually such as with Moses, Aaron, David, Job, and others; and I would come to understand these events were not just discipline for sin, but were actually discipline building events aligned with the sanctification process.

John the Baptist talking about Jesus in Luke 3:16 stated, "He will baptize you with the Holy Spirit and fire." This is followed with the description of Jesus with the winnowing fork in His hand separating the wheat from the chaff. I understood baptism by the Holy Spirit and that the Holy Ghost is often synonymous with "fire," but why were they separated here with the conjunctive "and"? What is this baptism with fire? As I reflected on this I contemplated that the Holy Spirit we receive by baptism in Christ not only seals us as God's and separates us as holy, but He also rebukes us and teaches us. Along with rebuking and teaching, He also convicts us of sin and sanctifies us, but how does that sanctification work? In Mark 10:38 Jesus asked two of His disciples, "Are you able to drink the cup that I drink, or to be baptized with the baptism with which I am baptized?" referring to His impending crucifixion. In another teaching He tells us that in the world "you will have tribulation" (John 16:33) and in Acts 14:22 Paul stated, "That through many tribulations we must enter the kingdom of God." That "baptism" Jesus was speaking of in Mark 10:38, those trials and tribulations we face can be from a variety of sources and often they may be related to temptations we face in our attempts to conduct ourselves in a righteous and holy manner in our walk with God while in this world, but as I stated earlier, Jesus taught those temptations we face would not only happen, but were in fact "necessary." In the Old Testament, "fire" is often used to describe the presence of God such as Exodus 3:2; 13:21; 19:18; 24:17, Deuteronomy 4:12, Isaiah 66:15 and in many others. It is also used to describe God such as Deuteronomy 4:24 which states, "For the Lord your God is a consuming fire." In other verses fire references a cleansing and purification process and others a discipline/punishing process or a display of God's power such as 1 Kings 18:24–38 or 2 Kings 1:12 and 14 and Psalms 50:3. Other verses describe God's judgment on sin or evil such as Job 15:34; Psalms 97:3, Isaiah 66:16; Lamentations 2:3–4, Amos 7:4 or God's cleansing and sanctifying process such as Isaiah 10:16–17; 26:11, Jeremiah 15:13–14; Lamentations 4:11 and 22, Malachi 3:2. In the New Testament, God is still described as a consuming fire (Hebrews 12:29) and the Holy Spirit is represented as tongues of fire in Acts 2:3. In observing all these verses, we see, ultimately in one way or another, fire is quite often used not only to describe God, but frequently describes the purification process of believers. In addition to the testing and sanctifying process of believers, fire will also test our works such as 1 Corinthians 3:13 or be used in the judgment of unbelievers and the wicked which may be an attempt of conviction and calling within itself as well as punishment. All that being said, 1 Thessalonians 4:3 reveals to us the will of God which is our sanctification and 1 Thessalonians 4:7 says that "God has not called us for impurity, but in holiness." It is my contention that much of our progressive sanctification while still in this earthly body is obtained through enduring trials and testing of various types which purges us of our evil inclinations and purifies us as one purifies gold through fire, and that is the fire referenced in conjunction with the Holy Spirit in Luke 3:16. The fiery trials we endure are part of the work of the Holy Spirit as He sanctifies us and purifies us through these various means, by rebuking us and convicting us of our sin while undergoing testing and trials of various types.

> But if *anyone suffers* as a Christian, he is not to be ashamed, but is to glorify God in that name. For *it is* time for judgment to begin with the household of God; and if *it begins* with us first, what *will be* the outcome for those who do not obey the gospel of God? And if it is with difficulty that the righteous is saved, what will become of the godless man and the sinner? Therefore, those also who suffer *according to the will of God* shall entrust their souls to a faithful Creator in doing what is right. (1 Peter 4:16–19, emphasis added)

Matthew Henry commented on 1 Peter 4:16–19[5] saying,

> "That these judgments will but *begin* with you that are God's house and family, and will soon be over: your trials and corrections will not last long."
>
> "The best of God's servants, his own household, have so much amiss in them as renders it fit and necessary that God should sometimes correct and punish them with his judgments."
>
> "But, if we take the salvation here in the highest sense, then we may learn, [2.] It is as much as the best can do to secure the salvation of their souls; there are so many sufferings, temp-

tations, and difficulties to be overcome, so many sins to be mortified, the gate is so strait and the way so narrow, that it is as much as the righteous can do to be saved. Let the absolute necessity of salvation balance the difficulty of it. Consider, Your difficulties are greatest at first; God offers his grace and help; the contest will not last long; be but faithful to the death, *and God will give you the crown of life,* Rev. 2:10."

"All the sufferings that befall good people come upon them *according to the will of God.* (2.) It is the duty of Christians, in all their distresses, to look more to the keeping of their souls than to the preserving of their bodies."

"The only way to keep the soul well is to commit it to God, in well-doing. Commit your souls to God by solemn dedication, prayer, and patient perseverance in well-doing, Rom. 2:7. (4.) Good people, when they are in affliction, have great encouragement to commit their souls to God, because he is their Creator, and faithful in all his promises."

Our God is the righteous judge of nations and peoples and exacts His ongoing judgments against sin in our temporal time, but He does it for the sanctification of His children. Examples of these temporal judgments and the purposes behind them can be seen throughout the books of the prophets. It is important to understand that the temporal judgments of believers, both His chosen in the Old Testament and the believers of the New Testament, are not in any way related to punishment. God will reveal His anger and wrath against sin, but His actions are disciplinary in nature rather than vengeful. Punishment is vindictive in nature, is initiated as a payback for a wrong done, and has no redemptive value. Though God's mercy filled chastisements done out of love can be observed in the Old Testament, it ultimately reveals itself in the New Testament when

Jesus died on the cross (Eph. 1:5–7; 2:4–7). When Jesus died on the cross as a propitiatory sacrifice for us He took all the punishment of God toward the believer upon Himself (Rom. 3:22–25). God does not and will not punish the believer because of Christ's sacrifice for our transgressions. What we must understand is that God's temporal judgments of the believer are not a punishment but are rather disciplinary in nature as a loving father disciplines his child in order to train, correct and help us grow and mature. God's discipline is always out of love for His children and is only geared toward our future benefit and welfare. Using me as an example, God's judgment of my sin, His loving disciplinary chastisement through my trial and affliction in the hospital in order to correct my mindset and behavior, was what finally got my attention and my return to God. Although discipline can often feel like punishment, it is not. Discipline is out of love and for correction but unfortunately it took a disciplinary act of that severity to get my attention. I had hit a low, but God in His mercy was seeking my return, and by His grace, He had, upon my repentance, allowed me to recover much further than anticipated. My substantial recovery was simply another undeserved mercy He extended to me based upon my repentance. All total I was in the hospital for eight and a half months, and as Dr. Kowalske predicted when I left the hospital, I was able to use a walker to walk short distances, and through the use of cochlear implants, I can now hear. After leaving the hospital, I was in outpatient rehabilitation for about another year and a half. Once I was in outpatient rehabilitation, I continued to progress. In fact, things were progressing so well the doctor felt that someday I might even be able to use a cane instead of the walker. I praised God for my improved condition, and I cannot help but feel that my response of repentance upon God's revelation of my sinfulness and recognition of my shooting being His work in answering my prayers led to this improvement. If I had chosen the other way of thinking, the worldly way, not giving God credit, I wonder what might have happened then.

But I did respond to recognizing God's hand, and I believe God rewarded me for that by allowing me to progress quite well. Things were beginning to look up, and I was also confident that I would be able to progress to a cane someday. My SWAT team members even bought me a cane fashioned out—of all things—a bull's reproductive organ. I cannot begin to imagine why they would give me a cane made from that and wondered if they were implying I was bullheaded or something. In any case, I loved it and hoped to be using it someday.

My progress in rehab was going that well. But then, like Job, I had another tribulation. For some unknown reason, my physical abilities began to decline. The decline began in outpatient therapy, and it was believed I had just peaked at my recovery, and therapy stopped. At first, after getting home, I exercised every day and still continued to progress until I could walk almost two thousand four hundred feet with a walker. Granted, it took me about a half hour to make that walk, but I did it daily. I still maintained an ambition of getting to a cane and maybe even walking a one-mile walk/run event someday, even if it took all day. However, the decline that manifested in therapy surfaced again at home. At first the walking became hard. I struggled to walk the twenty-four hundred feet, and eventually I struggled to even walk two hundred feet. It was later determined by doctors that my body, basically my brain, was blasting too many nerve signals, thereby overloading the nerve receptors and so basically overwhelming my system and causing my muscles to be rigid; they were contracting but not releasing, and so I could not "step." As a result, I underwent another surgery to install an intrathecal baclofen pump. At first that seemed to help, and after a few months, I had progressed back to walking about a thousand feet. But that is where the progress stopped, and the decline started again. As time progressed, I could only walk short distances with extensive hands-on assistance, and now I cannot walk at all. Though I could not walk, for a while I could at least stand for about fifteen minutes at a time and watch my son's baseball game or some other event. I eventually even lost the ability to be able to stand erect, and when I did try to stand, it took great effort, and I am in a crunched or bent position rather than standing, and the "standing" I did was attributed almost exclusively to arm strength. Now I cannot even do that. It was very disheartening to lose those physical abilities I had once regained.

However, as I reflect back on Job's tribulation, I cannot help but feel that physical regression I was experiencing was a further testing of my faith and a perfecting process to get me where I need to be with God. "But though our outer man is decaying, yet our inner man is being renewed day by day. For momentary, light affliction is producing for us an eternal weight of glory far beyond all comparison" (2 Cor. 4:16–17 NASB). Our bodies are only temporary vessels anyway. Our physical bodies will expire whether through illness, trauma, or just getting worn-out through age. But during our affliction, just like Job, we are being taught, shaped, and prepared much like a potter shaping a clay vessel (Jeremiah 18:3–6). For those being afflicted, *if* we are paying attention and respond properly, the afflictions we face help bring our focus to God and shape our character and, more importantly, train our spirit to get it where God wants it to be. It may be that I was likely becoming too prideful in myself again rather than properly giving all the credit to God, similar to Moses and Arron at the waters of Meribah (Numbers 20:9–13). My thoughts on this possibility are simply my way of understanding it, but certainly there are no limits to God's plan and purpose for it, and they may extend far beyond just me. But I do consider that God is still in the molding and perfecting process and is still killing that conceited pride within me. He is still humbling me into complete trust and reliance on Him and into giving Him *all* the glory.

Our God is a loving God who is full of grace and mercy, but our human fleshly ideas of grace and mercy are not necessarily God's, and He thinks far beyond our ability to contemplate or imagine. The Bible tells us that every good and perfect gift comes from God (James 1:17) and that God does not tempt anyone (James 1:13). Catch what these verses are saying, because only good comes from God, then He does not do evil to anyone, but the Bible also reveals to us that God is in ultimate and complete control of everything. Since God is in ultimate control of everything, in essence, when we suffer by some means, it is from God. I am not saying that God is the actor of the suffering, because suffering is caused by Satan and living in a fallen world, but in the ultimate picture, since God in His sovereignty is in control of everything, in a way, it is from Him because He has allowed Satan to cause it; but even though He has allowed it, He has done so with limitations and for His good purpose. He does not Himself afflict us, but He will allow us to be afflicted. What many people do not understand is that the bad we endure, the trials and afflictions that God allows are actually for our ultimate good—that is, they are allowed for one reason or another in order to benefit us in our sanctification and potentially others beyond us. Though we might suffer in some form physically or emotionally, and we perceive and define that as bad, when we realize it is actually for our benefit spiritually than what we perceive as bad, it is actually fully good. The problem is not with God's providential workings but with our definition of bad and good. In other words, what I am saying is that what we see as bad because it causes us to suffer, God actually sees and knows it to be good because it improves us spiritually even if we may not perceive how, and therefore, in the end, it means our suffering is in reality a good gift from Him. Our God is righteous and just, and He loves us so much He will chastise us and cause us distress in order to save us.

> For My thoughts are not your thoughts, nor are
> your ways My ways," says the Lord. "For as the
> heavens are higher than the earth, so are My ways
> higher than your ways, and My thoughts than
> your thoughts. (Isaiah 55:8–9)

In the book *WHY, O GOD? Suffering and Disability in the Bible and Church*, by Larry J. Waters and Roy B. Zuck,[6] they identify many of the reasons for our suffering. I will paraphrase their list and also show how many of the list connect to my ordeal:

1. Preventive Suffering—which was to keep one from perpetuating a sinful, false theology but also shows this type of suffering was not a rejection of them by God but instead an acceptance and training of them. This type of suffering warns and instructs, keeps the sufferer from wrongdoing and sin, keeps a person from pride and arrogance, saves a

person from the pit, and saves them from divine discipline. It is instructive, directive, and salvific. It warns, urges obedience, humbles, and guides the believer down the right path.

I believe I somewhat fell into this category partly because God was preventing me from escalating my sins in a manner that would have created more problems for myself and also harmed others including my children. Prior to my shooting I had experienced preventive suffering throughout my life that certainly had humbling and instructive effects, but for the most part I was not mindful of or alert to the spiritual instruction intended by those events and basically ignored them. I was also engaged in the belief of a false theology in that anything I did would have no consequences because of my professing of faith in Christ. He would awaken me to the truth through this and additionally prevented me from escalating into certain sins through the desire for obedience itself. Though I did eventually endure God's divine discipline through my shooting, it was because I elected not to hear and be guided by His warnings provided by His earlier efforts of preventive suffering.

2. Correctional or Disciplinary Suffering—It is the alternative to heeding the warnings of preventive suffering. It also serves to warn and direct the sufferer who refuses to forsake some sinful trend when confronted with preventive suffering. It is a step beyond just warning in that it escalates to actual chastisement.

This was what I had suffered while going through the shooting and hospitalization where God confronted me directly with my obstinate sinful behavior. I had experienced the preventive suffering through previous trials, but I did not listen to them. I also feel God was preventing me from escalating to future sins, which would have negatively affected my family and others. Because I did not heed the previous preventive suffering, I was escalated to correctional suffering which would indeed correct my sinful behavior and redirect my focus to God.

3. Educational Suffering—It teaches humility, God's will, obedience and self-control, patience and perseverance, and encourages a life of faith and looking to future glory. It teaches us to share in the sufferings of Christ and to represent Him and our faith to others, to pray and give thanks in times of trouble because of all the sanctifying benefits of it.

This Educational Suffering followed along with my Correctional Suffering. Once I had awakened, was humbled and repented, I truly began to learn about God, who He is and what He desires from us with regard to His will, obedience, self-control, and sharing in the suffering of Christ as we resist and endure temptation, trials, and afflictions by numerous causes. Because of all the sanctifying benefits I sustained as a result of His correctional actions and the growth in the awareness and knowledge of God, I could indeed give thanks for my time of trouble.

4. Glorification Suffering—Suffering can bring glory to God as the sufferer remains faithful and even praises God as he endures his suffering.

At the time, I did not recognize I was doing this because in my eyes I considered myself a complete failure with regards to my duties to God. But my faith, as weak as it was, became much stronger after God's confrontation and apparently displayed itself to others as I went through my physical therapy and afterward. I had been so grateful for His undeserved mercy and the about-face away from sin and returning to God, it caused me to give God all glory and praise for the outcome of His correctional discipline. I am so grateful to Him for not giving up on me and for taking His corrective action. Although I am still confined to a chair and have a life that will remain in physical suffering, I am so grateful for His actions, which caused my repentance, that I tell everyone how good and wonderful God is; and though I would desire to still have some of my initial recovery back, I in fact would not change a thing, if God so wills, because of what it has done for me and is still teaching me. God's work of righteous justice along with His loving mercy was displayed on me, and that can do nothing other than bring God glory.

5. Revelational or Communicational Suffering—This type of suffering helps the sufferer gain a deeper understanding of God's relational attributes of faith, love, and mercy. God forgives; He turns His people back to the right path and persuades to proper action.

I have seen God in His justice and faithfulness will exact certain chastising judgments, but in doing so, He will still extend His love and mercy by not making those judgments as severe as they could or should be. During these events, God will reveal not only the reason we are facing our events, but through them He will also communicate certain aspects of His majesty. Until my event, I had not recognized the full scope and extent of God's righteousness and justice. Remember His purpose in doing this is ultimately for our good as He wishes all to come to repentance and be saved. God in His holy righteousness and justice and in His deep love and desire for our salvation has and often will reveal and communicate His purpose and reason, often before the event, later while going through our event or afterward as we begin to recognize the purpose and benefits of why we went through our suffering event.

6. Organizational Suffering—This type of suffering can be God's method of teaching us what is important and prioritizes one's life and relationship with God. This type of suffering forces the believer to become dependent on God, to number his days and use his time wisely, and to focus the

sufferer's mind and hope on the grace to be revealed upon Christ's return.

I like to refer to "the numbering of days and using time wisely" aspect as "redeeming the time," realizing each day is an extra day God has given me, and using my time now redeemed to me to place God as the first priority of my life and do good works and make up for all the lost time I spent in my sins. I now realize each day is a gift and that all I have is from God and there is no promise of tomorrow and so each day should be used wisely and not wasted.

7. Relational Suffering—Relational Suffering can be used to develop a sufferer's relationship with God. Those suffering will cry out to Him, and in the midst of their suffering, He will deliver them by giving them "peace beyond understanding." This peace can not only make the sufferer grateful for their suffering, but it develops and deepens their faith and trust in Him. It also reveals the Father's love for us and confirms they are His child. This peace, the improvement of the personal relationship through increased faith and trust, can cause the person suffering to even praise God and rejoice in the suffering.

I can completely ascribe to this relational suffering; as I had made those prayers to be restored to Him prior to my shooting, I then cried out to Him in the hospital after being confronted with my sins, repented, and begged for another chance. I subsequently, by His mercy, recovered physically more than the prognosis predicted, my relationship with God is stronger than it ever was, and I rejoice in my suffering because of its effect upon me and because it proved to me beyond a shadow of a doubt, as noted in Preventive Suffering, that I was His child (Hebrews 12:4–7). I would like to clarify that even though we may have peace with our suffering and can even rejoice because of the various benefits derived from it; that does not mean we enjoy our suffering. Our sufferings can be hard and quite unpleasant. There is not a joy in suffering, itself, but there is a joy in the spiritual benefits obtained as a result of it.

8. Proclamational or Declarational Suffering—This type of suffering magnifies God and displays His judicious and wise nature.

God is true and faithful and will bring about what He says He will do, whether that is a blessing or a curse. He will do it for the sufferer's good even if that good is caused through chastisement, and He will do it for His own namesake. Nothing He does, no matter how hard it is, is either unfair or unjust, nor does He owe us anything. God pointed out several times in Ezekiel that He was going to punish Jerusalem and Judea because they were profaning His name, and He would not allow His name to be profaned. I would also fall into this category because prior to my suffering, though I might have professed myself a Christian by belief, I was living in very un-Christian ways. I was in essence profaning God's name, and He was not going to let that continue. As I stated earlier, I in fact brought my discipline upon myself as God had proclaimed or declared "life or death, blessing and curse" based on our chosen's actions, (Deuteronomy 30) and subsequently, as a result, He revealed His just, wise, holy and sovereign nature through it.

The short of it is God very often uses afflictions and tribulations to draw our focus to Him. It is through these afflictions and our distress that we lean on God for help and comfort. Jesus set the example for us when He went through His afflictions both during and even before His crucifixion; "while being reviled, He did not revile in return; while suffering, He uttered no threats, *but kept entrusting Himself to Him who judges righteously*" (1 Peter 2:23). We, like Christ, must have faith in God's *purposes* in our affliction. Unlike us, Jesus suffered tremendous and undeserved affliction that God the Father not only allowed but orchestrated. But the purpose for that affliction, God's plan with complete agreement and cooperation of Jesus, His Son, from the beginning of creation, was for Him to be a *perfect* and unblemished sacrifice in order to make atonement for the sin of mankind, which God knew was to occur and abhorred and not only would not, but could not, righteously accept without just punishment. Jesus's sacrifice was the just punishment necessary for our redemption and salvation if only we will have faith in Him and accept Him as our Lord.

Just as Jesus accepted His affliction without using abusive language or having contempt for His situation or hating those who were carrying out the crucifixion, we also need to trust God's plans for our lives and respond as Jesus said in Matthew 26:39, "My Father, if it is possible, let this cup pass from Me; nevertheless, not as I will, but as You *will*." We need to follow Christ's example by putting our trust in Him and enduring our affliction even if it leads to the death of our fleshly bodies. It is important that we recognize we are being trained and prepared "for glory beyond all comparison" (2 Corinthians 4:17). Let me emphasize this again: this tribulation is being *allowed* to occur and has a purpose, even several purposes that we ourselves may never know or understand, even partially. I cannot explain why each and every person goes through something, but for myself and from the testimony of several others, after their experiencing their afflictions, I do know it has brought both mine and their focus back on God. I also know that my afflictions are training me, crushing my pride, humbling me unto submission and reliance on God, and preparing me for a future I cannot even begin to imagine, just as it is written in 1 Corinthians 2:9, "Things which eye has not seen and ear has not heard, and *which* have not entered the heart of man, all that God has prepared for those who love Him" (NASB). Can you grasp that? God, by His Spirit, revealed the plan of salvation that was through Jesus Christ and revealed all the benefits to be obtained through faith in Christ while still here on earth. Things and ways the heart, mind, and eyes of man—by his own power—could not have imagined but are revealed through the Holy Spirit alone. In that same manner, we cannot really even imagine what heaven, or the glory we are being prepared for, will be like. We only have a basic concept of heaven that we can only begin to grasp from our mortal experience and understanding, but heaven itself, in the presence of God, will be much more than we can even imagine. Nothing we have seen, nothing we have any concept of, or can even contemplate on, even begins to compare to what God has prepared for us.

Share in Suffering

It was not long until it became clear to me that strongly related to and intermingled with the progressive sanctification and the testing of faith, which we undergo, that there was also a directive; in essence a command—to "share in the sufferings of Christ." When God became manifested to us, when He took on the human fleshly form so He could be seen in a fleshly body and thereby relate to us, He did so in order to speak to us directly and to bring clarity of understanding to His laws, which generations of priests had not fully understood or had misapplied. He came in bodily form to provide a visual example of how we are to live to God, by displaying it through actual example while enduring the human condition just as we do. Some say He had to experience the human condition in order to understand the fallen human nature, but I do not believe that is quite accurate. God knows all things and He understands the fallen human nature even though He cannot Himself be tempted. He pre-ordained Christ's manifestation and sacrifice on the cross because He knew what sin is and knew in advance that man would fall and that we could not overcome our sin nature ourselves. I am simply saying He did not have to experience the human condition in order to understand it, because He created it He already knew it. God did not create humanity perfect and flawless, and in addition, He created them with choice in order to test their love for Him. It is my opinion that He created them with free will because He did not want robots but instead wanted communion with His creation that "chose" by free will to love Him, and that love is proven through obedience and trust (1 John 2:3, 5). In his book Delighting in the Trinity, Michael Reeves defined sin as a misguided love in that Adam and Eve's love turned in on themselves rather than remaining an outward love of God and each other. That is something we in our fallen sinful nature tend to do still do today, to love ourselves and our desires more than God. After describing the essence of sin by using Adam and Eve as an example, Mr. Reeves then noted Paul's letter to Timothy in which Paul described the corrupted condition of the fallen human nature: "Lovers of themselves, lovers of money, lovers of pleasure rather than lovers of God" (2 Timothy 3:2–4). Christ's purpose in taking on the flesh, besides being the perfect sacrifice without sin, was to provide a visual example we could understand with regard to loving and trusting God and doing His will rather than our own. We then had another chance, just like Adam, at another choice. By becoming manifest in the flesh God not only communicated with us in a direct manner we could actually observe and hear and comprehend, but by enduring temptation in the flesh and dying a perfect and sinless sacrifice, He in the body of Christ would be our advocate and mediator in the Day of Judgment. He would show us the way to live and strive and suffer against sin by our choice, and our choice to have faith in Christ and to suffer against sin as He did, would result in our future glory with Christ just as Christ was glorified in His sufferings. First Peter 1:6–7 says, "In this you rejoice, though now for a little while, if necessary, you have been grieved by various trials, so that the tested genuineness of your faith—more precious than gold that perishes though it is tested by fire—may be found to result in praise and glory and honor at the revelation of Jesus Christ." This glory and praise and honor will be for us in response to our faithfulness as it is revealed at the judgment. Christ also by His suffering and resurrection would defeat Satan and destroy for the believer the fear and power of death Satan wielded. By faith in Christ, death would not have power over us and because by our faith we already have eternal life. Hebrews 2:9–10 says, "But we do see Him who was made for a little while lower than the angels, *namely,* Jesus, because of the suffering of death crowned with glory and honor, so that by the grace of God He might taste death for everyone. For it was fitting for Him, for whom are all things, and through whom are all things, in bringing many sons to glory, to perfect the author of their salvation through sufferings."

Hebrews 2:14, 18 further describe this purpose of His taking on the body of flesh: "Therefore, since the children share in flesh and blood, He Himself likewise also partook of the same, that through death He might render powerless him who had the power of death, that is, the devil." "For since He Himself was tempted in that which He has suffered, He is able to come to the aid of those who are tempted." (NASB)

While Jesus lived among us in the flesh, He was not only still God, though He had for a period of time "emptied Himself" (Philippians 2:7) by taking on the human form and leaving His place of glory and certain attributes that He had with God the Father, but He was also truly and completely human. He was still divine in His essence of being God, but He was now also human and could in His human aspect be tempted, and therefore, by enduring temptations of every kind, He could provide a visible example and demonstrate how we should respond to our temptations, tests, or anything we faced. We all know that Jesus suffered on the cross and through the tortures that immediately preceded it, but do you realize that Jesus suffered way before that? He in fact suffered in His fleshly existence in every way just like we do, including teenage adolescence and everything else. He would be hungry, tired, and thirsty and so feel all our physical needs, but He would also deal with temptations involving tests of pride, anguish, and all other emotional struggles.

The Bible directly documents three of His temptations, which He suffered when it describes Jesus at the start of His ministry. Just after His baptism, Jesus was led out to the wilderness by the Holy Spirit where He fasted forty days and nights and was being tempted during the entire forty days. We do not know how or what He faced during the forty days, but we learn after the forty days He was hungry. During that time of physical hunger and weakness, Satan then tempted Him with His hunger pangs by trying to entice Him to turn stones into bread (Matthew 4:1–3). But notice the *if* in verse 3: "And the tempter came and said to Him, 'If You are the Son of God, command that these stones become loaves of bread.'" Satan was not only tempting Him with a food option to satisfy His physical hunger, His desire for food, but he was subversively trying to get Him to succumb to pride. "If You are the Son of God." Jesus of course knew who He was and could have, in His human nature, been tempted by pride to prove it. But Jesus, though He was tempted by Satan with the pride enticement, would not allow Himself to fall to pride but instead stayed humble and responded with scripture. His temptation to pride was then again attacked directly in verses 5–6 of Matthew 4 when the *if* challenge from Satan to His status of deity came in again. And then finally Satan tempted Him with riches and comfort (Matthew 4:8–9). In all these temptations, Jesus refused to sin and responded with scripture, but undoubtedly His temptation to prove Himself, to satisfy His hunger, and to enjoy wealth as well as earthly and bodily comfort of every kind existed, especially after this period of fasting. Because of His human nature, I believe these temptations caused Him bodily and emotional suffering in resisting those temptations. I also took note of the verse of Luke 4:13 of 4:1–13, which also describes this event. It stated, "When the devil had ended every temptation, he departed from Him until an opportune time." Satan had tempted Him with *every* temptation and he departed from Him *until an opportune time.* The temptations for Jesus were not nearly over. Hebrews 4:15 reveals that He endured every temptation we face: "For we do not have a high priest who cannot sympathize with our weaknesses, but one who in every respect has been tempted as *we are, yet* without sin." He was *tempted in "every respect."* Now it must be understood that Jesus may not have faced cancer or internet porn or social media or other "modern" things, but every temptation we face finds its source from one of three areas and are even the sources of Adam and Eve's temptations. The three areas of all temptations are the lust of the flesh, the lust of the eyes and the pride of life and just like us, Jesus was tempted in these three areas.

Throughout His entire ministry, Jesus was challenged with many things in many ways and ultimately with rejection and crucifixion. In the Garden of Gethsemane, He was greatly grieved and distressed and prayed for a way out if there was another way, yet He still submitted to the will of God. He could have refused the cross, and I am sure Satan was there trying to plant that seed, but He refused to sin by turning from the will of God (Matthew 26:36–39, Mark 14:32–36, Luke 22:41–44, Matthew 26:52–54, John 18:11).

Just as Jesus suffered throughout His life in the flesh by resisting sin and temptations and enduring afflictions even to death without ever committing sin, I found I was also as a Christian supposed to share in the same type of sufferings of Christ. That is, I was also supposed to resist sin in every form or fashion that I would encounter, whether that temptation to sin came through elements of a fallen world or by persecution for being a Christian as a result of either (1) other people or (2) Satan's own efforts against me. Though I would have failings due to my weaknesses, I was obligated not to practice sin or to allow myself to easily fall to sin, but was instead to resist my temptations just as Jesus did. Whether due to pride or desires of the flesh or through any physical affliction I might suffer, I was to resist and patiently endure and thereby share in the sufferings of Christ. Christ gave Himself as an example of how I was to live and even die, and that example was to be in total obedience to, in communion with, reliant on, and fully trusting in God and not myself. I had an obligation to resist sin and by adhering to that conduct I would prove my love for God (1 John 2:5; 5:3). Hebrews 12:4 says, "In your struggle against sin you have not yet resisted to the point of shedding your blood." There are a multitude of verses that detail our fellowship with Christ in sharing in His sufferings, and those sufferings were not just physical and from being persecuted, though they certainly could be a part of it. Satan himself is the great persecutor of Christians and no matter how we may suffer, our suffering, though God allows it, comes from him, so all suffering of any type is the result of Satan persecuting us. My shooting was the action of Satan, but God by His wisdom and power, knowing what was necessary to get my attention, not only allowed it but then used it for good just as He did with Job. The fact is that much of Christ's suffering involved the resistance of sin and improper or overabundance of fleshly comfort. We were told Jesus suffered through temptations and trials in all things, and this suffering was not just through His crucifixion but also in His resisting the temptations of the flesh. I found this to be supported by Luke 22:28 when Jesus told His disciples, "You are those who have stood by Me in My trials"; this was at His last Passover meal just before His arrest, so His physical suffering of the crucifixion had not even begun, but the reference to His trials were all those temptations He faced during His time of ministry while with the disciples up to that point. This is vaguely supported by Hebrews 2:18, "For because he himself has suffered when tempted, he is able to help those who are being tempted." I interpret the phrase "because he himself has suffered when tempted" to be inclusive of all the temptations and trials He faced even before His arrest and crucifixion, and since He was tempted "in every respect," He is able to help us in any temptation we face—if we will only turn to Him.

The apostles, particularly Paul and Peter, instruct us to suffer as Christ suffered; and I believe that suffering is directly related to the resistance of sin. It is my opinion that our suffering and enduring through the resistance of sin while also still yet trusting and relying on God proves our faith, our salvation, and our love for God. The apostle Paul alludes to this suffering in the flesh in Romans 7 regarding agreeing with the law of commandments by living in the Spirit and hating the sin our body of flesh wants to commit. I also noticed again the conditional *if*, the second *if* occurring in Romans 8:16–17, "The Spirit Himself testifies with our spirit that we are children of God, and if children, heirs also, heirs of God and fellow heirs with Christ, '*if*' indeed we suffer with *Him* so that we may also be glorified with *Him*" (NASB). It is my understanding that the conditional *if* could be translated as *whenever*. Try reading the verse substituting *whenever*. This suffering by striving against sin is also supported by 1 Peter 4:1–2, which states, "Since therefore Christ suffered in the flesh, arm yourselves with the same way of thinking, for whoever has suffered in the flesh has ceased from sin, so as to live for the rest of the time in the flesh no longer for human passions but for the will of God."

When we make the decision for Christ and accept Him into our lives, we are supposed to make a decisive effort to live as He lived and to follow the examples He provided. While in the flesh, we have a corrupted and sinful nature full of lust and desires of physical comfort, always trying to put our benefit first even if it might appear to be putting others first. Often we will placate others, but the real motive is to make things easier for ourselves, sort of like "if mama ain't happy, then nobody's happy." We men may not want to empty the trash or help with the dishes, but we do it to keep our wives happy, and we do that to benefit ourselves because if our wives are happy we have peace in the house. Our physical fleshly desires are contrary to Christ's way, and it can truly sometimes feel like suffering when we resist sinful creature comfort temptations and even when we sincerely put others' needs first especially when it may be a large inconvenience. In addition to suffering with what I will call normal fleshly temptations of the spirit, we may also face physical suffering in many forms or fashions, but we should face those physical issues with the same perseverance and trust in God, even if it is to death.

Paul in 2 Thessalonians 1:4-5 commended the Christian Thessalonians on the endurance and patience in which they suffered persecutions, for their Christian faith in particular, but also, as I read it, for other afflictions of life in general. Along with Christian persecutions, some may also have faced physical infirmities which they not only had accepted as God allowing them, but they accepted them with a peaceful faith which exhibited God's power, similar to the manner of Job. They endured these tribulations with the peace only God could bestow and displayed a continuous righteous mindset and love for one another and others. God does not allow us to face more than we can handle and Paul encouraged them by telling them this was "evidence of the righteous judgment of God *that you may be considered worthy of the kingdom of God.*" Their suffering was not in any way earning a debt of heaven, but by their godly endurance in suffering through whatever they were dealing with, it revealed their true character as children of God and that it was proof that God considered them worthy to suffer for His kingdom as soldiers for Christ, and by their endurance they glorified and witnessed of God who can give a peace in suffering only He could provide. Philippians 1:29–30 supports this when Paul explains, "For it has been granted to you that for the sake of Christ you should not only believe in him but also suffer for his sake, engaged in the same conflict that you saw I had and now hear that I still have." Our trials in life reveal our true character.

They expose or reveal, both to us as well as to others, the strength of our faith or lack of it. If our faith is real, the manner in which we respond to our trials is a witness and testimony to others even if we ourselves are not actively trying to witness, and as such, even by our quietly displayed faith, we are still soldiers for Christ. This proof of being considered worthy as soldiers for Christ is supported by Christ's own teaching as in Luke 6:22, "Blessed are you when people hate you and when they exclude you and revile you and spurn your name as evil, on account of the Son of Man! Rejoice in that day, and leap for joy, for behold, your reward is great in heaven; for so their fathers did to the prophets." In essence, I believe Christ is implying that just as the prophets were called to their task and faithfully suffered for His kingdom and will be blessed and rewarded in doing so, we also may, as soldiers for Christ, be called to endure our sufferings by faith. If we are called to such suffering, in whatever manner they may occur and we faithfully endure, and we will be in some manner or another, we should rejoice because God considers us worthy to suffer for His kingdom. In other words, we see, by enduring, accepting the bad along with the good in a righteous manner, especially if our suffering is obviously or directly related to persecution for Christ, we are not only sharing in the sufferings of Christ, but we are witnessing as we are conforming to the image of Christ and glorifying God even in our suffering whether others will accept our witness or not. When we endure and share in Christ's sufferings, no matter what that might consist of, we have evidence that God considers us His children and we are considered worthy of His kingdom.

Scripture Speaks

IN SOME OF THE PRECEDING chapters, I have made statements about judgments of both a temporal and eternal nature, statements of rewards won or lost, and other comments without going into much or maybe any detail about those comments. Some Christian readers may be confused and alarmed at those statements and may even question them because they have been unheard-of by them, or they had been taught differently. I thought maybe I should explain my points of view and how I came by them so the reader could, I hope, at least see how I concluded my understanding from biblical scripture and see my comments, even if they might disagree with them, were not just pulled out of the air. The reader could give consideration to my statements and then search through the scriptures themselves. The truth is, in the years I have attended church, I do not recall ever having heard a sermon or Bible lesson even mention Christians facing judgment. I knew of the judgment for unbelievers, but not for believers. I was naïve to a judgment for believers other than when God confronted me in the hospital regarding making an accounting, but upon studying the Bible, there it was. Since I had never heard it spoken of, but I had found it through my own Bible studies, I felt it was something that should be brought to the surface and exposed for others to see and give consideration. Interestingly, as I sought to study and to clarify my points, additional information and questions developed. I therefore will present those questions and the answers as I believe they are presented by scripture. I will also then present possible scenarios in response to certain questions in which I could find no firm answers but rather strong possibilities in order to stir the reader's contemplation and meditation.

I had worked under several of the police department's top police chiefs during my tenure on the department as well as many lower-ranking chiefs. Several were good, but one of those whom I considered one of the best and coincidentally also my last was David Kunkle. Chief Kunkle was not the most charismatic leader as some would rate personalities. He was quiet and reserved, and he did not give an opinion or speak quickly without thought. He liked to listen and fully consider, and then he would reach a decision and provide an opinion. Because he was quiet and reserved, anyone who met him for the first few times might consider him somewhat dry and humorless or even standoffish. But as I began to get to know him, and as he began to accept me into his trust, he opened up, and I saw he actually had a sincere concern for doing what was best even if it was not the most popular. He displayed a strong sense of fairness for both officers and citizens, and I found he actually had a great sense of humor but he just rarely shared his humor with you unless he knew you and was comfortable around you. Getting to know Chief Kunkle and observe his work was very beneficial, and one thing that impressed me about him was his logical thinking, but even more impressive to me was his willingness to explain the logic of his decisions and how he derived them. Many in the power structure would expect you to follow their commands and decisions without providing an inkling of justifying them. Chief Kunkle was rare in that he sought not only to explain, but he was also open to even hearing opposition to his decisions. I think he knew no one is perfect, even himself, and due to that human error factor, he was open to the possibility there might be logical considerations he had not dealt with. He did not take offense easily and was willing to listen both to his command staff as well as others, who served as a sounding board. On most decisions he reached, I agreed with him, but even on those times where I disagreed with a decision, when he would explain why and how he came to them, I could see they were well-thought-out and quite logical. Though I might still disagree with his decision because of a different stance on priorities, I could not question his logic from his own view of priority. The fact he was so well-thought-out yet also willing to explain made him a great leader in my opinion. Though I might have still disagreed with a decision or direction, because they were logical with regard to his priority stance, it made me more willing to carry out his directives. That is what I want from the reader, to hear my logic on the following thoughts and see how I arrived to that point. The reader might not agree nor would I dare to be so arrogant to claim that I am correct in all points, but I would hope if they did not agree at the onset, they would at least give my view consideration and contemplation and be willing to review their own understanding more thoroughly with an open mind.

Along with explaining the logic for my statements, I am also going to ask some questions about theological possibilities that I believe the reader should give serious thought to. The fact is there are certain areas where I am just not completely sure of the answer, and it appears the scriptures have kept certain parts a mystery, but I also believe it is best to be cautious and conservative when it comes to God and spiritual matters as a cautious and conservative attitude will assist in walking more uprightly. I have discussed these issues with some whom I was confident were well-versed in the Bible and with regard to a certain issue that will be presented later, they agreed scripture did not reveal the answer clearly and my views had possibilities.

It all started one Sunday morning in my Sunday school class when a lesson prompted the question about judgment regarding Christians. The lesson was not about judgment itself, but the content of the lesson caused the question to be raised. I had already developed my views as discussed in other chapters, but I had not talked about them with my Sunday school nor did I know anyone else's view. But when the question arose, I observed the discussion revealed an almost even split among the class. Half the class felt Christians would face judgment while others thought no judgment would occur because of Christ's propitiatory sacrifice. Both sides quoted scripture regarding their views, and so I felt compelled to take a more intense look into the matter as I did not want to propagate any unsound theology. I will admit right up front that personally I believe Christians will be judged, and because of that, a question that arose in my mind was this: "If there is a judgment for Christians, what in particular is being judged and given consideration?"

Something we as Christians should be leery of is being too willing to accept too easy or convenient an answer. We should all fear our fallen nature, and because of the wiles and traps of Satan, we can easily be too willing to quickly accept certain beliefs simply for our own comfort and convenience or merely accepting them because that was what we were told. Many Christians feel they are not skilled or trained to properly interpret scripture, and thus they rely on their church leaders to instruct them. The thing is, as we delve into and study the Bible for ourselves, it will be the Holy Spirit who teaches and instructs us, that is part His job, and as we continue to apply ourselves, He will continue to teach and instruct. Because of this, we actually have no reasonable excuse for not studying the Bible for ourselves other than our own laziness or insecurities. That is, we may avoid personal and daily Bible study because we are afraid of what might be revealed to us and it would interfere with our comfort zone. We naturally want to feel good and be comfortable with ourselves, but when I say "naturally," I am referring to our fallen human nature and its susceptibility. Because we want to be at ease, most of us might seek a church where we are comfortable with what it being said rather than be convicted or challenged, and we might prefer not to believe in judgment either temporally or eternally, and we do not want to think our eternal rewards can or will be affected by any judgment that might occur. We most certainly do not want to think our rewards can be affected by certain—what I will refer to as—pet sins, which are those sins we might be secretly harboring and engaging in because we have never mortified them and maybe never even tried or which we may have justified as not necessarily being a sin or at least "not that bad of one." Our fallen nature is a very dangerous thing, and Satan subtly and quietly attacks it and its instability. It also concerns me what many modern preachers and theologians are saying today as compared to those who spoke just a short time ago and those things being taught and practiced today by many that I feel are most assuredly contrary to God's word and sound doctrine.

As I said earlier, as I began to dig into the scriptures, more questions developed. I will pose those questions and discuss the answers and present possibilities as revealed to me by scripture and for contemplation; but before we address the other questions that arose, I think it is first imperative to discuss even if there is a judgment for Christians because if there is not, then the other questions would be moot.

Question: Is there a judgment for Christians?

The more I researched the scriptures, the more I became convinced and was convicted that judgments do occur both temporally and eternally. Though Christ died on the cross for our sin and *we are/will* be forgiven by faith in Him and have salvation, I was to discover that His sacrifice, though it atones for our sins, does not preclude an accounting for our lives here on earth. I say I was convicted because, not only was I convinced by scripture, but I felt grief and had remorse because I realized all the shortcomings I had committed throughout the years after my baptism and felt I would have to give an accounting for even if I would be absolved of them and I was convinced that my current circumstances were in fact God's temporal judgment, that is His chastisement of my grievous and continually willful sinning, but it was a chastisement out of righteous love that He would use for my spiritual benefit as well as the benefit of others. As I continued to review scripture, I found there were many more scriptures that spoke of judgment for "all" or "each" or some other phraseology, as compared to those verses that indicate all sins would be forgiven and forgotten and we would be presented pure, verses such as Hebrews 4:13, "And no creature is hidden from his sight, but *all* are naked and exposed to the eyes of him *to whom we must give account*" (emphasis added). I came to believe there is also a Timing Factor involved with our sins being forever forgiven and forgotten, but that will be addressed later. Two of those scriptures in the New Testament I found to be most direct are Romans 14:10–12, "Why do you pass judgment on your brother? Or you, why do you despise your brother? For we will *all* stand before the judgment seat of God; for it is written, 'As I live, says the Lord, every knee shall bow to me, and *every tongue shall confess* to God.' *So then each of us will give an account of himself to God*," and 2 Corinthians 5:10, "For we must *all* appear before the judgment seat of Christ, so that *each one* may receive what is due for what he has done in the body, whether good or evil" (Many translations use *bad* instead of *evil*; emphasis was added). All three of these verses, Hebrews 4:13, Romans 14:10–12, and 2 Corinthians 5:10 as well as many others were written to believing Christian churches and their congregation and were instructing these Christians to be careful in their Christian walk because each one of us and what we do or do not do here in this life will all be accountable to God. Other New Testament verses showing judgment are Matthew 16:27, 1 Corinthians 3:8, 1 Peter 1:17, Revelation 22:12, Hebrews 9:27, and James 2:12; and these are just a portion of New Testament scriptures that reveal judgment for all, including Christians, but there are several more. The fact is, none of these verses were written to a general audience but were written to believing Christian churches with the exception of Matthew 16:27, which was Jesus talking directly to His disciples. Again, these verses were written to these church members in order to warn them about apathy towards sin, to be attentive to their conduct as well as to encourage them to walk uprightly, to engage in good works, and to attempt to be holy just as God is holy because there would be an accounting and a just recompense would be given. It therefore seems obvious in my opinion by proofs of scripture that there will be a judgment for all persons and that our conduct here on earth would be held to account and we would reap what we had sown. The next question then arises.

Question: If Christians will be judged, exactly what will be held to account?

This question may be one of the most difficult to answer clearly. The main question within the question is will our sins be part of the judgment, and I believe the answer is both yes and no. They will be seen, and they will have an effect but not in the way we might imagine. Clear as mud, right?

It is clear that the Bible teaches us that Jesus died on the cross as the propitiatory sacrifice for our sin. When we say He died a propitiatory sacrifice, we are saying He paid the just price to satisfy the demand of payment for our sin, and thus turned away the wrath and punishment of God for our sins; and through that sacrifice, redeemed and reconciled our relationship to God (Ephesians 1:7; Romans 6:23; 1 Peter 1:18–19; 1 Peter 2:24; Revelation 5:9; 1 Corinthians 1:30; 2 Corinthians 5:21; Romans 5:8–9; Titus 2:14; 1 John 2:2; Isaiah 53:5; Romans 5:18; Galatians 1:4; Galatians 4:4–5; Colossians 1:14; Romans 3:24; 1 Timothy 2:5–6). There are several more verses that help prove the point that Jesus died for our sins and paid the price in order to redeem us to God, and it is through these verses that we can confidentially know that we will not face punishment for our sins, either now or in the judgment, because the price and penalty of sin has already been paid.

The question remains, however, if our sins in this life will be seen at the Judgment Seat of Christ? According to some theologians, there are up to as many as six different future judgments, ranging through varying times for varying purposes. Other theologians do not separate and identify various judgments but simply affirm one judgment, in which all will be in attendance. I'm not certain of these various judgments occurring at different times as some are proposed, though there seems, in certain ways, to be some support for them. Although I find these numerous judgments as proposed could themselves occur in function, I question the proposition of them as necessarily being so separated. What I do see however is that are two different judgment seats which are specifically named. These judgment seats are the Judgment Seat of Christ that is referred to by name in 2 Corinthians 5:10, which is for believers, and the Great White Throne Judgment mentioned in Revelation 20:11, for unbelievers.

Though these two judgment seats are mentioned, I do not necessarily separate them in time frame myself. Several commentaries I have read separate these two judgments as occurring after the rapture and after the millennial reign, but I find there are complications with that separation. Those complications may be why the other judgments are argued to occur, but I also find some verses that seem to imply the judgments though separate in function, occur simultaneously such as John 5:28–29, "Do not marvel at this, for an hour is coming when *all* who are in the tombs will hear his voice and come out, *those who have done good to the resurrection of life, and those who have done evil to the resurrection of judgment*" (emphasis added). There is much debate regarding these judgments, and how or when they occur because there are also debates even about the rapture and the millennial reign itself, and it can be quite confusing. I am not even going to delve into this debate very much because I have not studied it intently, but even more so, because I really don't think it matters in the whole scheme of things. What I do see is the Judgment Seat of Christ for believers, and this judgment for believers is what 2 Corinthians 5:10 and Romans 14:10–12 and other verses appear to be speaking.

The Judgment Seat of Christ is just what it says it is: it is Christ judging and what He is judging is His church, the true believers. As Paul is writing to his fellow Christians in Corinth, he is telling them that their actions here on earth will be judged, whether good or bad, and they will be recompensed, that is, rewarded or a just compensation made, regarding their eternal heavenly status based on their conduct, actions, or decisions in this life, and how those actions affected others, and more importantly, reflected on God and the advancement of His kingdom. Paul, in his letter to the church in Galatia, describes it this way, "But let *each* one test his own work for *each* will have to bear his own load. Do not be deceived: God is not mocked, for *whatever one sows, that will he also reap*" (Galatians 6:4, 5 and 7; paraphrased). The judgment at the Judgment Seat of Christ is for believers only, and each one of us will have to make an accounting for our actions in this life. Though there may be a variance in reward for each person based upon the judgments of those life decisions, because of our professed faith in Christ and His sacrifice, there is in fact no condemnation or a risk of hell. It is important to understand that this is a judgment of how we conducted our lives here on earth, especially after we became a Christian. One might use the term "accounting," such as Paul in 2 Corinthians 5:10, or we might even use the word "evaluation," in that our lives and conduct will be evaluated and just rewards, given or not, depending on what we did or did not do, but whatever term we might choose to use, it is still a judgment, and that is why it is called the "*Judgment* Seat of Christ." All those at the Judgment Seat of Christ—who are being judged or evaluated—already have salvation through their faith in Christ; they are all part of His kingdom and will all be in heaven, and there is no punishment for sin because Christ already paid the penalty for our sin. That is how Romans 8:1 can state, "Therefore there is now no condemnation for those who are in Christ Jesus"; their judgment is not a risk of losing salvation, but it is a just evaluation and accounting of their conducts, decisions, actions, and motives of the heart while here on earth, and just rewards will be given as a result of that accounting.

Here is the complication as I see it and why I answered that it certainly appears we would see our sins at the Judgment Seat of Christ. Many theologians take verses like 2 Corinthians 5:10 and try to relegate the "good or bad" to simply what we have done—good or bad—as it relates to promoting the kingdom of God and deny that sins would be addressed at all since Christ died a propitiatory sacrifice on the cross for our sins and already paid the penalty of our sin. It is absolutely true that Jesus paid the penalty of our sins, and because of that, our sins are forgiven, and we will not be condemned, yet that being said, forgiveness of sin does not necessarily negate accountability for them. As we have discussed, and I hope you agree, we already know we will face a judgment. Granted, though we will face a judgment, this Judgment Seat we believers will stand before is in Greek called "the Bema" as compared to the Great White Throne Judgment for unbelievers. Historically, the Bema is a raised platform in the Jewish synagogues where scripture is read, and it also refers to a raised platform where rewards are given after ancient Roman Olympic-type contests. But according to 2 Timothy 2:5, "An athlete is not crowned unless he competes according to the rules" which reveals the contestants must compete according to the rules in order to win the prize, and the judge on the Bema Seat will determine if the contestants competed according to the rules or not, and rewards will be given or withheld accordingly. So the Bema is not only about rewards but about evaluation and just rewards.

On the day of Judgment, all our works, which includes our acts of sin, will be evaluated. Those works will include acts of commission and omission, as well as our thoughts and the motivations of our heart. We need to understand, however, that the review of our sins is not about punishment, but simply about potential gain or loss of rewards that we caused by our own choices, by what we sowed to in this life. As a temporal example of what I mean, we can look at Moses, who led the children of Israel out of slavery in Egypt; he brought them to Canaan, but due to a lack of faith on Israel's part, they were not allowed to enter Canaan and had to wonder the wilderness for forty years. Moses led these people that entire time but then, because of his sin at the waters of Meribah, he himself was not allowed to enter Canaan when the time came. Moses sinned, and though we know he was saved because he was at the transfiguration with Jesus in Matthew 17:1–8; he was still held accountable for that sin. This is, of course, a temporal and earthly example, but who can say for sure that our sins will not be held to account, not only now, but also in the future? Even part of what we may likely view in our judgment is what God did with regard to His chastisement of our sins in our temporal life and our responses to that chastisement.

If we are at the Judgment Seat of Christ, we have salvation. Our eternal security in Christ is not in question. At the Judgment Seat of Christ, He will not enact punishment for sin, but rewards will be justly given or lost, depending on how we lived our lives for the Lord, and our sins will be part of that evaluation. When we consider the "good or bad," I do not feel we can just relegate our evaluation to what we did or didn't do to advance the kingdom of God. For example, on a certain occasion, we shared our testimony and the gospel message. Okay, good, we get a reward for that, but on another occasions, when we could have shared the gospel, we declined to do so, and that would be considered bad and a reward might be withheld. But now consider if our sinful behavior, particularly if it was habitual and practiced sinful behavior, caused the kingdom of God to stall or take a step back so to speak. What if our behavior caused someone to reject Christ or dishonored God, do we think that will not be held to account? What if, in a prideful Christian mindset, we cause a younger or weaker Christian to stumble and fall into sin? Paul says if we cause a brother to stumble, we "sin against Christ" (1 Corinthians 8:12). Would we not have to answer for that, and would it not affect our rewards beyond salvation itself?

As I consider again what will be judged, I reflect back on 2 Corinthians 5:10 and "the deeds done in the body, whether good or bad." Upon reflection, it seems relatively easy to gather the good, though that could be more confusing than we might think. Did we profess to love God? Did we go to church almost every Sunday, and did we tithe regularly? Did we help the poor and needy, or the prisoners? Were we honest in all our dealings, whether at work or leisure, and did we share the Gospel of Christ and our testimony? Did we promote His kingdom in any way? Did we walk in good works, which God prepared for us to do? (Ephesians 2:10). It is confusing because, believe or not, there might be certain aspects of our "good" that will actually be found to be faulty. We will come back to that, but for now, let us assume we did all these things and more; the question then arises, "What is the bad?" or "What bad will be held accountable for the Christian?"

When we became Christians, at any age, we started a new contract, so to speak, or rather a new covenant agreement. A covenant is actually much stronger than a contract. When God makes a covenant, He is faithful to that covenant and does not break it. It, along with the terms of the covenant, will stand because God will make it stand. Humans, on the other hand, often violate the terms of the covenant agreement, and thus face consequences for their actions. The difference between covenant and contract is that a contract can be rescinded, broken, or absolved by mutual agreement or otherwise, such as a marriage contract and divorce, but a covenant agreement cannot. A covenant is set in stone, and though new covenants can be made that supersedes other covenants, the old covenant's promises still exist and are effective and is why the covenant with Abraham and the covenant promise with Israel will still come to fruition and be fulfilled though their complete fulfillment is under the new covenant of grace. That new covenant of grace is accepting Christ Jesus as our Lord, and in return, receiving forgiveness, salvation, and imputed righteousness by faith alone in Christ Jesus. Christ, by His sacrifice upon the cross, has paid the penalty for all our sins—past, present, and future—and made us holy, pure, and righteous to God. Jesus paid the penalty of sin "once and for all" (Hebrews 10:10, 12), and we are justified in the eyes of God by that payment. God, by sending His Son as a sacrifice for sin, did not just ignore or overlook our sin, but by His Son's sacrifice, God Himself, in the body of Jesus, actually paid the penalty of sin; and since the penalty has been paid, God's righteousness does not fall into question when He justifies the sinner by faith alone in Christ.

Remember however what I said before, that forgiveness does not prohibit or exclude accountability. Forgiveness does not mean getting off scot free; it means not getting what one deserves. In this case, sin against God rates death, but because of Christ's sacrifice, if we have repented and confessed our sin, God will forgive us and not give us what we deserve but will, instead, provide us salvation through our faith in Christ. Though we are forgiven, we are also warned and reminded repeatedly of the conduct and bearing we should have in Christ and warned that unrighteous and ungodly conduct would have consequences. Paul spoke about the conduct and bearing we should have as Christians in Romans 6; 7:4–8; 12:1–2, and the Apostle Peter warns against apathy and the licentiousness being taught by false teachers (2 Peter 2) and states to walk in control and godliness and love having escaped corruption by taking on the divine nature, but He also warns to be "diligent to make your call and election sure" (2 Peter 1:3–10) and warns of an upcoming future judgment (2 Peter 2:9; 20). These warnings and cautions are made numerous times in various places in the Bible and seem to reveal not heeding them and conforming to them would bring undesirable ramifications.

Understanding Christ's work on the cross but also seeing the continuous exhortations about the believer's conduct and bearing, as noted above, I contemplated, if not only our behavior but willful or unrepentant sin after baptism and confession of faith might be held to account, though not to the degree of loss of salvation. Willful sin is a behavior that conflicts quite badly with God's righteousness. Can we willfully engage in sin after knowing the truth and not face repercussions? Paul asks if we should sin more under the covenant of grace so grace may abound and answers to say emphatically, "By no means!" (Romans 6:1–2, 15). God did not allow willful and belligerent sin in the past under the old dispensation and God does not change, so why do we think He would allow it even under the new dispensation of faith in Christ?

I have already discussed our progressive sanctification and how we, out of God's love for us, are often chastised in order to further sanctify us and mold us into righteousness and the image of Christ. We now, in our lifetime, face certain judgments of God for our sanctifying benefit. As 1 Peter 4:17 says, "For it is time for judgment to begin at the household of God; and if it begins with us, what will be the outcome for those who do not obey the gospel of God?" You see, upon accepting Christ into our lives, we are to be dead to our flesh and now living for Christ, and by the power of Christ through his Holy Spirit, we can resist and overcome sin and temptation, and that ability to overcome our temptation and refuse to participate in sin is our freedom in Christ. But unfortunately, because of our sin nature, if we are not careful, we fall susceptible to the schemes of Satan, and we fall into the same apathetic mindset of Israel by thinking "I am a Christian, one of God's chosen, and so it doesn't matter if I sin because I'm already forgiven." That is a very dangerous mindset for a Christian; instead, we should be mourning over our sin.

Remember what I said about there being a fine line between being a prodigal but saved believer and a professing believer but one who was never saved in the first place? We should be very concerned if our profession of faith was real if our engaging in sin is no big deal to us. Even if our profession was sincere, if we are not careful and diligent, we may find ourselves, by our free will, choosing to sin in various ways—either actively by commission or inactively by omission—and it is possible that though Christ died for all our sins, that any sin we willfully commit in this life will be held to account as one of those "bad things," which could affect our eternal life. In the gospels, not only John the Baptist but Jesus Himself taught repentance of sin was a necessary step in receiving forgiveness. Repentance of sin is a main theme in the Bible and runs all the way through Revelation 2 and 3. A righteous God will not tolerate blatant willful sin, especially by His children, and He will justly address it. He did not tolerate it from His chosen in Israel, and I doubt—though Jesus died for all our sin and as such they will be forgiven—that He would tolerate it from us now, and we will have to face and account for our sin choices. I think much of this debate will center on if we practice sin, which means it has not been truly repented of, or whether our sin is an occasional slip, but one in which we will confess and repent of almost as soon as it had been committed or repented of later when one recognizes it as having been committed in ignorance. A child of God may actually find themselves slipping into practicing sin, but God will take corrective action in order to gain His child's repentance. God will look at the heart and the intention of the heart and any obstinate sin will bring repercussions. It may be argued that sin itself is not the only "bad" that can bring repercussions in judgment, but as I see it, in a way, all bad things we do—even things like not sharing the gospel message when we could—have their foundation in the fallen and sinful nature, and are thereby, in essence, connected to sin.

Though we have discussed certain easily identifiable bad, and there is much more, let us go back to our good actions for a minute. When we go to church, is it because we want to and we want to worship God? Or do we go because it is expected of us? Do we think going to church and tithing will earn us salvation or treasure in heaven, or is it that it makes us look good in others eyes, and that is really the only reason we do it? Insincere worship is appalling to God and also condemned by Him. Are all the good deeds we may do, such as helping the poor and needy, done with the right motives? Is our heart sincere? If our heart is not sincere, if our motives are wrong and we did not do these deeds out of love, then all these good deeds we think we have done are worthless in the sight of God because we did them for the wrong reasons (1 Corinthians 13:1–3). If we did them for the wrong reasons, most likely we did them because we felt compelled or just wanted a tax break or some such motive, in other words, our motives were insincere. The scary truth is, if in fact our deeds are insincere, they are more than worthless and may actually be considered as bad.

In 1 Corinthians 3:10–15, Paul talked about our work being "tested by fire," and possibly being burned up and worthless. He said we would be saved, but our works would be lost and of no value. In the verses of Matthew 7:21–23, where people said, "Lord, Lord" and mentioned all their "good works" and Jesus denied knowing them, I suspect it was because their heart was insincere, their faith was not real, and their piety, their acts of religion and reverence for God, were untrue and only for show. That is something to think about; what is our motive? Because of the verses in scripture that say we will face judgment and be held accountable for our lives, I still continued to try and reconcile my understanding of this and if our sins after baptism would be held to account.

In studying to see if our sins would be held to account, I read numerous commentaries that varied in opinions. Some commentaries denied Christians would face any judgment at all, while others believed there would be a judgment. But whether they agreed on a judgment or not, all were consistent in agreeing that all our sins—past, present, and future—were forgiven due to Christ's atoning sacrifice on the cross. Where they varied, however, was that some who declared there would be a judgment felt sins would not be brought up at all, and others felt we would face our sins but be acquitted. Some commentators that agreed we would face judgment stated sins would not be addressed at the Judgment Seat of Christ, but only what we did or did not do to advance the kingdom of God. But my question by that train of thought was, "Isn't our sin a 'work,' and wouldn't our sin fail to advance the kingdom of God, or maybe even do it harm, and thus be held to account?" As such, I tried to conduct a deeper study, and even to conduct a Greek-word study on such terms as forgiven, forgive, and will.

I will state again, I am not a Greek scholar by any means, and thus I am sure there may be certain nuisances I may have missed, and I am also certain I have probably missed reviewing certain applicable verses. All that being said, what I discovered in what I did review seemed quite applicable to resolving the question. Colossians 2:13–14 (NASB) states, "When you were dead in your transgressions and the un-circumcision of your flesh, He made you alive together with Him, having forgiven us all our transgressions, having canceled out the certificate of debt consisting of decrees against us, which was hostile to us; and He has taken it out of the way, having nailed it to the cross." The verb tense of "having forgiven us" appears to be written in the aorist tense, which is past tense in meaning, and basically means it has been done. Additionally, Colossians 1:13–14 says, "He has delivered us from the domain of darkness and transferred us to the kingdom of his beloved Son, in whom we have redemption, the forgiveness of sins." The verbs tenses of "He has delivered us" and "transferred us" are also in the aorist tense, meaning again that it has been done. God has already rescued us through Christ, if we accept Him into our lives as our Lord, and our sins are forgiven by faith in Him. This is for all intents and purposes; the gospel message in that we have salvation and eternal life by the blood of Christ Jesus and all our sins are forgiven. This is the focus of modern teaching, and it is, in fact, true and correct, but unfortunately, I feel it is also an avenue that Satan has used to invade the church and cause some Christians to become apathetic or complacent about sin and their duties to God. You see, forgiven does not necessarily mean forgotten. Now when I make that statement I want to clarify that our sins will in fact be forgotten as is pointed out in Psalms 103:12 in that our sins will be removed "as far as east from the west", but I believe that occurs after the judgment itself. I will talk more about that later.

God created us with free will and, in my opinion, with the bonds of sin broken, it is our choice in choosing what we will and will not do; and therefore, we will face the repercussions of our choices. James 2:12 reminds us we will be judged by "the law of liberty" and that law of liberty is by our choices in the liberty or freedom from the bondage of sin Christ has given us. Since we will be judged by our freedom of choice in Christ, and though I sincerely believe our sins—even those willfully engage in—will be forgiven, that does not mean we can abuse the gift of grace and just willingly commit sin. We will still face and account for our decisions on the day of final judgment and that accounting will have eternal results, but Satan has somewhat blinded us to that and so some have lost the sense of the sting of sin, thinking it no longer matters. Christians will in fact be judged, but they will not be condemned; they will be acquitted of guilt.

As King David declared in Psalms 32:5, "You forgave the guilt of my sin." Though we will be forgiven, it appears our sins will still be reviewed, along with our good works, or lack thereof, and they will have eternal repercussions. I will say it again: it appears, though we will not be condemned, those sins, along with our other deeds—whether good or bad—in one way or another will still be judged and held accountable, and they will affect our eternal future. David Powlison in his book *Good and Angry* stated, "Forgiveness means you don't get what you deserve," and "True forgiveness looks wrong in the eye. It makes no excuses. But it does not hold the offense against you." I considered that to mean that our sins, though they will be forgiven, will still be brought up, recognized and addressed, and they will have an effect, though not the awful affect they would have had. God has never justified sin, and He never will. He calls things as they are and confronts us with truth and will even spank us for correction, but He will still forgive us through Christ.

This description of being confronted with our sin, but yet forgiven, seems to fit right in with the story of King David's circumstances, as well as others. For instance, the story of 2 Samuel 12:1–14 has a spiritual allegory relating to the judgment. In this story, God confronted David with his sin regarding Bathsheba and Uriah the Hittite through the prophet Nathan, and He did not hold back the wrong of it. He then allowed David to suffer temporal consequences of that sin yet did not kill him as David knew he deserved. Though David was confronted with his sin and did suffer repercussions, he was still in God's grace and was saved. This was a sanctifying lesson for King David as we witness in Psalms 119:67–68. In a similar way, we will see the sins of our life displayed, and we will see we are deserving of death, but God will forgive us because of the grace He offered through faith in Christ, if we accepted that grace. We will be held to account, and our lives evaluated, but we will not get what we deserve; we will be forgiven of the guilt of our sin, which is death, and instead have life. I read in a periodical, a well-esteemed Bible scholar quote another scholar named Anthony Hoekema, "The failures and shortcomings...of believers...will enter into the picture on the day of judgment. But—and this is the important point—the sins and shortcomings of believers will be forgiven sins whose guilt will be totally covered by the blood of Christ."

As I continued in my Greek study, I reviewed other verses. These verses were Matthew 9:2 (cross-reference Mark 2:5 and 9), Matthew 9:6, Matthew 12:31–32, Mark 3:28, Luke 12:10, James 5:15, Romans 4:7, Luke 7:47, Ephesians 4:32, 1 John 2:12, Mark 11:25, Matthew 6:14–15, Luke 11:4. Upon analyzing the verbs of these verses, I discovered something I considered very interesting. I also looked at the word "will," as in Revelation 3:5, where Christ states, "I will confess his name before my father." Other "will" verses I reviewed are Hebrews 10:17–18, Hebrews 8:12, and Matthew 10:32–33. Here is what I discovered. Ten of these verses contained verbs written in the future tense, meaning just what it sounds like, that these events would be occurring in the future. These were verses like Matthew 12:32, "And whoever speaks a word against the Son of Man will be forgiven, but whoever speaks against the Holy Spirit will not be forgiven, either in this age or in the age to come," and Matthew 6:14, "For if you forgive others their trespasses, your heavenly Father will also forgive you." Seven other verses were written in the aorist tense. The aorist tense is typically a past tense connotation denoting an event that already occurred and is completed. One example of a verse in the aorist tense is Romans 4:7, "Blessed are those whose lawless deeds are forgiven, and whose sins are covered."

Four of the verses were written in the present tense, which denotes an event or action that is occurring in the present time and is continuous in action but has not been completed yet. Such a verse is Matthew 9:2, "And behold, some people brought to him a paralytic, lying on a bed. And when Jesus saw their faith, he said to the paralytic, 'Take heart, my son; your sins are forgiven.'" Finally two of the verses were written in the perfect tense. The perfect tense, unlike the present tense, denotes an event that has occurred, and is continuing to occur, yet it is a completed event. The perfect tense in

Greek means it is an action which is a completed event, yet though it is a completed event, it has an ongoing result which is continuing to occur. This is the sense in which all sins—those of the past, the present, and the future—are all forgiven. These verses are Luke 7:47, "Therefore I tell you, her sins, which are many, are forgiven—for she loved much. But he who is forgiven little, loves little," and 1 John 2:12, "I am writing to you, little children, because your sins are forgiven for his name's sake."

But in general, with all the verses reviewed, the completed action of forgiveness, being transferred to Christ's kingdom, and Christ confessing us before His Father on the Day of Judgment, though already done in a sense and continuing in a sense, are also still future events to be completed in full. Our salvation and transfer into the kingdom of God, by faith in Christ, is done. Our forgiveness of sins and not getting what we deserve because of our sins by faith in Christ is done. Yet none of this means we will not face our choices and make an accounting or that those sin choices, though forgiven, will not have eternal repercussions. That is, that God preordained and completed our forgiveness and salvation by faith in Christ Jesus; and Jesus, by His sacrifice, facilitated that forgiveness of us and covered our sins through our faith in Him and His blood sacrifice. This forgiveness has, in one sense, already been done, and is completed by God's preordained plan. As Jesus said on the cross, "It is finished." It is done; we are rescued by faith in Christ and His atoning sacrifice. We are transferred to His kingdom. Yet in another sense, though done, it is yet to be fully completed until a future time, which is the Judgment Day. Though these verses show we are forgiven even now, they do not, in themselves, in any way, preclude or nullify a future judgment. Because the Bible contains numerous verses that reveal there is a future judgment, I think we must look for the middle ground.

It is my opinion, on that day, we will indeed see all our conduct here on earth, and we will see the seeds we have sown—whether to the flesh or to the Spirit—and we will reap what we have sown, but because we accepted Christ into our lives, though we will receive the fruits, whether good or bad, from the seeds we have sown, we will still already be acquitted by our faith in Him and His propitiatory sacrifice. God through Christ Jesus will forgive us of every sin, even our obstinate willful sin. By faith in Christ, it is already done, finished, and completed. We have salvation in Christ. Yet in another sense, it is not yet completed because, though we have salvation already sealed, we must still make an accounting of our lives and actions and thoughts we engaged in after our baptism and confession of faith, and that accounting, evaluation, judgment, or whatever term you wish to use, will affect our heavenly eternity in some manner. We will not get what we deserve because of our sins, which is death. Instead of death, we will have eternal life, but our forgiven sins, though not ending in death, will have some type of eternal effect. Our judgement is not a punishment, but instead a just recompense.

Though I am sure of the Judgment Seat of Christ for believers and the Great White Throne judgment for nonbelievers, I truly have no idea exactly how or when they will occur. What I am certain of, what I am convinced of in my mind, is that for believers, there will be recompense of rewards—given or lost—and an accountability made according to how we lived our lives. I certainly may be wrong because certain commentaries did build their arguments, but I tend to lean toward there being one final judgment, consisting of the Judgment Seat of Christ and the Great White Throne Judgment working simultaneously, and both the saved and the unsaved will be present together, though we will be separated as the sheep from the goats as described in Matthew 25:32.

Yes, there seem to be certain rewards related to the millennial kingdom and so forth, but again, all the various arguments related to the judgments, even my own, really make no difference. It will all come out in the wash as it should, and there is nothing we can do about it. But let's agree, for a moment, that the judgments are simultaneous. Here is a proposed scenario: once we are gathered, Christ will separate the saved and the unsaved (Matthew 24:31; 25:32, Revelation 14:14–19). The Book of Life and the Book of Remembrance are brought out (Revelation 20:12). We will witness everyone's life on earth, including our own, and every thought, spoken word, action and inaction, and their repercussions will be displayed. The audience will see that even as Christians, we had many sins, and even some sins that might have been of a worse nature than some unbelievers. Satan accuses us of all our wrongs, and our heart and conscience also either accuse us or defend us (Romans 2:15–16). We realize no matter how good we thought we were in life, we now see all our wrongs, and their effects are revealed. Nothing is hidden from God, and everything will be revealed (Hebrews 4:12–13). The unbelievers will also see our lives were just as messed up as theirs in many ways, and as the Apostle Paul pointed out in Romans 3:10, 23, no one is righteous, "for all have sinned and fall short of the glory of God." But as our life trial closes out, Jesus, our advocate, who has already kept us separate since we are already saved but allowed us to watch the review of our lives and face the rebukes, will then declare our faith in Him, and affirm He paid the penalty for our sins by His death and blood sacrifice, and He will welcome us to eternal life. Most theologians believe this portion of Revelation 20, the Great White Throne Judgment is only for unbelievers, however the "if" seems to indicate that at least some names at this judgment are in the Book of Life and I believe these are the sheep (believers) who are sep-arated from the goats (unbelievers). Jesus will profess us at this time, just as He said He would and He will do this before all the unbeliev-ers, and all knees will bow to God—both believers and unbelievers in humility—but for different reasons.

Our salvation by faith in Christ alone will be a testimony and witness to the justice and righteousness of God. The righteousness of God will be seen because He would not tolerate sin, and reparation had to be made. The justice of God will be seen because sin had to be atoned for, and it was atoned for by Christ's blood sacrifice and thus reparation for our sin was made. Then finally, the grace of God will be seen when He freely offered salvation by faith in Christ and His atoning sacrifice alone. Those who declined to accept Christ, or felt that something additional to faith alone in Christ's sacrifice had to be done in order to earn salvation, will be judged guilty and con-demned. They will see the grace that was offered by God and given to believers, but that they declined. I think, for them, that will be one of the worms that will never die in their torment (Mark 9:48). But for those who chose faith in Christ, God then bangs His gavel and declares us "not guilty." I believe it is, at that point in time, at the time of His declaration on Judgment Day, that all our sins are forever forgiven, and there is a verdict of no guilt. In my opinion, it is at that time our sins are removed "as far as East is from the West," and they will never be remembered again. It is at this time, though we are already saved in Christ while here on earth and though Christ has already paid the penalty and forgiveness is already ours, it is at this point in time when everything takes full effect, and we will truly be presented pure and holy in the sight of God for eternity.

Due to the verse of 2 Corinthians 5:10 and the myriad of other verses which state we will all be held to account for our lives, that there is no doubt in my opinion about a future judgment. Incidentally, for the verse of John 5:24, the King James Version, as well as other translations, use the word condemnation rather than judgment: "Verily, verily, I say unto you, He that heareth my word, and believeth on him that sent me, hath everlasting life, and shall not come into condemnation; but is passed from death unto life." There is a variance between these two words in the different translations, and I like how one translation seemed to melt them together by translating it, "will not be judged guilty." The translation of not coming into condemnation, however, seemed to me more accurate as it concurs with Romans 8:1, "Therefore there is now no condemnation for those who are in Christ Jesus." There would be a judgment, an accounting so to speak, at the Judgment Seat of Christ, but since He paid the atoning sacrifice, there would be no condemnation. All our sins are covered and forgiven by the blood of our Lord Jesus Christ. We will be presented holy to God. The answer to the question with regard to when our sins are forgiven and fully erased is that, technically, they already are by our faith in Christ, but though technically already done, the full effects of that forgiveness are still future. Because of our faith in Christ, our sins are even now forgiven. I would like to think I would not have to face my sins in any form or manner, but I do not perceive that to be the case. Though I have the desire not to face my sins, especially willful sin, and have them illuminated for all to see, the fact is I made those choices and therefore the subsequent exposure are on me.

All I am saying is that there are indications that though we are forgiven, we may yet see our sins and their repercussions, and we may even face some rebuking during the judgment proceeding, though there will be no risk of damnation. After all, our sins, particularly willful and practiced sin, are part of our "works" as much as anything good we might do. They are just bad works. I want the reader to understand that sin, even though forgiven, has consequences now in our time, and I believe, especially if not repented of, will potentially have eternal effects in the final Judgment Day. I am just asking the believer to be very cautious of your attitude toward God and sin. Consider the possible consequences of sin, especially willful sin. Sin certainly has repercussions in our earthly life, such as disrupted communion with God, lost blessings, and often undesirable consequences that make life less enjoyable and harder. It may be that our sins in our lifetime will only affect our earthly life experience and will have no effect whatsoever on our eternal life, but it in my opinion, that doesn't quite float, and I feel sins will affect the Christian's eternal state at the judgment, as well as here. Though they are forgiven and we will not get what we deserve because of our sins but will have eternal life, Satan wants to deceive you into believing there are no forthcoming eternal consequences for sin. Are you willing to take the risk and continue to be complacent or apathetic about willful sin if that sin, though not leading to condemnation, might still be held to account and affect your eternity? Are you willing to continue in willful sin and risk that your sin won't even be addressed? I'm not.

Remember that I consider myself quite the sinner, and for years I had strayed from God's path and was willfully engaged in sin. But our God is merciful, and He took action and did not willingly let me die in my mountain of sin which I had accumulated over almost thirty years. Instead of letting me die in my sinful state and face my accountability as a whole, God displayed His mercy just as He did to Israel. He disciplined me because of my sinfulness through the shooting and then confronted me in the hospital over my sins. I then had a choice. Because of this act of mercy and discipline, I did repent of my ways, confessed my sins, and begged for forgiveness. I know my sins will indeed now be forgiven, though I perceive I may still have to give an accounting for them. All my sins have been covered by the blood of Christ and are forgiven sins and I will not get what I deserve because of them. I will have to give an accounting for them and reap certain potential results, but I will not be condemned because of them. As 1 John 1:9 says, He is faithful to forgive us our sins once we confess them. But I want to make it clear that I am not saying that though they are forgiven, that they won't still have an effect, but He will forgive and not hold us guilty unto condemnation. At the very least, He has turned my ways back to Him and has provided me an opportunity to do good deeds that He created us for (Ephesians 2:10) and to accumulate a treasure in heaven rather than just the straw and stubble I had accumulated thus far (1 Corinthians 3:11–15). As I reflected back on my hospital stay I am further convinced I would have to account for my sins because, if my sin was of no account, why would God ask me while in the hospital how I would account for all my sins if I died that day?

The wonderful news is that God, along with being a righteous God full of judgment, is also a God of great mercy. God by His grace had given me an opportunity in my affliction and was testing me to see which way I would go. In truth it was by God's grace being presented to me that I became a Christian at sixteen, it was by His patience and grace I did not die in my long period of sinfulness, and it was by God's grace I was disciplined through my shooting, survived, and was subsequently confronted by Him in the hospital. It was simply by His grace I was even allowed an opportunity to confess and repent, and I believe such opportunities, though maybe not as severe, are in some manner given to all Christians at some point, but especially wayward Christians in some way or another.

Let us consider how many times in the New Testament alone are we warned and exhorted about our conduct, our holy walk, and staying alert and leery of the devil's schemes? I did not count these warnings specifically, but I know it is over a dozen times. Why would these cautions be made unless our walk and conduct on this earth, whether good or bad, would indeed have an effect on our eternal life? The passage of Titus 2:11–14 tells us "the grace of God appeared… training us to renounce ungodliness and worldly passions, and to live controlled, upright, and godly lives in the present age" and that God's grace through Christ has given us the power over sin to do this because He "gave Himself to redeem us from all lawlessness." First Peter 1:18 says, "You were ransomed from the futile ways." What they are telling us is we were empowered to say no to and to fight against sin. But God has not made us robots; He has broken the bond of sin, but it is still our freewill choice to engage in sin or other activities, which are contrary to God or not, and as such, I believe there will be an accounting for our decisions.

We should be careful to reconsider our way of thinking and be open to possibilities that we could be misunderstanding or misinterpreting certain factors, especially after over two thousand years have passed. We have discussed—and I pray you now agree due to the numerous verses that speak of it—that there will be a judgment for all man, including Christian believers. The reality is we just do not really know everything the judgment will consist of. And because we do not know, it is in our best interest to take the warnings and instructions of the apostles to heart and to walk as well as possible, doing good deeds out of love and avoiding any even potentially questionable activities.

We might consider it like a speeding ticket where we are brought before the court. We know we are guilty because we left home in a hurry late for an appointment. Because we were in a hurry, we were neglectful of the speed limit sign and our speedometer. When we see the officer (death/sin), it is too late; and looking down at the speedometer, we confirm for ourselves (our conscience) that we were speeding and in the wrong. Subsequently the officer issues a citation for the violation accusing us of wrong (sin) and we face the penalty. But as the trial ensues, a technicality arises (in this case Christ), and that technicality causes the radar gun and its accuracy to be questioned, and thus the judge declares us not guilty and absolves us of any and all guilt, and we are free to go, never to be confronted with the speeding ticket again. (Okay, not a great analogy, but work with me here.) Let's try another one. A man is accused of murder and he stands before the judge's bench for trial. The prosecution, who is Satan, presents all his evidence against him in support of the murder and it looks bad. But then the defense, who is Jesus, presents His evidence and in this case shows that He by grace offered to pay the penalty for that murder by His death upon the cross and taking the sin upon Himself, and the accused accepted that offer. The judge, hearing all the evidence and seeing propitiation, that is, the payment of the penalty has already been made, then declares the defendant not guilty. We must remember that whether we are found guilty or acquitted, we have all still stood before the bench, made an accounting, and been judged. Judgment means to make a distinction or ruling. It is a censorial power over a situation that can allow or suppress evidence and determine a proper outcome. What I am trying to say is that judgment occurs in many forms, but judgment does not necessarily result in condemnation. Both decisions—guilt or acquittal—are a judgment. Although we do not know exactly how judgment will be handled in heaven, and though some of these propositions may not be fully accurate or provable, I believe if I am wrong, it is better for us to err on the side of caution rather than be too liberal with our thinking.

Since it certainly appears we will in fact face a judgment, the next question that arises is what will be the effects of our judgment? We now address the topic of rewards.

Question: What will be affected by our judgment if salvation is ensured?

As implied by the question, salvation is here ensured, but that being said, I believe it is fair to say that salvation is itself the baseline of reward for faith in Christ. Some people may be unwilling to accept the idea that there will be a variance in heaven and feel that would somehow be unfair. Those that resist that concept will often point to the parable of The Laborers in the Vineyard located in Matthew 20:1–16 in that the laborers hired toward the end of the day for one hour of work were paid the same as those who were hired early and worked all day in the sun. But my understanding of this parable is that it is related only to salvation itself. A person who finds and confesses God on his deathbed will receive the same salvation by faith as the person who has served God his entire life as well as anyone along that spectrum who confesses Jesus as the Christ. But though they will be equal in having salvation, that does not mean they will necessarily be equal in heavenly rewards. First Peter 1:5 states that we "by God's power are being guarded through faith for a salvation ready to be revealed in the last time." He states again in verse 9 the salvation of our souls is the end of our faith. Though our faith will earn us salvation, nowhere is it stated that salvation is the end-all be-all of heaven. We will be saved by faith, but I believe God has more in store than salvation as is supported by the apostle Paul who says in 1 Corinthians 2:9, "What no eye has seen, nor ear heard, nor the heart of man imagined, what God has prepared for those who love him." I know I cannot even begin to imagine what heaven will be like. Sure, I can imagine, dream and contemplate, but my thoughts of it and its rewards will not even be close.

If "once saved, always saved" or rather the eternal security of the believer is true, then salvation itself cannot be lost. I will not debate that particular subject as some denominations believe you can fall from grace, but let us accept the argument for now that salvation is secure. If salvation could be lost, then we know exactly why Satan continues to hound the Christian. But assuming it could not be lost, we must ask what is affected. As I pointed out earlier, the Bible appears to show there will be what I will call a variance of hell for lack of a better way to describe it. Everyone in hell will be tormented and separated from God, but there appears to be some type of difference for some. Call it, for lack of a better way to describe it, levels of hell. I do not know if it will be a Dante's *Inferno* type of thing, but I reflected on the gospel of Matthew in Matthew 11:20–24 where Jesus stated the day of judgment "will be more tolerable" for the sinful cities of Tyre and Sidon and the land of Sodom (which was destroyed for its sinfulness in Genesis) than for Chorazin or Capernaum. In the same way as there appears to be a variance or a degree of leniency in hell, there also appears to be a variance in heaven beyond salvation. I would not go so far as to say there are "levels" of heaven but a variance. We will all be in heaven and all have communion and access to God, all live in the New Jerusalem, all have our own mansions and all will be eternally happy. Yet with that being said, the Bible clearly reveals there are rewards and placements in heaven that can be gained or lost. For example there are at least five crowns that are identified, such as the crown of life, the crown of glory, or the crown of righteousness. These crowns or others can be won by our decisions and conduct here on earth when we are tempted by Satan or tested by God or by what we decided to do when certain acts of providence are presented by God or so forth. In the same manner, they can also be lost. The apostle John in 2 John 8 warns us, "Watch yourselves, so that you may not lose what we have worked for, but may win *a full reward*," and in Revelation 3:11, Jesus states while addressing the church of Philadelphia, "I am coming soon. Hold fast what you have, *so that no one may seize your crown*" (emphasis added).

Though I certainly cannot speak authoritatively about what it will actually be like in heaven or hell, it appears there are additional rewards and placements in heaven beyond just gaining or losing crowns. In the Parable of the Guests in Luke 14:7–11, Jesus describes placements of honor and being humble and being moved up to a better seating position rather than embarrassed by assuming a place of honor and being told to move down a bit for someone more honorable. This parable was a slam against the proud and arrogant Pharisees, but I believe it may also have a spiritual interpretation alluding to a place of closer communion with Christ in heaven that can be gained. This would blend with how Jesus responded to the question asked of Him by James and John in Mark 10:36–40 regarding sitting at His right and left hand and that the placement they were requesting was "for those for whom it has been prepared." There also appears to be thrones of ruling with Christ and other similar rewards such as the number of cities one could have authority over as well as other possibilities. We need to remember that our God is fair and just in all things and though by His grace we may all have salvation by faith in Christ no matter at what point we confessed that faith, I doubt that I will have all the same rewards as say, Mother Teresa or Billy Graham. Jesus clearly taught that the one who wants to be the greatest or first in heaven must be humble like a child (Matt.18:1–4) and servant to all (Mark 9:35). We should also recognize for there to be a greatest, there must be those who are less and least, and for there to be a first, there must be those who follow. Now I am sure there will be no unhappiness or sorrow in heaven, and no one will take issue with why someone has more crowns than them. In heaven, all sin will be abolished, and coveting or envy will not even exist. Even the crowns we earn we will be casting to the feet of Jesus because it was He who gave us the ability to earn those crowns in the first place. But with everything considered, it seems to me that in some manner, the experience of heaven will be greater for some than for others, and that will be Christ's just reward for how we lived this life. I doubt we will necessarily know others' experience as they will not know our experience, but heaven will still be beyond all our imagination, and we will all be happy and satisfied because we will have seen what we truly deserved yet were rescued from. But all that being said, in my opinion, there does appear to be a variance, and that variance is a just recompense according to what we did, either good or bad, right or wrong. Recompense is a repayment or a requital, that is, something given or done in return. Remember 2 Corinthians 5:10, "So that each one may be recompensed for his deeds in the body, according to what he has done, whether good or bad."

As I briefly stated earlier, I have read some commentaries that say only those things we did or did not do with regard to the promotion of God's kingdom will be addressed at the Judgment Seat of Christ related to rewards and that sin by the Christian would not be addressed at all due to Christ's sacrifice on the cross. Yet my question to that theory goes back to Ezekiel 36:20-23 and Israel profaning God's name due to their sinful rather than holy activities which I discussed earlier in another chapter. If the Christian sins, especially practiced intentional sin, and it causes God's name to be profaned and the advancement of the kingdom of God takes a hit so to speak, do we not think we will be held accountable for that? Isn't the sin that hinders the advancement a "bad" thing and as such wouldn't it affect our eternal rewards though not our salvation since our salvation is secure in Christ if our profession of faith was sincere?

I want the reader to understand that I am not questioning salvation by faith alone in Christ by any means. I am not questioning the sufficiency of His ability to cleanse us of all sin nor His ability to present us pure and holy before God. But what I am questioning is our attention to the details and duties we have while living here in the flesh and what effects our diligence, or lack thereof, will have. If we are paying attention to our duties and obligations, we will live in a true reverent fear of God. These duties and obligations do not in any way earn us anything regarding salvation, but they are instructions, duties and works God has given us to perform out of obedience to Him, and He expects us to obey and do them (Ephesians 2:10). If we do not, there will be repercussions. Adam and Eve had several instructions regarding their duties for tending the Garden of Eden, and one command of what not to do. They violated that command and paid the consequence. It is very similar to how earthly parents instruct their children in life and expect them to be obedient to those instructions and to complete any chores given to them. If they are disobedient they do not stop being your children and you still love them, but you will discipline them for disobedience and for their good. The Israelites, God's chosen people, strayed while going from Egypt to the borders of Canaan the first time in approximately a year. They were disobedient and unfaithful to trust God and enter into Canaan as He instructed them because they were scared of the Canaanites strength. As a result, God chastised them by making them wander the wilderness until that unfaithful generation died off (Numbers 14). But even after the new generation faithfully entered Canaan under Joshua's leadership, it only took the Israelites a genera-tion after finally entering Canaan to again stray from God. Even after God would again chastise them for forsaking Him and eventually they would return to Him, they would still then subsequently stray again within another generation or two. Just read the book of Judges alone and see how habitually they strayed. After kings were given to Israel, each discipline enacted on Israel and its kings under the Old Testament were to be an example to us who are now God's chosen in the New Testament. God was chastising Israel and its kings out of love and for the purpose of sanctifying them. They were His chosen nation. Although they would subsequently, many generations later, reject Christ Jesus and the door of salvation would be opened to the Gentiles, these acts of discipline towards His chosen people of Israel are examples of how God still works even today for believers under the new covenant of grace. The point is, God does not change, and Christ's sacrifice and the gospel being presented to the Gentiles was planned from day one, so nothing has changed about God or His expectations or how He works. Though we are under the new covenant of faith, the examples of discipline provided in the Old Testament are still in effect and He will discipline us just as He did Israel. We are now over two thousand years since Christ's crucifixion and resurrection; is it possible we in our fallen human insufficiency might have muddled things up and misconstrued things some? Maybe we did not do it intentionally but simply failed to heed the Holy Spirit as fully as we should have because of our own fallen character. Look how many denominations have developed over the last two centuries and even how many denominations there are within denominations. Over the centuries, man's corruption has subtly been played by Satan, our fleshly nature has, due to our ignorance or lack of focus, succumbed to his traps, and it appears many of us have slowly yielded in our reverence for God, and thus we have slowly been conforming our standards of conduct and what we deemed as acceptable behavior to the world's views. I believe our subtly conforming to worldly ways has slowly and incrementally increased generation after generation, causing us not only to be too liberal in our modern-day thinking in relation to God and spiritual matters, but in also becoming so indulgent and permissive to not even recognize anything out of order. I cannot help but simply look back at the difference between the Puritan writers of the sixteenth century as compared to those of today and see a vast difference in biblical thought and piety.

Here is the deal: we are not and cannot be perfect in this world while we still occupy these fleshly bodies, and we know that. It is a fact that we will sin. God introduced the commandments and laws as a guideline of moral behavior we should follow and also in order to prove that salvation could not be gained by our own efforts but by His grace alone through Jesus Christ. Incidentally, those commandments are fulfilled in the law of love though we still love imperfectly while living in our mortal bodies. James taught, "For whoever keeps the whole law but fails in one point has become accountable for all of it" (James 2:10). The apostle Paul stated he did not know coveting until the law said, "Thou shalt not covet" and then he coveted everything (Romans 7:7) and that "we all have sinned and fall short of the glory of God" (Romans 3:23). Though we may still have sin involved in our lives because we will never be perfect until that day, it is still our obligation, out of love to God and to each other, to battle against and resist that sin as best we can, and we should be mournful of the sins we commit as well as the sins of the world itself. That is incidentally the meaning of Matthew 5:4, "Blessed are those who mourn, for they shall be comforted." We should hate our sin and the offense to God that it causes. We should therefore be diligent to confess our sins as we come to recognize them and obediently repent of them in our holy walk with God. Our sin interrupts communion with God as we feel guilt for them because our conscience tells on us and nags us. But if we confess our sins and repent of them, we can know God will gladly forgive our sins, and thus we will restore our communion with Him because we know we are forgiven. 1 John 1:9 says, "If we confess our sins, he is faithful and just to forgive us our sins and to cleanse us from all unrighteousness." Though we know we will be forgiven our sins upon confession of them and not be held guilty, it is not now while living in the flesh that we should not feel guilt and remorse over our sin, but it is later after our eternal judgment in which we will then be declared without guilt because of our faith in Christ. God Himself will proclaim us to be without guilt, and because sin will no longer exist, we will no longer be tempted or fail again. Looking at the continually displayed attitude of God towards sin and the high probability we will be held accountable, how can we realistically expect willful or unrepentant sin to not have an effect on the rewards of our eternal state? Though Christ died for our sin, and as such, we will have salvation, our sins, particularly willful and practiced sin in defiance of God, will certainly reap some type of repercussions. Do not let the schemes and lies of Satan deceive you and draw you into a false security and complacency about sin and its effects. It is debatable as to when our confessed and repented sins are officially forgiven because of the question of the timing as discussed earlier. I liken it to be similar to positional sanctification and progressive sanctification in that we are by all technical standards forgiven at the exact moment we confess and repent, but the full effect of the forgiveness is still progressive and in the future; but regardless, it is highly probable that non-repented or willful sin will be one of those "bad" things referred to in 2 Corinthians 5:10, which will have unknown costs with regard to our recompense and eternal standing in heaven.

We are often compared as soldiers for Christ and as athletes in the race who must compete by the rules if we expect to gain the prize. We have commandments and instructions of those things we are not supposed to do but we also have guidelines and commandments of what we are to do. These are the rules of the race for the prize. We are told our greatest duty is to love God with all our heart, and the apostle John tells us our obedience to Him is proof of our love of Him. "But whoever keeps His word, in him the love of God has truly been perfected" (1 John 1:5). That "love of God" is not God's love to us but our love to Him. Jesus Himself says in John 15:10, "If you keep My commandments, you will abide in My love; just as I have kept My Father's commandments and abide in His love," and in verse 14, Jesus states, "You are My friends if you do what I command you." Note the conditional *if* in both verses. What is His command? He tells us in verses 12 and 13, "This is My commandment, that you love one another, just as I have loved you. Greater love has no one than this, that one lay down his life for his friends." We must lay down our fleshly, sinful lives *for* Him and begin to live holy lives *to* Him in brotherly love *towards* others. Apathy toward and about sin and even more so a willful participation in sin even if it is just a small little sin does not mix with the holiness and righteousness of God and our love for God is not complete. We should not allow ourselves to fall into the schemes and traps of Satan by making us think that though all our sins will be forgiven, that they will have no effect on our eternal standings. I do not mean to be so repetitive, but I feel this point is important and really must be recognized and understood. The apostle John points out that if we practice sin, meaning to willfully and habitually engage in sin, we do not know God (1 John 2:4–5) or love Him as we should. Upon reflecting back, though I was baptized at a young age and I believe it was sincerely, I apparently did not love God as purely and completely as I should have because I strayed terribly. It was not until years later after the confrontation in the hospital and my subsequent reawakening that I truly found Him and loved Him. It was not until the age of forty-four I truly felt God in my heart and not just my mind. I had much to answer for, and my wrongful conduct would have many unknown ripple effects that I will see at the judgment and which will have affected rewards I would have received if I had lived more righteously. What I am trying to say is, if our initial baptism into Christ was sincere at whatever time it occurred, and though we may find ourselves straying, our salvation is not lost, but our communal relationship with God can be interrupted and the experience of our eternal state can still be affected, and Satan wants desperately to affect our eternal state. Think of it this way: upon our confession and baptism, all our past sins have been erased and we have started a new life in Christ (Romans 3:25). We have entered into a new life contract of sorts and subsequently any new sins, whether they are private or public, and their effects are marked down and written in the Book of Remembrance. Those sins will not affect our salvation but will affect our rewards at the judgment. As I said, we will not lead a perfect life, we cannot, but if we become complacent in our duties, our complacency will haunt us on Judgment Day. It is quite certain because Christ died for our sins and paid the punishment that we will not be found guilty and thus condemned to hell, yet we will still be held to account and otherwise reap the results of our choices. We will not be punished as we might define punishment here on earth, and we will be saved, but we will also be fairly and justly recompensed, which means additional rewards beyond salvation will be lost or gained.

It is simply my desire for the reader to give serious consideration to the points I have presented. It is my hope that the reader will then search through scripture for themselves, alone or with others, diligently and with an open mind for the whole and complete truth. Our hearts and minds need to be open to the full message of scripture, and we should cautiously be as conservative in our interpretations as possible. Though I am older in age, I am still yet a baby

Christian in experience and understanding. As such, I am not saying I am right about all these issues, but I strongly and sincerely believe there will be a judgment in which we must give an accounting, and that should be a concern for us; and as such, we should give serious thought to what will be held to account. I cannot say everything the judgment will consist of, but I think it is best to try to stand before God with as clear a conscience as possible. To stand before God with a clear conscience we must constantly evaluate ourselves and our conduct and be diligent to enact proper changes in our behavior and way of thinking in order to be as honestly righteous as possible. As the apostle Paul stated in 2 Timothy 1:3, "I thank God, whom I serve with a clear conscience," and 2 Timothy 4:6–8, "For I am already being poured out as a drink offering, and the time of my departure has come. *I have fought the good fight, I have finished the course, I have kept the faith*; in the future there is laid up for me the crown of righteousness, which the Lord, *the righteous Judge*, will award to me on that day; and not only to me, but also to all who have loved His appearing" (emphasis added). The apostle Paul, though he admitted struggling with sin, affirms he strived to his best ability to do everything that was expected of him and therefore had a clear conscience. We should be cautious to do the same.

It is also my desire in the writing of this chapter to prompt thinking upon these issues in order to bring the reader into a true reverential fear of God. I am not talking exclusively about the reverent awe of God as most people understand "fear" related to Him in scripture, but an actual true fear. This fear is not so much of God specifically because God is truly love and very merciful, but the fear must be of ourselves and our corrupted nature and what actions— our apathy toward sin and our holy duties—might incur or provoke from a holy, righteous, and just God. Our fear of God should be about what He will do in judgment and chastisement for our conduct or irreverent attitude here temporally and what their effects may have eternally. The apostle Paul appears to address temporal consequences for wrongful behavior to a degree in 1 Timothy 1:20 when he speaks of some false teachers at the church in Ephesus, "whom I have handed over to Satan that they may learn not to blaspheme," and in 1 Corinthians 5:5 regarding an adulterer, in which he stated, "You are to deliver this man to Satan for the destruction of the flesh, so that his spirit may be saved in the day of the Lord." I do not relish being a quadriplegic, but I do praise God's love in that He would chastise me physically even this severely in order to get my undivided attention and to correct me and to save me spiritually by turning me back to Him in sincere love and dedicated obedience. Look on me as an example of God's temporal judgment, His temporal judgment chastising me, not only as a loving father regarding the disobedience of one of His children, but also for the purpose of breaking the bonds of my sin in order to sanctify me. We should fear our conduct that would cause God's temporal chastisement, but then also be concerned for the effect our actions will have on our eternal rewards beyond salvation in God's, just recompense to our choices and other actions in this life. We should have concern over even what we might consider relatively small things. For example, do we not count our failure to testify and share the gospel message with others a bad thing? We should—God commanded us to do so, and failure to do so might be a sin of omission. God is faithful, righteous, and just—and out of love—He will respond to our decisions, either by blessing or chastising us to the degree necessary for our sanctification in this life. For me, God's heavy temporal chastisement to gain my attention and devotion after several less-intense attempts failed resulted in my being a quadriplegic before I finally reawakened to Him. I have been blessed, and God has given me grace and mercy even through my chastisement, even as He did Israel and others He chastised, but being chastised, though beneficial, is not enjoyable. I do not derive pleasure in being a quadriplegic, and I am asking you to please be cautious about your life and decisions and fear letting it have to go that far or worse for you. As Jesus told the crippled in John 5:14, "Behold, you have become well; do not sin anymore, so that nothing worse happens to you."

NEW HEART, NEW MIND

AS I REFLECT BACK ON this whole incident almost twelve years after it occurred, I see a much fuller picture, from everything that occurred years before, to those things leading up to the incident, and after. God in His infinite love and extreme patience had answered my prayers in a most amazing way. Even as I tarnished His name He continued to remain patient with me and worked on me, trying to correct my path and to answer my prayers in a much less-severe manner. God gives us free will to make choices and though we may stray, He does not abandon us. Rather than abandon us because we turn away from or stray from Him, He instead continues to present events which promote opportunities for us to make the choice to repent and return. Sadly I was unresponsive to those lesser attempts, and it took this incident to get my attention. Once He gotten my attention, I still had a choice; God in His love was patiently willing to show me the errors of my ways in order to allow another free will choice opportunity. I could still have refused to return, or I could repent; the choice was mine and my choice would reap an outcome one way or another. Thankfully, I made the right choice, but how tragic for me that I had become so hard-hearted in my sin that I would not listen to Him sooner. The fact is however, that God is omniscient, which means He knows everything from beginning to end. Though I had free will and could have and should have made different choices with regard to all those previous opportunities prior to my shooting, He knew what I would and would not do. Nothing is a surprise to Him, but in all that disobedience, He was using my actions and decisions in other ways and for other purposes. Someday we will get to see a review of our lives showing all the ripple effects of all our decisions and how each decision and ripple affected the lives and decisions both for ourselves as well as others, and how God used those decisions and ripples for His own reason and design. It will be a show of epic proportions that will stun and amaze us.

It took over two years for the trial to begin for my shooter. During the trial I was not allowed in the courtroom to hear the testimony. I really wanted to hear it because I had lost my memory of that whole week preceding the shooting and many days after the shooting, and I was hoping the testimony would jar some remembrance of those days I had lost before the shooting. After the testimony had been completed, I was allowed to hear closing arguments; and after her sentence of guilty was declared, I was allowed to be present for sentencing testimony and even to hear from the defendant herself. During her sentencing testimony, she pled to me for forgiveness, but I was not given an opportunity to reply. So here in this book is my reply.

After my shooting, I was of course sedated and not really conscious for a while, and even after regaining consciousness, I was still not thinking much about anything except recovering. Then after God's confrontation with me, which brought me to my repentance and the subsequent recovery that He graced me with, I still had very little thought about my shooter. I did not think along those directions at all. My focus was totally on regaining what I had lost both physically and spiritually. The reality is, however, that I did not even begin reading and studying the Bible again until after I had been released from the hospital.

Eventually as time progressed, after my release and return home from the hospital, I was confronted with the issue of my shooter as I was being interviewed about what I could recall regarding what happened. As stated earlier, I could not really remember anything; and in fact, the last thing I really remembered was taking my family to the State Fair of Texas the week before. The little I thought I could remember was just a blur at best, and the rest was gone completely. It is the same even today. But the one thing I could not find in my heart with regard to my shooter, either during the interview or afterward, was any hate or anger, and I found that I had already forgiven her. How could I not be angry with my shooter, and how could I possibly forgive her? The answer to both questions is simply by the power of God. He had changed my heart. After being confronted by God and realizing my total guilt before His eyes, upon being forgiven by Him, how could I not return that forgiveness? When I say I have forgiven her, I am not saying that she should not have been prosecuted for shooting me or for her other illegal activities, certainly she should, forgiveness does not mean forgetting or allowing wrong. But I also recognized just as I had been caught up in my sinful activities, which were illegal in God's court of law, and had been forgiven, she was also caught up in her sinful lifestyle, which ultimately led to her shooting me and I needed to forgive her as well. God had mercifully forgiven me my continuous affronts to Him, and I had discovered it was incumbent upon me by His command, that if I was to be forgiven, that I must also forgive (Matthew 6:14–15; Mark 11:25). But what amazed me was that by the power of His Holy Spirit, I had already done so in my heart even before my mind was consciously aware. It is by the power of the Holy Spirit I had been convicted of my sin and recognized my need for forgiveness, and it was by His power that I was able to and had already forgiven in return. This concept of the necessity of forgiving was also explained in the parable of the Unforgiving Servant in Matthew 18:21–35, where a servant who owed a king a great debt, had been forgiven that debt which he could never repay, but then refused to show mercy and forgive a man who owed him a small debt. Subsequently, because he refused to forgive in return, he was then imprisoned until he paid his debt in full. If God has forgiven me for the great debt I owed Him for my sins, how could I not also forgive? Verses 32–35 really strikes home when it reveals that our failing to forgive others after being forgiven ourselves would reap severe consequences. This parable and these verses about forgiveness being necessary in order to be forgiven should raise alarm bells for the professing Christian who finds himself unable to forgive.

You see, the Bible talks about the necessity of forgiving others sincerely from the heart, and it is only by the power of the Holy Spirit we can do so. If we do not have the Holy Spirit working within us, it would be almost impossible. If we claim to have been forgiven of our sin but refuse to or seemingly cannot forgive someone else of their offense against us, than likely, we do not have the power of the Spirit in us at all, and we are only fooling ourselves about our own relationship with Christ. Forgiveness can sometimes be difficult. I understand. The fact is, the harm and hurt someone has caused cannot just be forgotten. The memory of the event will always exist, but forgiveness is not about forgetting, but about not holding a grudge, which is more harmful to you than to them. Forgiveness is a choice, and the lack of forgiveness of others, especially if we obstately refuse to forgive, may be an indication that our relationship in Christ does not exist like we think it does, and our own forgiveness may be in question (James 2:13, Matt. 6:14–15). In other words, if we cannot recognize and be grateful for the huge amount of sin of which we are have been forgiven and in turn then willingly work towards forgiving others, the power of Christ is not in us, and we may find we are disqualified for forgiveness. If however we find we can forgive, even if it is not easily, but especially if it is easily, it is proof the Holy Spirit is at work within us. If you find yourself unable to forgive in the sincerity of your heart, you need to question why and spend much time in prayer, reflecting not only on the sins in your life and your need for forgiveness, but also recognizing God's continued blessings even though you are sinful. You should pray and reflect on these things until such a time as your heart is finally humbled and you can finally and honestly release your anger and forgive. When you can, you can also have confidence in your own forgiveness. God knows if you have forgiven from your heart or not. As I pointed out earlier, what is important to understand, and I think the misunderstanding of this is the obstacle for many, is that forgiveness does not mean forgetting or condoning someone's wrongful or hurtful actions. Forgiveness means choosing not to continue to hold onto those actions in anger or hatred but releasing them and giving them to God to sort out as He deems best. But what I found most interesting in my case is that by the power of God, it was easy for me. During my early stages of Bible study at home, I had apparently already reached that decision to forgive and that decision really displayed itself at the time of the interview. I had no hate or anger toward her whatsoever. I did not know her personally; to me, she was just another unknown criminal offender. Though I did not appreciate being shot, I did appreciate what God did for me as a result of the shooting, and upon recognizing God's hand was involved in the entire incident, it did not take long for me to realize she was just an instrument He was using to get through to me. In addition, even seemingly more amazing to me, was that through my change of heart that was manifested by the power of the Holy Spirit, I found I was not satisfied simply with being able to forgive her, but that I actually found myself concerned not so much for her prosecution, but for the condition of her soul. I found myself concerned about whether she had ever heard the gospel message.

God had answered my prayers through the shooting and, true to His promise, changed my heart of stone into a heart of flesh and answered my prayers to return me back to Him. I quickly realized how trapped in sin I truly had been and how God was using the affliction of my shooting to reawaken me, to cause my repentance and my return to His path. Because of this knowledge, I could not be angry at Him but instead only grateful. God had moved me into my position where I would be shot, and just as He had allowed and even orchestrated my shooting to occur for the purpose of rescuing me, I believe He also orchestrated events in such a way as to place my shooter in the position to shoot me and face prosecution. That is, God allowed that shooting, and He allowed it in order to get my attention, but why would I limit His work to me alone? I cannot say for certain of course because no one knows the mind of God, but I often wonder if I was the only person in play in this action. I doubt I was. Because I recognized my need for forgiveness, long before the trial ever started, I had already forgiven my shooter. Indeed because of my forgiveness by God and my changed heart, I had even taken measures to ensure she heard the gospel message because I had no idea of her religious knowledge or upbringing.

I contacted a friend of mine and made arrangements with him to ensure that she had heard the gospel message of Christ Jesus. We did it rather anonymously because the trial had not even been set yet, and I did not want to risk attorneys trying to twist my desire to save her soul into some kind of courtroom theatrics in front of a jury and mislead them. Like I said, I felt she should have to face the penalty for her illegal actions, but my primary concern was for her soul, and no time should be lost as the trial delayed because we do not know what the future holds. When God presents an opportunity, however seemingly strange it might seem to us, we should pursue that opportunity in obedience to Him. The Bible tells us to love our enemies and pray for those who persecute us, and I believe, in forgiving my shooter and seeking her salvation, I was doing just that in the best way I could. The fact is I am still a sinner, we all are, and as strange as it may sound, I feel, in the eyes of God, I am absolutely no better than any other person. As the apostle Paul pointed out, we all, every one of us, fall short of the glory of God. We often want to compare ourselves and grade our sins against the sins of others, all the while ignoring certain sins we have justified to ourselves, and for some reason, we never seem to think our sins are as bad as others' sins. But the truth is, sin cannot be graded because all sin is a violation of God's laws, they are affront to His holiness, and all of them are worthy of death, and in that sense, all sin is equally sinful. That is one reason why I consider myself no better than others, because like it or not, my sin is just as bad as theirs. Our job as Christians is not to judge others or try to compare ourselves against others, but to realize we are all fallen creatures. When we finally recognize and accept that truth, we should be cautious to remain humble, and remember we are saved only by grace and in turn share that grace that comes through faith in Christ alone with everyone, including those that might be classified as our "enemies." I heard back from my friend who told me that she did claim to know Christ and that she stated she had accepted Him into her life at a young age. That was good news to hear, but it also seems obvious, due to the circumstances as a whole, that she had strayed from her commitments to Christ as well. Just as God used the shooting for my good, I wonder if He was using it for her good also.

She has been sentenced to prison for a long time. She has her full health and physical ability but will be in the confines of the prison system for most if not even her whole life, similar to how I will be confined to my broken body the remainder of my life. But I wonder if in doing so, God is not also trying to get her attention and trying to get her to return to His fold? I wonder if He was trying to mitigate her circumstances by breaking a dysfunctional cycle for her and also for the sake of the child since both she and the father will be in prison for a while. The grandparents or some other family members will hopefully raise the child outside the lawbreaking and drug-using environment and hopefully raise it in a law-abiding and church environment instead. I wonder sometimes just how many lives God has planned changes for, all out of this one incident.

All this was going through my head and heart before I really got the chance to read through the Bible very well, much less study it well, but one thing I did recall becoming starkly clear at that beginning stage was the importance of, or better said, the necessity of forgiveness, and not just for our friends and family but for our enemies as well. Hate the sin but love the person and forgive their sins and trespasses against us because we all need to. be forgiven somehow in some way and most in a multitude of ways. (Matt. 5:44; 6:12, 14–15; 18:21–22; 18:32–35; Mark 11:25; Luke 6:37; Eph. 4:32; Col. 3:13).

Now, after several years of Bible study and drawing ever closer to God, upon seeing God as I never knew Him, a very personal and fully involved God who intervenes in our lives in many ways in order to try and save us and mold us, my forgiveness to my shooter as well as everyone who might offend me is stronger than ever. God does not force anyone to return to Him, but He makes and presents opportunities time and again. If they never return, they were probably never His to begin with. He has given us free will, and in that way it is up to us to respond accordingly. He does not quit on us, and He is very patient and loving and will always be glad to receive us upon our repentance from sin and acceptance of Christ. Once we make that decision, He never stops molding and shaping us from common clay into an honorable vessel, no matter how far we may have strayed. I dare say, that many of the temptations we face and the subsequent failures we experience, as well as the circumstances we endure, are all part of that molding process. God does not want us to be tempted, to fail, or to experience bad situations, but that is part of the fallen human nature and God will use those things to shape us, and if we are open and receptive to His workings, we will benefit from them. I am not saying if we are perfectly receptive to His molding that we will not still face other issues in the future. Because we can never be truly perfect in this life, God will continually shape us and may even use our bad circumstances to help mold someone else in some manner, but the more responsive we are to being formed, the more we benefit, and the less we may have to be spun and pounded before becoming the object He desires. The more resistant we are the more turmoil and shaping we will face.

I was reading the parables of Matthew 20:1–16 regarding the landowner, and Luke 15:11ff regarding the prodigal son, and I could not help but relate myself to these. I was the prodigal. I had become a Christian at the age of sixteen, but upon going to college, I became ensnared in worldly behavior. All of a sudden several years later, I realized my situation and wanted to come back home to God, but I was not only heavily ensnared in my sins, but I was feeling less than worthy of His continuing forgiveness because of my behavior, especially since I had strayed away after already accepting Him as a teenager. I guess I was feeling like I had made my bed by my own choices and now I had to lie in it. That unworthy feeling was something Satan was planting in my head. But God, being the patient and loving Father that He is, was more than willing, and I would say, even anxious, to welcome me back into His arms. Not only was He patiently waiting for me, but instead of waiting, He was actively pursuing me (Matthew 18:12–14). After He directly confronted me in that pursuit, upon my repenting, He has fully forgiven me and accepted me back. Upon my returning to Him, I yet felt unqualified for His grace and simply wanted to be His servant and be able to sleep under a tin roof. Like the parable of the landowner, I had not labored equally with the others and just like the prodigal son I was feeling unworthy. Yet despite my lack of duty and obedience, He has openly welcomed me back. Rather than just placing me with the servants, He has instead placed me in the same house with everyone else in the family, along with those who have been His faithful servants for many years, and He has given me a new spirit for Him. I can feel no less than blessed and humbled by His mighty love, and His continued display of love has caused me to love Him even more.

I can only think there are many prodigals out there. I do not think that way because I want to feel better about myself and say "I'm not the only one," but I suspect there are many who profess Christ but may have strayed just like I did. Maybe even my shooter. Satan will lie by trying to tell you that you cannot be forgiven again or that somehow you are unworthy. He will try to keep you so busy or keep you so entertained that you will be too busy to think about your sinfulness, God, or your need for His mercies. But it is time to slow down and think and realize the truth, that there is no sin too great that God cannot and will not forgive it if you simply and sincerely ask and repent.

As she pled to me for forgiveness that day, I wish I had been allowed to respond even if just privately and let her know that she indeed already had it. I had no anger toward her because I knew she had only been an instrument utilized for my benefit. Here's the thing though, I believe God is using her subsequent imprisonment to try to awaken her. He has removed her from the lifestyle she was in bondage to and taken away the temptations of drugs, money, and whatever else was drawing her away. Just as I had time to do nothing but stare at the ceiling until being confronted by God, she would also have plenty of time to reflect. I believe He is actually talking to her and trying to awaken her to repentance to gain her return back to Him even now. I hope she is listening, and I hope she is engaging in some type of prison ministry with others who are also finding their way back to Him; if so, though she will likely remain in prison for a long time, that awakening and her responding to His call will bring her peace and an acceptance of her situation, and she may even find a way to praise and glorify God for it and in it.

The apostle Paul in his letters to the Romans stated his earnest desire to come to Rome and see the Christians there. He stated in

Romans 1:9–10, "For God is my witness, whom I serve with my spirit in the gospel of his Son, that without ceasing I mention you always in my prayers, asking that somehow by God's will I may now at last succeed in coming to you." Paul had prayed "somehow," "by God's will," "I may now at last succeed in coming to you." Paul had it in his mind that he would be stopping by Rome on the way to his fourth missionary trip to Spain. Although he had indications he would face adversity when he returned to Jerusalem, little did he realize God had bigger plans for him besides going to Spain and he was about to be arrested and suffer imprisonment. God was in fact answering Paul's prayer to go to Rome, but it would be as a prisoner and not a missionary as he expected. However, while imprisoned in Rome, Paul wrote his letter to the Philippians and stated in Philippians 1:12–14, "I want you to know, brothers, that what has happened to me has really served to advance the gospel, so that it has become known throughout the whole imperial guard and to all the rest that my imprisonment is for Christ. And most of the brothers, having become confident in the Lord by my imprisonment, are much more bold to speak the word without fear." God moves in mysterious ways to accomplish His plans. God used and even organized Paul's imprisonment in Rome, partially to further mold, shape, and sanctify Paul for his good, but He did it also for the saving of others and He will do the same with us even through our affliction, because, "God causes all things to work together for good to those who love God, to those who are called according to *His* purpose" (Romans 8:28). In a similar manner, just as He used my shooting for my good, He can use it for her good if she will receive it. God has brought me back to Him in a much, much stronger fashion than my relationship with Him in high school and even in a much stronger fashion than I could have imagined. Not only have I become rededicated to Him, but through Bible study, prayer, and His Holy Spirit, I now know God as never before, and I see His righteous and just attributes in full display. He can do the same for you, as He will work good in even the largest storm of your life. God is so good, and I can only praise Him for His work and to now dedicatedly attempt to serve Him as best I can.

As I said in another chapter, during my first year and a half of recovery, things were going very well, but then I started having setbacks. I went from walking a decent distance with a walker to not being able to walk at all and now even to having extreme difficulty in transferring. Initially I prayed several times a day for recovery of what I had regained but then lost. I wanted it so bad and could not understand why it was going away. But as I was dealing with these issues, I read Paul's letters to the Corinthians. In 2 Corinthians 12:7–10, Paul talks about his "thorn in the flesh" and describes it as a "messenger of Satan" to keep him humble for the revelation he described in verses 1–5. He stated that God answered him and told him the thorn in the flesh would not be removed and that "My grace is sufficient for you, for My power is made perfect in weakness."

As I read this, I could not see but how it applied to me as God's grace in Christ to save my soul is all I truly need. God was displaying His power through my disability in many ways. He was showing His righteousness, displaying His power and control, revealing the peace He could bestow, and glorifying Himself in other ways. I lost physical abilities I had regained, and additionally, ever since I had been shot, I have lived in pain. You would think quadriplegics, paraplegics, and others who had suffered nerve interruptions and loss of feeling would not feel pain, but actually the opposite is true for many. I may not be able to feel many external sensations like needlesticks and bumps or other things, but the nerves have a way of creating pain where you would think there should be none, and the body will respond to pain even if a person is not consciously or physically aware of it. Not only had I prayed for the recovery of my lost abilities, but I had even more stringently prayed for an end to the constant pain. But as I read this and contemplated the power of God and what He not only had done for me but was still doing for me, I could do nothing but see that God's grace was more than sufficient and to just trust Him in everything as I recognized and was honored to be a useful instrument as He displayed His power through my weakness.

When Paul went to Rome as a prisoner, many more heard and listened to what he had to say than would have bothered to listen to him if he had gone as a missionary. People knew he was imprisoned for the gospel message, and so they wanted to hear what that message was, and as such, it truly advanced the gospel in a tremendous way. Although I believe the main purpose in my shooting was to cause my awakening and repentance, I found that it was causing other things to happen also. Because I did awaken and repent and because I was praising God for His work, suddenly I found I had a testimony, a testimony God had given me. Suddenly people were listening to my story, and I was invited to different churches in order to share what God had done in and through my suffering. People who were suffering or knew someone who was were hearing my story and felt I could truly understand and relate because they saw I was a fellow sufferer. They were not simply listening to someone who had never suffered, at least not severely, speaking about God's hand in suffering no matter how theologically correct they might have been. Because I was actually experiencing hurt and loss but was still praising God through it, my story carried weight, and God was using that. The truth is I have no idea just how far God's plan for me might go or just what God is using it for, but I do know that He has met my needs by rescuing my soul and that though I am weak and live in pain, God's grace is truly more than just sufficient for me and His power is being exhibited through my disability. Praise be to God for everything, and may His will always be done.

Through my Bible study, I have become personally convinced that not all things will be equal in heaven, and though we will be saved by our faith in Christ Jesus, we may not all live in the same size mansions. We will be happy in whatever state we land in, sincerely happy, but our rewards will be different. In fact, I consider myself to have wasted so much time in sin instead of godliness that I believe my "mansion" in heaven will be a pup tent in the back yard of someone else's mansion. I do not recall where I heard it, back in my youth, a hymn or what, but I heard that we here on earth accumulated lumber for our mansions in Heaven by our works. The Bible talks about accumulating treasures in Heaven (Matthew 6:19–20) but I'm not sure how the lumber analogy relates to that. If that analogy were true in some respect, I'm not sure I have accumulated enough lumber for a house much less one on my own lot. God willing I will remain on earth long enough to at least save up enough lumber for a good log cabin (I like log cabins).

The Bible teaches us of the grace, mercy and forgiveness of God which He offered to us as a free gift through faith in His Son Jesus Christ, and that Christ's redemptive sacrifice for the sins of man and reconciliation to God had been pre-ordained before the world or even time began. This is the gospel message that is primarily taught, that we have salvation by faith alone in Christ Jesus, it is a free gift of God, and all we have to do is accept it. But the Bible also teaches that all mankind will face judgment at the end of time and that God, who is just and righteous, will reward or recompense each person according to their life here on earth and the decisions they made. The saved, those that made the choice of faith in Christ, may share in the common decision to have faith in Christ, but even if they share the same faith, everyone will also decide, act and think in different ways, and so accordingly, in some manner or another, there will be a difference in rewards and recompense and as a result, a variance in heaven and our eternal life.

Many are uncomfortable with the concept of being judged, yet the Bible teaches that we will. Though we will face temporal judgments now that mold and shape us into the image of Christ, eventually we will face an eternal and final judgment. Bible scholar's debate regarding what that judgment will consist of. We will have salvation in Christ Jesus if we chose to believe in Him, and our sins may or may not be part of that judgment, but we will be judged in some way and just recompense made according to our life here on earth. James 2:12 tells us, "So speak and so act as those who *are to be judged under the law of liberty*" (emphasis added). Did you catch both portions of that statement? "Speak and act" addresses conduct and decisions and "judged under the law of liberty" addresses our freedom of choice regarding our decisions and conduct. Christ's sacrifice broke the bonds of sin and we are no longer bound by the power of Satan to commit sin. It is our choice and as such, if we accepted Christ as our Lord and Savior, we will face judgment not with regards to salvation or condemnation, but of the choices we made "under the law of liberty" by our own free will. We will reap in eternal life what we have sown in this life. We must take the teachings of the Bible as a whole and if we accept one part we must also accept the other and attempt to understand how these teachings coexist and harmonize with each other rather than conflict. When we do this, when we harmonize these teachings, we see a fuller picture of God and His holiness and recognize not only our salvation through Him, but also our duties and responsibilities toward Him.

Through my incident, I have now come to see God in 3-D, a whole complete picture as He has revealed Himself with all His attributes and traits displayed. I do not claim to know Him completely as I do not think any human can, but I now know Him more fully than I ever had and I see His many attributes and how they are working together. All His attributes and traits work cohesively and symbiotically toward one goal, the salvation of mankind and a redeemed communion with Him which we shared in the Garden of Eden before the fall of Adam and Eve into sin. God's characteristics reveal Him as a loving, merciful and forgiving God who is also holy, righteous, and just. He is all-knowing and all-powerful, and He is a jealous God full of wrath, fire, and judgment. There are other attributes I have not mentioned and probably more than He has revealed to us, but we must see, know, and accept God in all His attributes and traits, and recognize how each of them apply to us. To not know all His attributes as He reveals them to us once we recognize their existence, is to not know God and to reject or deny an attribute for whatever reason is to reject or deny God. If we reject certain aspects because they make us uncomfortable or because they keep us from pursuing our own desires and comfort, then we have placed ourselves above God and become our own idols. Remember however that God is a jealous God who will have no other idols before Him, and He will break our idols and us along with them if He must. Instead, we must take Him as a whole and love Him as our God who is to be held in highest reverence and awe and be praised and glorified for eternity. We must humble ourselves and rise to God's standards rather than try to bring Him down and bend Him to our standards.

There are some who cling to no judgment or accounting for sin of any type and see only grace, love, and mercy. There are others who feel anxiety because they see a whole future accounting for sin by a just and righteous God and are concerned for their eternal state. I think we need to avoid both extremes and meet together on middle ground to see and accept God in a whole complete picture. Though some of my findings regarding the forgiveness of sins might appear controversial to some modern teaching, I do not believe that is actually so. I feel if we will review those findings under the whole scope of forgiveness and salvation, along with a future judgment as a total package, they will actually harmonize. By faith in Christ, our sins, past, present and future, from the sin of Adam to Armageddon *are* forgiven both now already and yet are still future. That forgiveness, though complete in one sense, does not reach its total consummation until the future day of judgment. I think by observing this to be so, we will find that middle ground that has divided so many Christians and we can become more unified in our thinking. I hope so.

I suspect that for most people attending church, their knowledge of God comes from a twenty-minute sermon on Sunday mornings. I believe it is probably that way in many religions, cults and other such venues and is why people fall susceptible to certain ways of thinking, that is, to believing only what they were taught and in which they never bothered to take the time to look for themselves to search for the truth. I perceive that many who minister are strong in certain aspects but weak in others and in some ways, though they make the honest effort and so must be applauded and appreciated, the fact is, because of their strengths and weaknesses, they promote certain aspects while unintentionally missing others. The individual members of Christian community as a whole vary in gifts, talents and knowledge and should therefore gather together often in order to share their gifts and insights and thereby edify each other and teach each other in order to build toward a more full and complete knowledge of God (Romans 12:3–6, Hebrews 10:24–25), but it is also up to us to seek that knowledge for ourselves and not just rely on others. The apostle Paul taught in Romans 14:5 that "Each one should be fully convinced in his own mind." If we do not search for the truth ourselves we will fall to lies and divisions. That is one reason we are so divided as denominations and within our own congregations, and why such tragedies occur such as the Jonestown Massacre and the Branch Davidians in Waco. Many may get some additional learning at a Sunday school class, but that only equates to about an hour total one day a week and that simply is not enough for something so important and that our eternity hinges upon. Certainly we need guidance from ministers, teachers and others, but we must not be solely reliant upon them. We must search for ourselves and let the Holy Spirit guide us, and test what we have been told by others. The preacher for the most part can only give a general message on the Bible, usually does not have time to go in depth, and will very rarely speak of the wrath, jealousy, judgment, and righteous anger of God and how those attributes affect believers because they are topics that must be discussed in depth to be properly understood. As such, I believe it is imperative that believers read and study the Bible on their own time and be willing to ask questions about things they do not understand. That is the only way they will likely ever truly learn the whole God as He is, and I fear claims of ignorance will be no excuse because He knows the heart and knows if you truly wanted to know Him or if you were too busy on social media or other entertainment options or feigning ignorance as an excuse to pursue your own desires. God also gave us a moral code; it is instilled in our DNA, so we know right from wrong, and our conscience will testify either for or against us.

God has displayed Himself and His power throughout, amongst and within creation in a great and mighty way. God works in many ways to mold us and shape us including in and through our adversity. All His work is for our good both now and for eternity. We, the entire human race, are nothing but clay, just dust that will turn back into dust when our body dies, but our created soul is eternal, and God wants communion with our souls because, after all, He created them. I feel I now know, though still likely imperfectly, the complete God, or as much of Himself as He has chosen to reveal to us. I myself will continue in my efforts to know God even more completely than I do now and I am sure He will continue to reveal more of Himself as I do so. I love Him with all my heart, and I can only hope this book will bring Him the glory, praise, and honor He deserves or at least the best we can give until that day when we all will see Him as He is. This story is His story, not mine. I am simply conveying it, what He has done for me through my shooting and afterward, and some of the lessons He has taught me. Thank you for reading this book. I hope it has benefitted you and helped you draw closer to Christ and possibly enhanced your knowledge of God in some manner, and hopefully motivated you to dig into scriptures on your own. Let us give honor, praise, and glory to God our Father and His Son, our Lord Christ Jesus, the Savior of our souls.

The End

NOTES

1   John Owen, *The Mortification of Sin*, Abridged by Richard Rushing (Murrayfield Road, Edinburgh, UK: Puritan Paperbacks, The Banner of Truth Trust, 2009), 112.

2   Matthew Henry, "Hebrews," *Matthew Henry's Commentary on the Whole Bible* (McLean, Virginia, MacDonald, 1706), 902–903.

3   *Webster's New World Dictionary of the American Language, Second College Edition*, David B. Guralnik, editor in chief (Simon and Schuster, 1980).

4   Matthew Henry, "1 Corinthians 11:27–32," *Matthew Henry's Commentary on the Whole Bible* (McLean, Virginia, McDonald, 1706), 565–566.

5   Matthew Henry, "1 Peter 4:17–19," *Matthew Henry's Commentary on the Whole Bible* (McLean, Virginia, McDonald, 1706), 1032.

6   Larry J. Waters and Roy B. Zuck, *Why O God? Suffering and Disability in the Bible and Church*, (Wheatland, Il: Crossway, 2011), 119–122.

7   David Powlison, *Good & Angry* (New Growth Press, Greensboro, NC, 2016), 81, 83.

8   Michael Reeves, Delighting in the Trinity, (Intervarsity Press, Downers Grove, Illinois, 2012), 65

ABOUT THE AUTHOR

CARLTON R. MARSHALL CLASSIFIES HIMSELF as just the normal, average person. He was baptized into Christ at age sixteen but struggled with his Christian walk for many years. At the age of forty-four, he sustained a life-altering injury as a police officer, which resulted in quadriplegia. He now testifies how God had been pursuing him through his life struggles and worked through his incident in amazing and unforeseen ways to revive him spiritually. He is a husband and father and resides in Lancaster, Texas.

CPSIA information can be obtained
at www.ICGtesting.com
Printed in the USA
FSHW010505110221
78462FS